# ANATOMY
## FOR STRENGTH AND
## FITNESS TRAINING
# FOR WOMEN

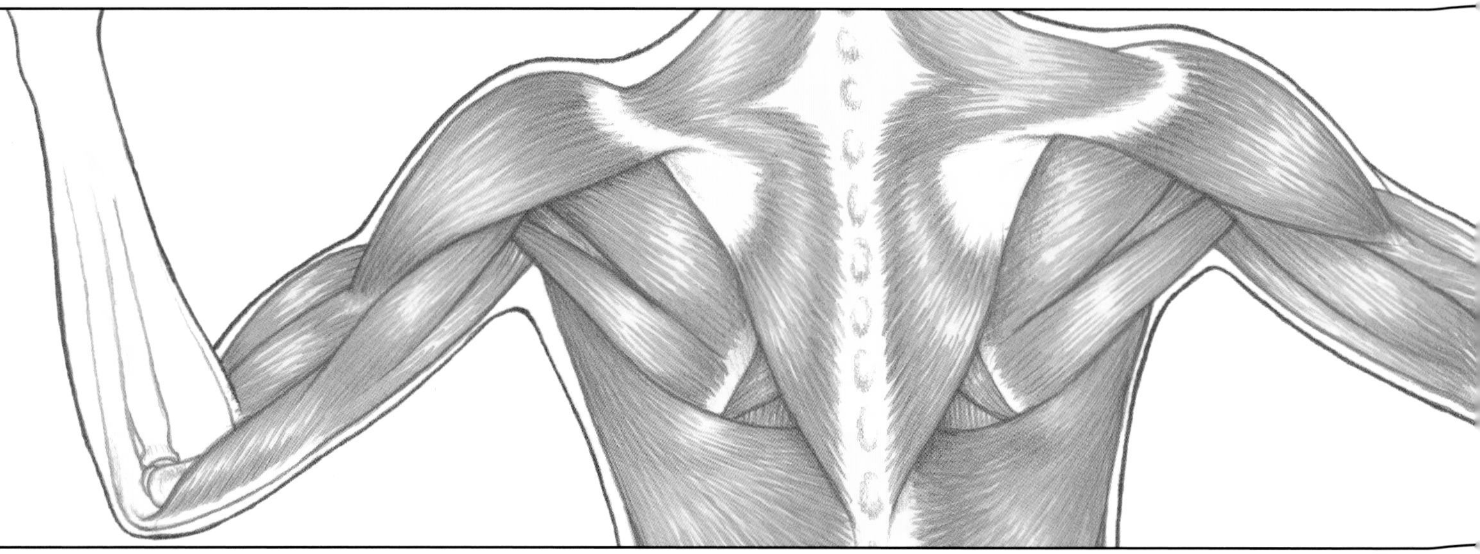

# ANATOMY
FOR **STRENGTH** AND
**FITNESS TRAINING**
## FOR WOMEN

### MARK VELLA

## Dedication
To my late parents, I wish you could have seen this one too.
This book is dedicated to you and your legacy. Time has not
faded the memories, but has made them stronger.

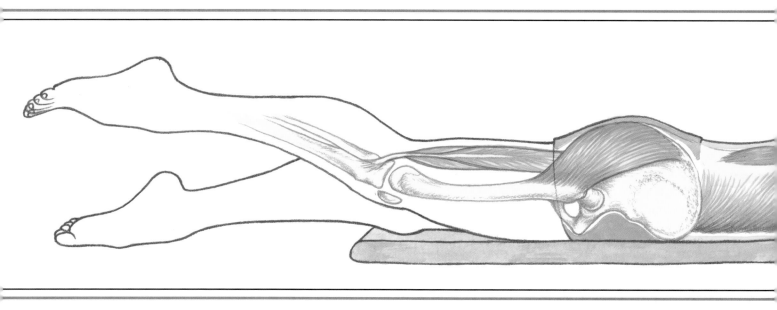

### Author's Acknowledgments
Over the past 19 years, my journey through the health sciences has been paved with brilliant teachers and students along the way. Thank you to my colleagues Sally Lee and Tanya Wyatt, two of the best health and fitness professionals I am likely to ever know, for raising the bar. This book is a creative collaboration. To artist James Berrangé, for your enthusiasm, insight and commitment in this project—without you, this book would just be a good idea. To the team at New Holland and McGraw Hill, thank you, thank you, thank you.

A book like this requires a lot of help. Abundant thanks are due to the following:
- For his mentorship, Professor Graham Louw, Department of Health Sciences, University of Cape Town
- For her generosity, Caroline Powrie, curator of the Anatomy Museum at Groote Schuur
- For making our lives simpler, Virgin Active Gym, Long Street, Cape Town
- Our fantastic models, Lara Turk and Terri Bruning of Cape Town City Ballet
- For her reliability, Glennis Harris of the ETA
- For their expediency and kind permission, David Brewer and Christa Dickey of the ACSM, David O'Brien and Gill Watson of Lippincott, Williams, and Wilkins.

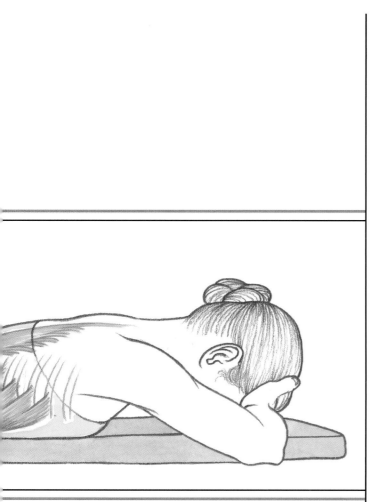

First McGraw-Hill edition, 2008

0 9 8 7 6 5 4 3 2 1

ISBN 978-0-07-149572-1
MHID      0-07-149572-X

The Library of Congress Cataloging-in-Publication Data is available on file.

The advice presented within this book requires a knowledge of proper exercise form and a base level of strength fitness. Although exercise is very beneficial, the potential for injury does exist, especially if the trainee is not in good physical condition. Always consult with your physician before beginning any program of progressive weight training or exercise. If you feel any strain or pain when you are exercising, stop immediately and consult your physician. As all systems of weight training involve a systematic progression of muscular overload, a proper warm-up of muscles, tendons, ligaments, and joints is mandatory at the beginning of every workout.

McGraw-Hill books are available at special quantity discounts to use as premiums and sales promotions, or for use in corporate training programs. For more information, please write to the Director of Special Sales, Professional Publishing, McGraw-Hill, Two Penn Plaza, New York, NY 10121-2298. Or contact your local bookseller.

Printed and bound in Singapore.

# CONTENTS

## PART 1

### ANATOMY AND EXERCISE PROGRAMS 8

Building a better you • Guide to anatomy • Exercise Analyses and Principles • Devising a Program • Exercise Programs

## PART 2

### THE EXERCISES

### 1. Aerobic Training 28

Walking • Jogging and running • Aerobics • Swimming and aqua-aerobics • Aerobic machines

### 2. Abdominals, Stabilization, and Balance 38

Posture basics • Seated ball balance • Transverse activation in four-point kneeling • Plank pose stabilization on ball • Shell prone ball roll-up • Abdominal stabilization program • Two-stage crunch • Reverse incline bench sit-up • Body-weight oblique crunch—ball between legs • Combination crunch • Hip flexor apparatus • Mid-back scapular stabilization on bench • Kneeling heel touch

### 3. Chest 56

Body-weight modified push-ups • Wall push-ups on bar • Bench press machine • Incline dumb-bell bench press • Barbell bench press • Body-weight dips • Incline pec deck machine • Dumb-bell flat bench flyes • Cable crossover

### 4. Legs and Hips 68

Squats with ball between legs • Free-standing barbell plié squats • Free-standing barbell squats • Machine incline leg press • Barbell reverse lunge • Free-standing lateral lunge • Bench step • Modified barbell bent leg deadlift • Double leg bridge with shoulder flexion • Ball bridge • Side-lying ball lift • Hip abductor machine • Hip adductor machine • Supine adductor stabilization with ball • Cable hip abductions • Prone hip extensions • Machine lying leg curl • Seesaw with ball • Yoga quad stretch with forward lean • Free-standing calf raise • Seated calf raise machine

## 5. Back and Shoulders 92

Machine cable front lateral pull-down • Chin-up assist machine • Standing cable pull-over • Standing reverse grip cable rows • Seated low cable pulley rows • Supported bent-over row machine • Dumb-bell bent-over rows • Prone back extensions on ball • Back extension apparatus • Alternate arm and leg raises on ball • Machine shoulder press • Dumb-bell seated shoulder press •Dumb-bell standing lateral raise • Rear deltoid machine •Seated bent-over dumb-bell raises on ball • Rotator cuff stabilization with theraband

## 6. Arms 112

Seated overhead tricep extension on ball with theraband • Supine bar-bell French curl • Tricep machine • Cable tricep push-down • Tricep rope pull-down • Standing barbell curl • Seated incline dumb-bell curl with supination • Dumb-bell concentration curl

## 7. Stretches and Flexibility 122

Neck and shoulder stretch • Standing chest and anterior shoulder stretch • Ball shoulder stretch • Seated side stretch on ball • Full-body stretch • Supine hip flexion stretch • Spine roll • Side-to-side hip rolls • Supine lying gluteus stretch • Supine lying single leg hamstring stretch • Seated stride into saw stretch • Supine lying deep external rotatators stretch • Standing Iliopsoas stretch • Gastrocnemius stretch • Plank to downward-facing dog • Child stretch

## Glossary 140

## Index 141

## Resources 144

Research in the last ten years has made it clear that a woman's body should be exercised differently from a man's. Additionally, due to the physiological differences and the distinct cycles of a woman's life, her training program should be adjusted to suit her body type and transformations as she moves through the various life stages. *Anatomy for Strength and Fitness Training for Women* combines valuable training information, exercise illustration, and analysis of female-specific exercises, as well as guides on how to do each exercise properly. It is a unique guide, reference, and education tool for any woman interested in understanding her own body and formulating a personal exercise program, as well as for practitioners involved in exercise science and anatomy such as trainers, teachers, and students.

## How to use this book

*Anatomy for Strength and Fitness Training for Women* is both a visual and textual analysis of common exercises, and a guide to how to do various exercises properly.

The introductory section offers an explanation of basic anatomical movement terminology and exercise analysis, as well as a self-assessment of fitness and body types that can be used in choosing a personal exercise program. The sample programs that follow illustrate how to choose a routine based on the needs you have established in the assessment.

The core of the book is the exercise section. It covers aerobic training, the development of the postural stabilizers, exercises for the chest, legs, and hips, back and shoulders, and arms, as well as static stretches. Each part begins with a basic introduction focused on the body part or type of training covered. Every exercise is covered independently, and defined and given some background. There is a "how-to" guide to doing the exercise, as well as a visual and technical exercise analysis describing which muscles are being used as mobilizers and postural stabilizers. The starting position is usually depicted in line drawings.

The adult human body has more than 600 muscles and 206 bones. In this book, emphasis is placed on the 70 or so main muscles involved in movement and stabilization. Many of the smaller muscles, as well as the deep small muscles of the spine and muscles of the hands and feet, are not given specific attention—if they were, it could take several pages to analyze just one exercise and movement.

**Schematic diagram of how the exercise pages are structured**

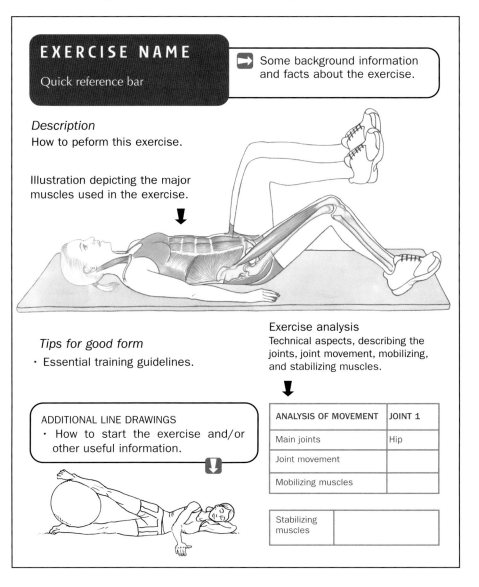

# ANATOMICAL DEFINITIONS AND TERMINOLOGY

Anatomy has its own language and, although technical, it is quite logical, originating mostly from Latin and Greek root words that make it easier to learn and understand the names of muscles, bones, and other anatomical parts.

## The musculoskeletal system

The body comprises an integration of approximately 12 distinct systems that continuously interact to control the multitude of complex bodily functions. This book specifically illustrates and analyzes the systems that control movement and posture, namely the muscular and skeletal system, which is often referred to as the musculo-skeletal system.

The skeletal system consists of bones, ligaments (which join bone to bone), and joints (technically known as articulations). Adults have 206 bones in a skeleton weighing about 18–20 lb (8–9 kg). The skeletal system acts as a movement framework. Muscles attach to bone and cross joints. Where they cross free-moving joints, contraction of the muscles causes joint movement.

The muscular system is made up of three types of muscle tissue, namely cardiac, smooth, and skeletal.

Cardiac muscle forms the heart walls, and smooth muscle tissue is found in the walls of internal organs such as the stomach and blood vessels. Both types of muscle are activated involuntarily through the autonomic nervous system and hormonal action. Of the 700 or so muscles in a woman's body, approximately 650 are skeletal muscles. On average, half of the body's weight is muscle, and three-quarters of this is water.

Muscles attach to bone via tendons. These attachment points are referred to as the origin and the insertion. The origin is the point of attachment that is proximal (closest to the root of a limb), or closest to the mid-line or center of the body. It is usually the least moveable tendon, and acts as the anchor point in muscle contraction. The insertion is the point of attachment that is distal (farthest from the root of a limb), or farthest from the mid-line or center of the body. It is usually the most moveable part and can be drawn toward the origin.

Knowing the origin and insertion points of a muscle, which joint or joints the muscle crosses, and what movement it effects at that joint or joints is a key element of exercise analysis.

## Anatomical terms
### The anatomical position

When learning anatomy and analyzing movement, we refer to the standard reference position of the human body, known as the "anatomical position." All movements and the location of the anatomical structures are named as if the person was standing in this standard position.

The anatomical position is described as follows: the body is in a standing position and facing forward, the legs and feet are together, and the arms hang loosely at the sides with the palms facing forward.

### Anatomical terms of position and direction

There are standard terms of position and direction that describe the position of body structures, or their relationship to other body parts. The human body is a complex, three-dimensional structure, and knowing the proper anatomical terms of position and direction will help you to compare one point on the body to another, and to understand where it is in relation to other anatomical structures. The terms are standard whether the person is sitting, standing, or lying down.

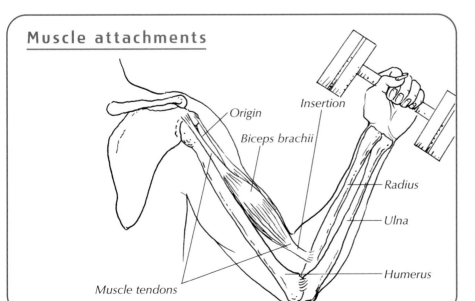

## Muscle attachments

*Origin*

*Insertion*

*Biceps brachii*

*Radius*

*Ulna*

*Humerus*

*Muscle tendons*

## Anatomical terms of position and direction

| Position | Definition | Example of usage |
|---|---|---|
| Anterior | Toward the front, pertaining to the front | The abdominal muscles are found on the anterior aspect of the body |
| Posterior | Toward the back, pertaining to the rear | The hamstring muscles are situated on the posterior aspect of the leg |
| Superior | Above another structure, toward the head | The shoulder is superior to the hip |
| Inferior | Below another structure, toward the feet | The hip is inferior to the shoulder |
| Lateral | Away from the mid-line, on or toward the outside | The outside of the knee joint is its lateral aspect |
| Medial | Toward the mid-line of the body, pertaining to the middle or center | The inside of the knee joint is its medial aspect |
| Proximal | Closest to the trunk or root of a limb. Also sometimes used to refer to the origin of a muscle | The hip joint is proximal to the knee |
| Distal | Situated away from the mid-line or center of the body, or root of a limb. Also sometimes used to refer to a point away from the origin of a muscle | The toes are the most distal part of the leg |
| Superficial | Closer to the surface of the body, more toward the surface of the body than another structure | The Rectus femoris is the most superficial of the quadricep muscles |
| Deep | Farther from the surface, relatively deeper into the body than another structure | The heart is deep to the ribs that protect it |
| Prone | Lying face downward | Prone back extensions are done, as the name suggests, from a prone lying starting position |
| Supine | Lying on the back, face upward | Abdominal crunches are performed from a supine lying starting position |

## Joint movements

Knowing and understanding the body's movements, and at which joints they occur, is essential in order to analyze an exercise.

## Types of joint

Some joints in the body are fixed or semi-fixed, allowing very little or no movement. For example, the bones of the skull join together in joint structures known as sutures to form fixed joints; but where the spine joins the pelvis, the sacroilliac joint is semi-fixed and allows minimal movement ("sacro" from sacrum, "iliac" pertaining to the pelvic crest). A third category, synovial joints, comprises free-moving joints that move in different ways determined by their particular shapes, sizes, and structures.

Synovial joints are the most common joints in the body. They are characterized by a joint capsule that surrounds the articulation, the inner membrane of which secretes lubricating synovial fluid, stimulated by movement. Typical synovial joints include the shoulders, knees, hips, and ankles, and the joints of the hands, feet, and vertebrae. Of all the joints, the knee joint is the largest, the hip joint is the strongest, and the shoulder joint is potentially the most unstable.

## Joint action

When performing an activity such as lifting weights or running, a combination of nerve stimulation and muscular contraction facilitates the movement that

ANATOMICAL DEFINITIONS AND TERMINOLOGY

occurs at the synovial joints. When doing a bicep curl, for example, the weight rises because the angle of the elbow joint closes as the bicep muscles, which attach from the upper arm bones to the forearm (radius and ulna), shorten in contraction, thereby lifting the forearm.

## Joint movement pointers

Most joint movements have common names that apply to most major joints, but there are some specific movements that only occur at one specific joint. The common joint movements occur in similar anatomical planes of motion. For example, shoulder, hip, and knee flexion all occur in the same plane. This makes it more logical and easier to learn about joint movements and movement analysis. In the table on the next page, common movements are listed first, followed by specific movements that only occur at one joint.

In general, movement is paired with the joint moved; for example, shoulder flexion, knee extension, spinal rotation, scapular depression, and so on. Strictly speaking, it is incorrect to name the movement and a limb or body part. For example, "leg extension" does not clarify where in the leg the movement occurs—at the knees, hips, or ankles.

Movements generally occur in pairs. For a "forward" movement there must be a "backward" movement to return to the original starting position. Typical pairs of movements are flexion and extension, abduction and adduction, internal rotation and external rotation, and protraction and retraction. You will notice these pairs of movements when you look at the analyses in the exercise section.

All movements are named as if the person is standing in the anatomical position as described on page 9 so, for example, "elbow flexion" is the same whether the person is standing, lying supine, or sitting.

## How a woman's body differs from a man's
### Skeletal differences

A woman's skeleton is usually smaller and smoother than that of a man. Overall she is 7 percent shorter and 8 percent smaller. However, skeletal proportions vary, so that a woman's torso is usually longer, and proportionately longer from waist to feet. With different somatotypes (see page 14) this shifts, with ectomorphs typically having longer legs than men of the same height. This increases leverage and injury risk on the knees. A woman also has a lower center of gravity than a man, giving her better balance.

## Muscle and connective tissues

Basic measures of body strength show that females generally have 30–50 percent less strength than males. This is mainly in the upper body, where men are about 40 percent stronger. Women typically have less muscle mass and more body fat. Additionally, a man's taller and wider skeletal frame provides a leverage advantage. However, "female muscle" and "male muscle" are exactly the same. There are no inherent gender differences in muscle quality or capacity, and women can generally generate the same force per unit of muscle as men. Furthermore, with training they make the same relative strength improvements.

In certain sports, such as climbing, dance, and aspects of gymnastics, the lower center of gravity, flexibility, strength-to-weight ratio, and shorter levers give a woman a better relative strength ratio.

## Fat tissue

Two types of body fat make up total body fat, namely fat stored mainly within the organs and muscles essential for the various body processes, and adipose tissue stored underneath the skin of the body. Excess fat is stored in adipose tissue.

High testosterone and growth hormone in men create greater muscle mass with higher basal metabolism-consuming energy. Men can therefore eat relatively more and expend more energy than women. Estrogen in women, on the other hand, increases fat storage in a woman's body.

Women have more essential body fat than men (12 percent as opposed to 3 percent), as well as greater body-fat percentages. For a woman in her twenties a healthy body-fat percentage would be 23–27 percent. The equivalent in a man would be 16 percent. After the age of 45, a healthy woman would have 32 percent body fat compared with 25 percent in a man.

In men, adipose fat deposition occurs mainly around the stomach. In women it is distributed between the hips and buttocks, in the inner thighs, and in small sites at the backs of the upper arms, around the navel, and medial knee. The breasts are also filled with fat, which encloses the mammary glands.

Women are more likely to experience weight fluctuations than men, particularly if they experience early menopause, or are sedentary or overweight to begin with.

Elevated fat levels are therefore a normal part of a woman's physiology. Exercise consultation should define excess versus healthy fat levels, and programming should set realistic goals and expectations of what is possible and healthy to strive for.

# Major joint movements

| GENERAL MOVEMENTS | Plane | Description | Example |
|---|---|---|---|
| Abduction | Coronal | Movement away from the mid-line | Hip abduction |
| Adduction | Coronal | Movement toward the mid-line | Hip adduction |
| Flexion | Sagittal | Decreasing the angle between two structures | Moving the forearm toward the upper arm. Standing Barbell Curl |
| Extension | Sagittal | Increasing the angle between two structures | Moving the forearm away from the upper arm. As above, downward phase |
| Medial rotation (internal rotation) | Transverse | Turning around the vertical axis of a bone toward the mid-line | Cable Crossover |
| Lateral rotation (external/outward rotation) | Transverse | Turning around the vertical axis of a bone away from the mid-line | Turning at the waist |
| Circumduction | All planes | Complete circular movement at shoulder or hip joints | Swinging the arms in circles |
| **SPECIFIC MOVEMENTS** | | | |
| **1. Ankle movements** | | | |
| Plantarflexion | Sagittal | Moving the foot downward | Free-standing Calf Raise (upward phase) |
| Dorsiflexion (Dorsal flexion) | Sagittal | Moving the foot toward the shin | Free-standing Standing Calf Raise (downward phase) |
| **2. Forearm movements (the radioulnar joint)** | | | |
| Pronation | Transverse | Rotating the wrist and hand medially from the elbow | Standing Dumb-bell Curl |
| Supination | Transverse | Rotating the wrist and hand laterally from the elbow | Making circular movements with your hand |
| **3. Scapula movements** | | | |
| Depression | Coronal | Movement of the scapulae inferiorly, e.g. squeezing scapulae downward | To stabilize the shoulder girdle, e.g. Hip Flexor Apparatus |
| Elevation | Coronal | Movement of the scapulae superiorly, e.g. hunching the shoulders | Dumb-bell Seated Shoulder Press (up) |
| Abduction (protraction) | Transverse | Movement of the scapulae away from the spine | Seated Low Cable Pulley Rows |
| Adduction (retraction) | Transverse | Movement of the scapulae toward the spine | As above |
| Downward rotation (medial rotation) | Coronal | Scapulae rotate downward, in the return from upward rotation | Machine Cable Front Lateral Pull-down |
| Upward rotation (lateral rotation) | Coronal | Scapulae rotate upward. The inferior borders of the scapulae move laterally and upward | As above |

*ANATOMICAL DEFINITIONS AND TERMINOLOGY*

| 4. Shoulder movements | | | |
|---|---|---|---|
| Horizontal abduction/extension (transverse abduction) | Transverse | Movement of the humerus across the body away from the mid-line | Dumb-bell Flat Bench Flyes |
| Horizontal adduction/flexion (transverse adduction) | Transverse | Movement of the humerus across the body toward the mid-line | As above |
| 5. Spine/trunk movements | | | |
| Lateral flexion | Coronal | Movement of the trunk away from the mid-line in the coronal plane | Seated Side Stretch on Ball |

## Joint movements

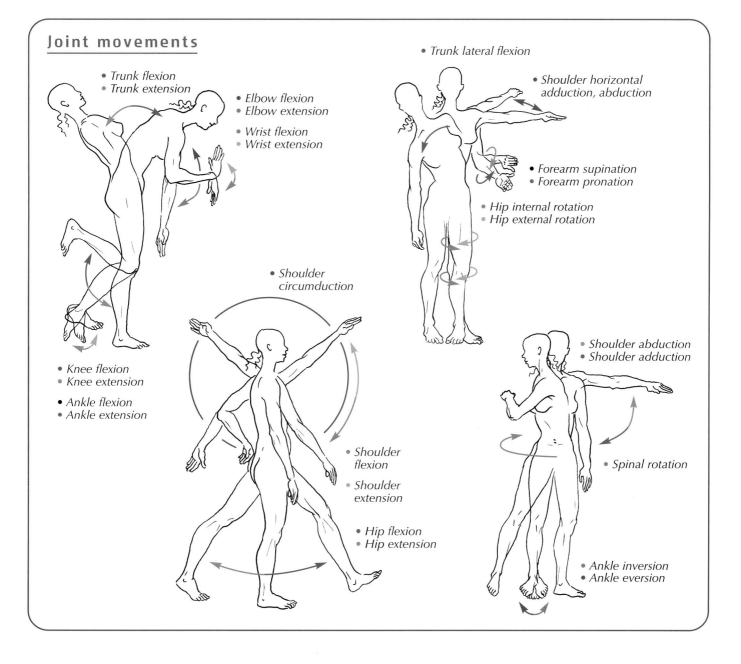

- *Trunk flexion*
- *Trunk extension*

- *Elbow flexion*
- *Elbow extension*

- *Wrist flexion*
- *Wrist extension*

- *Trunk lateral flexion*

- *Shoulder horizontal adduction, abduction*

- *Forearm supination*
- *Forearm pronation*

- *Hip internal rotation*
- *Hip external rotation*

- *Shoulder circumduction*

- *Knee flexion*
- *Knee extension*

- *Ankle flexion*
- *Ankle extension*

- *Shoulder flexion*
- *Shoulder extension*

- *Hip flexion*
- *Hip extension*

- *Shoulder abduction*
- *Shoulder adduction*

- *Spinal rotation*

- *Ankle inversion*
- *Ankle eversion*

## Purpose of exercise analysis

Analyzing an exercise enables you to understand what joints and muscles are being used in a certain movement and how they are moving. Changing the movement, or doing the movement incorrectly, affects both the muscles used to perform the exercise and how they are used. Exercise analysis can also help you to determine if the muscles you intend to train are, in fact, being utilized in the specific exercise being done, as well as whether you are doing the exercise correctly.

## Somatotyping

The word "somatotyping" literally means "body typing." The term is used in a system of classification of human physical types, according to which human beings can be grouped in terms of three extreme body types. Endomorphs tend to relative fatness, mesomorphs to relative musculoskeletal robustness or muscularity, and ectomorphs to relative linearity or slenderness. Assessing your somatotype will indicate what your particular mix of these three types is. In turn, the somatotype will suggest certain traits—for example, ectomorphs often show better aerobic ability than endomorphs, who show better power and strength capacity.

## Endomorphs

Female endomorphs tend to be pear-shaped (which means that they carry weight mainly around the hips), and convert to more of an apple shape after the menopause. This is due to increased intra-abdominal fat being laid down in the abdomen at this time. Male endomorphs tend to be apple-shaped, that is abdominally obese. Overall, endomorphs struggle to lose weight and tend to gain it more easily than the other somatotypes. Women are more likely to be endomorphic than men.

## Mesomorphs

Female mesomorphs tend to be hour-glass shaped, with smaller waists compared with the bust and hips, which are the same size. This shape, although popular, is less common in women than in men.

## Ectomorphs

Ectomorphic women struggle to gain weight and have less curvature and shape than the other somatypes. While they recover relatively quickly from exercise, their longer levers and reduced muscle mass increase their need for postural and strength conditioning.

## Starting out

As you kindle the exercise habit, expect to go through three distinct phases. Knowing these will help put your feelings in each phase into perspective. It is quite normal for progress to seldom be smooth from one phase to another. It is common to have lapses and relapses, but with consistent perseverance you will move through them. If you get bored easily, introduce some variation to your program. It may also be an idea to train, initially at least, with an exercise partner.

## The three phases of motivation

### Resistance phase

In this initial phase, which lasts 6–12 weeks, expect your motivation to be relatively low and your resistance to exercise to be high. The key is to try to be consistent. Keep your workout appointments. The program should be fairly uncomplicated and err on the conservative side, but challenging enough to feel worthwhile. This phase often reveals what the assessment did not, and may lead to you to reconsider your goals or choice of program. While you might not be seeing much physical change, you should feel some improvement by the third week. Most people report better sleep as the first change.

### Transition phase

In the second phase, which lasts some 3–6 months, physical results should have started to show. You may start to over-train because you are tempted to try for more changes. Instead, keep trying to get maximum results from minimum effort. Use your three-month fitness reassessment to make necessary adjustments in your program based on how your test scores have changed. You should also begin to become more aware of the subtler aspects of your fitness and health. Training frequency usually reaches its peak by this stage.

### Intrinsic phase

This point is reached when your motivation to exercise comes from the inside and is an established lifestyle habit. You may by now have homed in on some aspect of training you enjoy, such as aerobics or swimming, and be including exercise as an established part of your diary. To offset a training plateau and prevent getting into a complete rut, try to vary the program every three months or so. This may also be a good time to consult a specialist trainer to further individualize your training, or acquire more technical information and skills.

## Principles you should know

Functional training involves using your body in a way that is similar to day-to-day movement. Most functional training employs compound exercises, namely those that use more than one muscle group and joint at a time, and that are generally close-chain and weight-bearing. Functional training is a part of health-related fitness, which is a part of everyday health, ensuring optimum quality of life for everyday demands. It is usually defined by the variables of cardiovascular fitness, flexibility, strength, strength endurance, and flexibility, with cardiovascular fitness being regarded as the most important because it has the greatest influence on our health. The definition has begun to also consider and include aspects such as postural strength.

The principles of exercise are based on the laws of nature. Understanding them will help you exercise in a safe and effective manner, and ensure the best results.

### SAID principle

According to the principle of Specific Adaptation to Imposed Demands (SAID), your body will change predictably, through an adaptive process, in response to the exercise demands that are placed on it. This means that if you stretch regularly (stimulus) it can improve your flexibility (response), as your body becomes more supple (adaptation) to handle the increased range of movement demands placed on it. Each component of physical fitness can be developed and trained. The adaptation is also specific to the response. If you run regularly, you will become a better runner. If you cycle regularly, you will become a better cyclist. Your training program should thus be specific to the desired response.

This principle also illustrates why it is important to train in postures and functional positions, and in a manner that is closest to the demands of your life. For example, exercising in standing positions contributes to strengthening the spine and trunk, and leg stabilizers, contributing to their fitness for everyday activities. How fast adaptation will occur varies between individuals, but those just beginning to exercise or in the low ranges of functional capacity are likely to improve the quickest.

### Overload principle

In order to gain improvement in fitness, the body must be stimulated beyond its current capacity. Therefore, if you wish to gain strength, you must train with a weight stimulus that is higher than your current capacity. This amount of stimulus is called the overload. Too great an overload can, however, cause injury.

### FITT principle

There are four major variables of overload to any training plan or exercise prescription. These are frequency, intensity, type, and time or duration. Your training program will be incomplete if these are not incorporated into your plan. To maximize overload you can increase training in any of the four major variables.

### Progression principle

Over time, adaptation to the initial training stimulus occurs. To overcome this plateau, the overload must further increase.

### Reversibility principle

It is often said, "Use it or lose it." This is a simple illustration of the reversibility principle. Adaptation made through training stimulus may be lost if the stimulus is discontinued.

### Rest/effort balance principle

Rest and recovery periods are as much a part of training as is training itself, and must be balanced with training. Resting too much results in regression, whereas training too much results in overtraining.

Health-related exercise programs should include a good range of variety, especially as you get fitter, and a training program should balance safety and effectiveness.

## A note on nutrition

For consistent training effort you need sustainable energy. To achieve this you must give your body the nutritional quality and quantity it requires. Wholefoods such as grains, pulses, fruits, vegetables, seeds, and nuts are completely or only minimally processed and refined. They contain a relatively balanced and complete nutrient profile. Make sure you include plenty of them in your diet. Minimize commercially processed and refined foods rich in additives and preservatives, fried and fast foods. Moderate your intake of caffeine, alcohol, refined sugar, and dairy and animal proteins, and drink fresh water on a regular basis.

Minimizing the substances and influences that rob the body of potential nutrients is important. These include smoking, alcohol, stress, medications, and pollutants, which can inhibit absorption, increase nutrient requirements, and promote poor digestion. Eating habits like chewing food slowly and thoroughly, not skipping meals, allowing time for digestion, and having a healthy attitude toward eating are as important as what you eat. Avoid manipulating a nutrition plan to justify what are obviously unhealthy habits.

There is no such thing as the perfect program—but there is the perfect program for you; one that best suits your needs and goals, based on improving your present weaknesses, and optimizing your strengths. In order to measure your present physical fitness objectively, some basic health-related fitness tests should be done. Subjective measures ("I look or feel too fat," or "I need to lose 20 pounds") are often inaccurate because they tend to be driven by our emotions rather than by objective reality.

Professional fitness testing is a service worth paying for if you have access to a gym or health center that offers tests from qualified instructors. A qualified health professional can also help you to obtain a more accurate interpretation of the results of your tests, and offer more specific and individualized advice.

To get started, use the basic five-part assessment shown opposite. This has been adapted from standard protocols. It assesses body type and four important components of health-related fitness that will help you determine which exercise program is best for you. From the interpretation of your results you will be directed to a suitable program for your needs.

## Step 1: Pre-exercise Screening

This will help you clear and confirm your readiness for exercise. Before commencing a test or exercise program it is important to check your physical fitness. If you answer "yes" to any of the questions in the following questionnaire, you should contact your doctor for clearance before starting any fitness test or exercise routine.

1. Are you female and above the age of 55?

2. Does your family have a history of heart attacks or sudden deaths before the age of 55 in first-degree males (brother, father), or before 65 in first-degree females (sister, mother)?

3. Do you have any diagnosed or suspected heart or lung disease?

4. Are you HIV positive?

5. Do you have any neuromuscular, musculoskeletal, or rheumatoid disorders that would be exacerbated by exercise?

6. Do you currently smoke or have you quit within the last six months?

7. Is your blood pressure over 140/90 mmHg (taken at least twice on separate occasions) or are you on anti-hypertensive medications?

8. Is your total serum cholesterol more than 200mg/dL or are your high-density lipoproteins less than 35 mg/dl?

9. Have you been diagnosed with insulin-dependent diabetes mellitus?

10. Are you currently physically inactive?

11. Do you have episodes of fainting, unusual fatigue, pain, shortness of breath, palpitations, or dizziness?

12. Have you been advised not to exercise by a health-care professional?

13. Do you have any other illness or injury that may be aggravated by physical activity?

14. Are you pregnant, or have you given birth in the last three months?

15. Have you had any surgery within the past three months?

16. Do you know of any other reason why you should not engage in physical activity?

## Step 2: Home Fitness Assessment

This will assist you in determining which program is right for you. Do the tests below and opposite on one day in sequence. Avoid having a heavy meal two hours before doing the tests, and wear comfortable, loose clothing. To be effective, the assessment should be done following the instructions precisely. Repeat the assessment in three months, and thereafter every six months to get a valid idea of improvements as well as possible adjustments that are needed in your program. If you feel faint or dizzy at any stage, stop and contact your doctor before repeating the assessment.

### Fitness assessment test

**BODY MEASUREMENTS**

**TEST Height (inches)**
Standing, without shoes. Take measurement perpendicular to crown.

RESULT Inches [..............]

**TEST Weight (pounds)**
Standing, without shoes. Preferably use a beam balance scale (found in many gyms).

RESULT Pounds [..............]

**TEST Body Composition – Body Mass Index (BMI)**
This is the measure of mass per height. Determine it by dividing your mass (in pounds) by the square of your height in inches. This gives a result measured in pounds per $in^2$.

RESULT lb per $in^2$ [..............]

## TEST Body Type

Choose the somatotype that applies most to you.

| Endomorph | Mesomorph | Ectomorph |
|---|---|---|
| Round shape: apple or pear | Hourglass shape | Ruler shaped |
| Waist and hips larger | Bust and hips same, waist smaller | Narrow waist and hips, small bust |
| Big-boned | Balanced limbs and relatively good shape | Fine-boned. Thin, linear appearance |
| Limbs relatively short | | |
| Comparatively small hands | Upright posture | Shorter upper body, longer limbs |
| High waist | Gains and loses weight with reasonable effort | Stooped shoulders |
| Overactive digestive system | | Struggles to gain weight |
| Gains weight easily | Physical character | Loses weight easily |
| Struggles to lose weight | | Intellectual character |
| Emotional character | | |

If you encircle your wrist with the middle finger and thumb of your opposite hand:

| Middle finger and thumb do not touch | Middle finger and thumb just touch | Middle finger and thumb overlap |
|---|---|---|

RESULT Body type [_____morph]

## TEST Resting Heart Rate

Sitting relaxed, take your pulse for one complete minute at the brachial pulse (wrist) or carotid (neck). Start counting at zero.

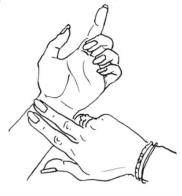

RESULT Beats/minute [_____]

## TEST Flexibility: Sit-and-reach

This test normally measures flexibility by assessing how far a person can reach along a sit-and-reach board. You can make your own makeshift board at home by taping a tape measure to the ground. Sit on the floor with your legs fully extended, feet upright, and shoes off. Run the tape measure away from you between your legs, with the mark in line with the base of your feet being 10 in (26 cm). Place one hand on top of the other and with fingertips aligned, reach forward with your arms and hands fully extended. Breathe out when bending forward and hold for three seconds at the farthest point. Note the distance in inches. Your score is the longest point reached after three trials.

RESULT Inches [_____]

## TEST Strength Endurance: Modified Push-ups to Fatigue

The aim is to perform as many modified push-ups in a rhythmic manner and with no rest as you can. In the "up" position the arms should be fully extended, and in the "down" position they should be 2 in (5 cm) from the ground. There is no time limit—stop the test when you cannot maintain proper technique and pace, or when there is forced strain. This test also gives an idea of postural strength. If you cannot perform the test with proper technique, i.e. with the shoulders, waist, and knees in a straight line, this indicates weak postural strength. Alternatively, you can do push-ups with the hips up and record your result, although this will over-estimate your strength endurance.

RESULT Repetitions [_____]

## TEST Aerobic: YMCA 3-minute Step

This is one of the most universally used fitness tests. It measures cardiovascular recovery and is based on the linear relationship between aerobic fitness and recovery. The quicker you recover, the fitter your aerobic component. You need a step-up box 12 in (30.5 cm) high, wide enough to place both feet on, a stopwatch and a metronome set to 96 beats per minute. Step up and down on the box for three continuous minutes to the 96 beats pace, i.e. 24 stepping cycles per minute. At the end of the three minutes, immediately sit on the box, and record the total number of pulse beats (see above) in the minute after exercise. You must start counting within five seconds of completing stepping.

RESULT Beats [_____]

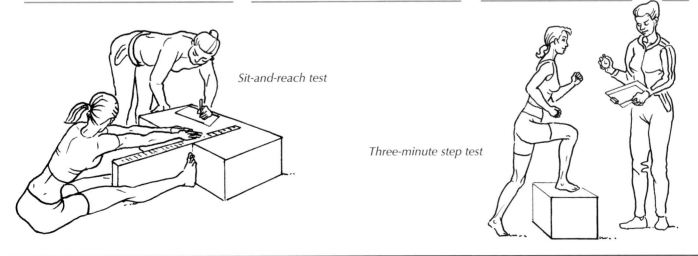

Sit-and-reach test

Three-minute step test

## Step 3: Test Scoring and Interpretation of Results

Use Tables 1, 2, and 3 below and opposite to find out how you score and rank relative to your age group. Write your results into Table 4 on page 20. The basic idea is to match an exercise program based on the results of the test. Use the guidelines in Table 4 to choose the program best suited to your needs.

Note that all tests are relative to the population being assessed and where the norms assessed against derive. In addition, estimation of body composition from BMI carries up to a 5 percent error margin.

## Table 1: Rating of Body Mass Index and Estimation of Body Composition (Fat Percent)

Find your BMI under the BMI column. To the left note the category, and to the right note the estimated health risk associated with your BMI. Then match your age and BMI to get your estimated body composition (fat percent). Write down the results and fill in Table 4. Note that the index does have limitations. The test is only a crude measure of heaviness. Scores tend to be less accurate with very lean, overweight, and abdominally obese individuals. If you can, get your body composition measured at your local gym or health center using the skinfold testing method. Special calipers are used to measure certain sites and body fat percentage is calculated using a formula.

## Table 2: Scoring, Ranking, and Category of Your Estimated Body Composition, Sit-and-reach Test, and Push-ups Test

Find the column matching your age group. Find where you score in each test. Find the rank and category matching that score by following to the left of the table. Take note of the results and fill in Table 4.

| Table 1 | | | | | |
|---|---|---|---|---|---|
| Category | BMI | Health Risk | 20–39 years | 40–59 years | 60–79 years |
| Underweight | <18.5 | Elevated | <21% | <23% | <24% |
| Normal | 18.5–24.9 | Average | 21%–32% | 23%–33% | 24%–35% |
| Overweight | 25–29.9 | Elevated | 33%–38% | 34%–39% | 36%–41% |
| Obesity, class: | | | | | |
| I | 30–34.9 | High | ≥39% | ≥40% | ≥42% |
| II | 35–39.9 | High | ≥39% | ≥40% | ≥42% |
| III | ≥40 | High | ≥39% | ≥40% | ≥42% |

Modified from Expert panel: "Executive summary of the clinical guidelines on the identification, evaluation, and treatment of overweight and obesity in adults," *Arch Intern Med*, 1998, 158: 1855–1867. Gallagher D., Heymsfield, S.B., Heo M., et al., "Healthy percentage body fat ranges: an approach for developing guidelines based on Body Mass Index," *Am J Clin Nutr*, 2000, 72: 694–701.

| Table 2 (20–49 years) | | Age 20–29 years | | | Age 30–39 years | | | Age 40–49 years | | |
|---|---|---|---|---|---|---|---|---|---|---|
| Category | Rank | Body Composition % | Sit-and-reach inches | Modified Push-ups | Body Composition % | Sit-and-reach inches | Modified Push-ups | Body Composition % | Sit-and-reach inches | Modified Push-ups |
| Well above average | 90%+ | <14.9 | ≥17 | ≥32 | <15.5 | ≥16½ | ≥31 | ≤18.5 | ≥15¾ | ≥28 |
| Above average | 70–89% | 19–15 | 15–16½ | 22–31 | 20–15.6 | 14½–16 | 21–30 | 23.5–18.6 | 14–15¼ | 18–27 |
| Average | 50–69% | 22.1–19.1 | 13½–14½ | 16–21 | 23.1–20.1 | 13–14 | 14–20 | 26.4–23.6 | 12–13½ | 12–17 |
| Below average | 30–49% | 25.4–22.2 | 11½–13 | 11–15 | 27–23.2 | 11–12½ | 10–13 | 30.1–26.5 | 10¼–12 | 7–11 |
| Well below average | 10–29% | 32.1–25.5 | 8¾–11 | 5–10 | 32.8–27.1 | 8½–10½ | 4–9 | 35–30.2 | 7½–10 | 2–5 |

| Table 2 (50–69 years) Category | Rank | Age 50–59 years | | | Age 60–69 years | | | |
|---|---|---|---|---|---|---|---|---|
| | | Body Composition % | Sit-and-reach inches | Modified Push-ups | Body Composition % | Sit-and-reach inches | Modified Push-ups | |
| Well above average | 90%+ | <21.6 | ≥15¾ | ≥28 | ≤21.1 | ≥37 | ≥25 | Adapted from: *Body composition data*, Cooper Institute for Aerobic Research (1994). |
| Above average | 70–89% | 26.6–21.7 | 13¾–15¼ | 13–22 | 27.5–21.2 | 31.36 | 12–24 | |
| Average | 50–69% | 30.1–26.7 | 12–13½ | 9–12 | 30.9–27.6 | 28–30 | 6–11 | Push-up and Sit-and-reach based on *Canadian Standardized Test of Fitness Operations Manual*, 3rd edition (1981). |
| Below average | 30–49% | 33.5–30.2 | 10¼–11½ | 3–8 | 34.3–31 | 24–27 | 2–5 | |
| Well below average | 10–29% | 37.9–33.6 | 7½–10 | – | 39.3–34.5 | 18–23 | – | |

## Table 3: Scoring, Ranking, and Category of your Resting Heart Rate and Step Test

Find the column matching your age group. In each test, find your score. Find the rank and category matching that score by following to the left of the table. Take note of the results and fill in Table 4.

| Table 3 (18–45 years) Category | Rank | Age 18–25 years | | Age 26–35 years | | Age 36–45 years | |
|---|---|---|---|---|---|---|---|
| | | Resting Heart Rate | Step Test | Resting Heart Rate | Step Test | Resting Heart Rate | Step Test |
| Well above average | 90%+ | ≤60 | ≤83 | ≤59 | ≤86 | ≤59 | ≤87 |
| Above average | 70–89% | 66–59 | 100–84 | 66–60 | 103–87 | 66–60 | 104–88 |
| Average | 50–69% | 72–66 | 112–101 | 70–67 | 116–104 | 71–67 | 114–105 |
| Below average | 30–49% | 78–73 | 124–113 | 76–71 | 127–117 | 78–72 | 127–115 |
| Well below average | 10–29% | 86–79 | 142–125 | 84–77 | 141–128 | 84–77 | 143–128 |

| Table 3 (46–65 years) Category | Rank | Age 46–55 years | | Age 56–65 years | | Age >65 years | |
|---|---|---|---|---|---|---|---|
| | | Resting Heart Rate | Step Test | Resting Heart Rate | Step Test | Resting Heart Rate | Step Test |
| Well above average | 90%+ | ≤60 | ≤93 | ≤59 | ≤92 | ≤59 | ≤86 |
| Above average | 70–89% | 66–61 | 106–94 | 67–60 | 106–93 | 66–60 | 104–87 |
| Average | 50–69% | 72–67 | 118–107 | 72–68 | 116–107 | 71–67 | 120–105 |
| Below average | 30–49% | 77–73 | 126–119 | 77–73 | 127–117 | 76–72 | 127–121 |
| Well below average | 10–29% | 85–78 | 138–127 | 85–78 | 142–128 | 88–77 | 135–128 |

Adapted from: *Heart Rate and Step Test: Y's Way to Physical Fitness*, Golding, L.A., PhD, Myers, C.A., PhD and Sinning, W.E., PhD, 2nd edition.

| Table 4 Fitness component | Test | Result/Score | | Rank | | Category | |
|---|---|---|---|---|---|---|---|
| | | Assess Date ............. | Reassess Date ............. | Assess Date ............. | Reassess Date ............. | Assess Date ............. | Reassess Date ............. |
| Somatotype | Visual estimation of body type | Always the same | | | | | |
| Body composition | BMI/percent fat estimation from BMI | | | | | | |
| Flexibility | Sit-and-reach test | | | | | | |
| Strength endurance | Modified push-ups to fatigue | | | | | | |
| Resting heart rate | 1-minute resting pulse | | | | | | |
| Aerobic fitness | Step-test post-exercise 1-minute recovery heart rate | | | | | | |

## Table 4: Record of Assessment Results

Using the information from the tables on the previous pages, fill in Table 4 above. Space has also been set aside for your reassessment date in three months' time. You can also compare the changes in your weight and body measurements.

## Step 4: Choosing a Program

After you have completed your tests, use the charts on the right to choose the right program for you. Within that program, choose the part that matches your body type. Use your second fitness test to determine your next program.

## Choosing the right program

**If your results were:**

Mostly below average or well below average (two out of three from the strength endurance, body composition, and aerobic fitness), especially if you are just starting at a gym.

**Choose:**

Program 1, beginner phase progressing to intermediate phase.

**If your results were:**

Mostly below average (two out of three from the strength endurance, body composition, and aerobic fitness), especially if you are just starting at a gym.

**Choose:**

Program 1, intermediate phase progressing to program 2 if your aerobic and body composition scores were lower, or program 3 if your strength scores were lower.

**If your results were:**

Mostly average or above, with poorer results in your aerobic fitness and body composition, and you are not a novice at a gym.

**Choose:**

Program 2, then use your second fitness test to determine your next program. This program is focused on helping you with weight loss and aerobic fitness goals.

**If your results were:**

Mostly average or above, with poorer results in your strength endurance and body composition, and you are not a novice at a gym.

**Choose:**

Program 3, then use your second fitness test to determine your next program. This program is focused on helping you with strength conditioning and toning.

**If your results were:**

Mostly average or above, with poorer results in your strength endurance and flexibility, and you are not a novice at a gym.

**Choose:**

Program 4, then use your second fitness test to determine your next program. This program is focused on helping you with postural and functional strength, and flexibility.

---

**If your results were:**

Mostly average or above, and if you are over 55 and/or want a specific home training program.

**Choose:**

Program 5, then if you consider joining a gym, use your second fitness test to determine your next program. This program is focused on helping you with postural and functional strength, and flexibility.

---

**If your results were:**

Flexibility was your poorest score at below average or below.

**Choose:**

Consider adding a specific stretching program to the end of your normal training routine. Choose 6–12 stretches from the final exercise section, and do them three times a week. Vary the stretches.

# EXERCISE PROGRAMS

The exercise programs contained in this section are sample programs. Each exercise chosen is included in Part 2. Although aerobic and strength components are included, stretches are omitted, except in program 5. Each program includes variations for the different body types. Choose the variation that matches your body type. Additional walking, running/walking, and running aerobics programs are included in the section on aerobic training, which begins on page 28.

Note that these programs take into account general needs, but cannot account for all specific individual needs. In the advanced phase, it is recommended that you consult a qualified exercise professional who can tailor your program to your needs.

Because of your genetic traits and the principles of adaptation, once an intermediate to advanced level of fitness has been reached, incremental improvements in fitness are smaller and more specific. Overload progressions are also smaller.

Once you have been using the same program for a while, you will reach a training plateau, when results will not be as noticeable as they were when you started the program. To overcome this, your programming should be more individualized, and there should be greater variation in the intensity, type, and duration of exercise. A trend of moderate seasonal cycles works very well. For example, during winter focus on building a good base of aerobic and strength fitness; in spring and summer focus more on toning and shorter, more intense workouts, all performed within the general trend of your individual program goals.

## General guidelines for strength training

· Include time for a proper warm-up, especially of those muscles and joints that will be worked in a specific training session. When doing aerobics training first, this will act as a warm-up.

· "Max" in the programs refers to doing the maximum repetitions possible using the correct technique.

· Figures for intensity are provided with each program. For a detailed explanation of training intensity, refer to page 28.

· To set weight, use a weight that allows you to do all repetitions with good form, with the last two repetitions being difficult, but not impossible. If you are feeling stiff the next day, ease off your training intensity. You should notice the effect of having trained, but it should not hinder you physically or give you pain. Learn the difference between "good pain" (training effort) and "bad pain" (injury). The latter is a warning sign that should not be ignored.

# PROGRAM 1: GENERAL CONDITIONING PROGRAM/Beginner Phase

## Endomorph Program

Suitable for gym beginners • Gym program • Frequency 3 x week (alternate days) • Intensity 4–6/10 • Faster repetition speed
• Rest periods 30–60 seconds

| Aerobic training: choose from stationary cycle, rowing machine, treadmill, elliptical machine, swimming (avoid step machine) | Weeks 1–2 6–8 minutes | Weeks 3–4 8–12 minutes | Weeks 5–6 10–20 minutes |
|---|---|---|---|
| 1. Wall Push-ups on Bar | 2 x 12 | 2 x 15 | 2 x 18 |
| 2. Squats with Ball between Legs | 1 x 15 | 2 x 12 | 2 x 15 |
| 3. Hip Adductor Machine | 1 x 15 | 2 x 12 | 2 x 15 |
| 4. Hip Abductor Machine | 1 x 15 | 2 x 12 | 2 x 15 |
| 5. Free-standing Calf Raise | 1 x 15 | 2 x 12 | 2 x 15 |
| 6. Double Leg Bridge with Shoulder Flexion | 2 x 12 | 2 x 12 | 2 x 15 |
| 7. Machine Cable Front Lateral Pull-down | 1 x 15 | 2 x 12 | 2 x 15 |
| 8. Dumb-bell Standing Lateral Raise | 1 x 12 | 2 x 8 | 2 x 12 |
| 9. Cable Tricep Push-down | 1 x 12 | 2 x 8 | 2 x 12 |
| 10. Transverse Activation in 4-point Kneeling | 1 x 12 | 2 x 8 | 2 x 12 |
| 11. Abdominal Stabilization Program | 1 x max | 2 x max | 3 x max |
| 12. Two-stage Crunch | 1 x max | 2 x max | 3 x max |

## Mesomorph Program

Suitable for gym beginners • Gym program • Frequency 3 x week (alternate days) • Intensity 4–6/10
• Rest periods 30–60 seconds

| Aerobic training: choose from stationary cycle, rowing machine, treadmill, elliptical machine, swimming (avoid step machine) | Weeks 1–2 5–8 minutes | Weeks 3–4 6–10 minutes | Weeks 5–6 8–15 minutes |
|---|---|---|---|
| 1. Body-weight Modified Push-ups | 1 x 12 | 2 x 8 | 2 x 12 |
| 2. Squats with Ball between Legs | 1 x 12 | 2 x 8 | 2 x 12 |
| 3. Hip Adductor Machine | 1 x 12 | 2 x 8 | 2 x 12 |
| 4. Hip Abductor Machine | 1 x 12 | 2 x 8 | 2 x 12 |
| 5. Free-standing Calf Raise | 1 x 12 | 2 x 8 | 2 x 12 |
| 6. Double Leg Bridge with Shoulder Flexion | 1 x 12 | 2 x 8 | 2 x 12 |
| 7. Machine Cable Front Lateral Pull-down | 1 x 12 | 2 x 8 | 2 x 12 |
| 8. Standing Barbell Curl | 1 x 10 | 2 x 8 | 2 x 10 |
| 9. Cable Tricep Push-down | 1 x 10 | 2 x 8 | 2 x 10 |
| 10. Transverse Activation in 4-point Kneeling | 1 x 10 | 2 x 8 | 2 x 10 |
| 11. Abdominal Stabilization Program | 1 x max | 2 x max | 3 x max |
| 12. Two-stage Crunch | 1 x max | 2 x max | 3 x max |

## Ectomorph Program

Suitable for gym beginners • Gym program • Frequency 3 x week (alternate days) • Intensity 4–6/10 • Slower repetition speed
• Rest periods 45–90 seconds

| Aerobic training: choose from stationary cycle, step, rowing machine, treadmill (avoid elliptical machine) | Weeks 1–2 6–6 minutes | Weeks 3–4 5–10 minutes | Weeks 5–6 6–12 minutes |
|---|---|---|---|
| 1. Body-weight Modified Push-up | 2 x 6 | 2 x 8 | 3 x 6 |
| 2. Machine Incline Leg Press | 2 x 8 | 3 x 6 | 3 x 6 |
| 3. Free-standing Barbell Plié Squats | 2 x 8 | 2 x 8 | 3 x 6 |
| 4. Free-standing Calf Raise | 1 x 15 | 2 x 12 | 2 x 15 |
| 5. Double Leg Bridge with Shoulder Flexion | 2 x 8 | 2 x 8 | 3 x 6 |
| 6. Machine Cable Front Lateral Pull-down | 2 x 8 | 3 x 6 | 3 x 6 |
| 7. Supported Bent-over Row Machine | 2 x 8 | 3 x 6 | 3 x 6 |
| 8. Standing Barbell Curl | 2 x 6 | 2 x 8 | 2 x 8 |
| 9. Dumb-bell Standing Lateral Raise | 2 x 6 | 2 x 8 | 2 x 8 |
| 10. Seated Tricep Machine | 2 x 6 | 2 x 8 | 2 x 8 |
| 11. Abdominal Stabilization Program | 1 x max | 2 x max | 3 x max |
| 12. Body-weight Oblique Crunch—Ball between Legs | 1 x max | 2 x max | 3 x max |

# PROGRAM 1: GENERAL CONDITIONING PROGRAM/Intermediate Phase

## Endomorph Program

Suitable for gym beginners • Gym program • Frequency 3 x week (alternate days) • Intensity 5–7/10 • Faster repetition speed • Rest periods 15–60 seconds

| Aerobic training: choose from stationary cycle, rowing machine, treadmill, elliptical machine, swimming (avoid step machine) | Weeks 1–2 15–25 minutes | Weeks 3–4 20–30 minutes | Weeks 5–6 25–35 minutes |
|---|---|---|---|
| 1. Machine Bench Press | 2 x 15 | 2 x 18 | 2 x 22 |
| 2. Barbell Reverse Lunge | 2 x 15 | 2 x 18 | 2 x 22 |
| 3. Double Leg Bridge with Shoulder Flexion | 2 x 15 | 2 x 18 | 2 x 22 |
| 4. Supine Adductor Stabilization with Ball | 2 x 15 | 2 x 18 | 2 x 22 |
| 5. Machine Cable Front Lateral Pull-down | 2 x 15 | 2 x 18 | 2 x 22 |
| 6. Supported Bent-over Row Machine | 2 x 15 | 2 x 18 | 2 x 22 |
| 7. Dumb-bell Seated Shoulder Press | 2 x 8 | 2 x 12 | 2 x 15 |
| 8. Cable Tricep Push-down | 2 x 10 | 2 x 12 | 2 x 15 |
| 9. Rotator Cuff Stabilization with Theraband | 2 x 10 | 2 x 12 | 2 x 15 |
| 10. Abdominal Stabilization Program | 2 x max | 3 x max | 3 x max |
| 11. Two-stage Crunch | 2 x max | 3 x max | 3 x max |

## Mesomorph Program

Suitable for intermediate level • Gym program • Frequency 3 x week (alternate days) • Intensity 5–7/10 • Rest periods 15–60 seconds

| Aerobic training: choose from stationary cycle, rowing machine, treadmill, elliptical machine, swimming, step machine | Weeks 1–2 12–20 minutes | Weeks 3–4 15–25 minutes | Weeks 5–6 18–30 minutes |
|---|---|---|---|
| 1. Machine Bench Press | 2 x 15 | 3 x 12 | 3 x 15 |
| 2. Machine Incline Leg Press | 2 x 15 | 3 x 12 | 3 x 15 |
| 3. Double Leg Bridge with Shoulder Flexion | 2 x 15 | 3 x 12 | 3 x 15 |
| 4. Cable Hip Abductions | 2 x 15 | 3 x 12 | 3 x 15 |
| 5. Machine Cable Front Pull-down | 2 x 15 | 3 x 12 | 3 x 15 |
| 6. Supported Bent-over Row Machine | 2 x 15 | 3 x 12 | 3 x 15 |
| 7. Dumb-bell Seated Shoulder Press | 2 x 12 | 2 x 15 | 3 x 12 |
| 8. Standing Barbell Curl | 2 x 12 | 2 x 15 | 3 x 12 |
| 9. Seated Tricep Machine | 2 x 12 | 2 x 15 | 3 x 12 |
| 10. Rotator Cuff Stabilization with Theraband | 2 x 12 | 2 x 15 | 3 x 12 |
| 11. Abdominal Stabilization Program | 2 x max | 3 x max | 3 x max |
| 12. Plank Pose Stabilization on Ball | 1 x max | 2 x max | 3 x max |
| 13. Two-stage Crunch | 2 x max | 3 x max | 3 x max |

## Ectomorph Program

Suitable for gym beginners • Gym program • Frequency 3 x week (alternate days) • Intensity 5–7/10 • Slower repetition speed • Rest periods 45–90 seconds

| Aerobic training: choose from stationary cycle, step machine, rowing machine, treadmill (avoid elliptical machine) | Weeks 1–2 8–15 minutes | Weeks 3–4 10–18 minutes | Weeks 5–6 12–25 minutes |
|---|---|---|---|
| 1. Machine Bench Press | 3 x 6 | 3 x 8 | 4 x 6 |
| 2. Machine Incline Leg Press | 3 x 6 | 3 x 8 | 4 x 6 |
| 3. Hip Abductor Machine | 3 x 6 | 3 x 8 | 4 x 6 |
| 4. Chin-up Assist Machine | 3 x 6 | 3 x 8 | 4 x 6 |
| 5. Supported Bent-over Row Machine | 3 x 6 | 3 x 8 | 4 x 6 |
| 6. Dumb-bell Seated Shoulder Press | 2 x 6 | 3 x 6 | 3 x 8 |
| 7. Standing Barbell Curl | 3 x 6 | 3 x 8 | 3 x 8 |
| 8. Tricep Machine | 3 x 6 | 3 x 8 | 3 x 8 |
| 9. Rotator Cuff Stabilization with Theraband | 2 x 8 | 2 x 8 | 2 x 8 |
| 10. Abdominal Stabilization Program | 3 x max | 3 x max | 4 x max |
| 11. Body-weight Oblique Crunch—Ball between Legs | 3 x max | 3 x max | 4 x max |

# PROGRAM 2: WEIGHT-LOSS AEROBIC FOCUS

## Endomorph Program

Gym program • Frequency: aerobics 4 x week, weights 3 x week (alternate days) • Intensity 4–7/10 • Faster repetition speed
• Rest periods 15–60 seconds

| Aerobic training: choose from stationary cycle, rowing machine, treadmill, elliptical machine, swimming (avoid step machine) | Month 1 8–20 minutes | Month 2 20–40 minutes | Month 3 30–50 minutes |
|---|---|---|---|
| 1. Machine Bench Press | 2 x 15 | 2 x 18–20 | 2 x 20–25 |
| 2. Barbell Reverse Lunge | 2 x 15 | 2 x 18 | 2 x 20 |
| 3. Hip Adductor Machine | 2 x 15 | 2 x 18 | 2 x 20 |
| 4. Machine-lying Leg Curl | 2 x 15 | 2 x 18 | 2 x 20 |
| 5. Machine Cable Front Lateral Pull-down | 2 x 15 | 2 x 18 | 2 x 20 |
| 6. Dumb-bell Standing Lateral Raise | 2 x 12 | 2 x 15 | 2 x 18–20 |
| 7. Cable Tricep Push-down | 2 x 12 | 2 x 15 | 2 x 18–20 |
| 8. Abdominal Stabilization Program | 2 x max | 3 x max | 4 x max |
| 9. Two-stage Crunch | 2 x max | 3 x max | 4 x max |

## Mesomorph Program

Gym program • Frequency: aerobics 4 x week, weights 3 x week (alternate days) • Intensity 4–7/10
• Rest periods 1–60 seconds

| Aerobic training: choose from stationary cycle, rowing machine, treadmill, elliptical machine, swimming, step machine | Month 1 8–15 minutes | Month 2 15–35 minutes | Month 3 35–45 minutes |
|---|---|---|---|
| 1. Machine Bench Press | 2 x 15 | 2 x 18 | 2 x 22 |
| 2. Free-standing Barbell Plié Squats | 2 x 15 | 2 x 18 | 2 x 22 |
| 3. Barbell Reverse Lunge | 2 x 15 | 2 x 18 | 2 x 22 |
| 4. Hip Adductor Machine | 2 x 15 | 2 x 18 | 2 x 22 |
| 5. Machine-lying Leg Curl | 2 x 15 | 2 x 18 | 2 x 22 |
| 6. Machine Cable Front Lateral Pull-down | 2 x 15 | 2 x 18 | 2 x 22 |
| 7. Machine Shoulder Press | 2 x 12 | 2 x 15 | 2 x 20 |
| 8. Cable Tricep Push-down | 2 x 12 | 2 x 15 | 2 x 20 |
| 9. Abdominal Stabilization Program | 2 x max | 3 x max | 4 x max |
| 10. Two-stage Crunch | 2 x max | 3 x max | 4 x max |

## Ectomorph Program

Gym program • Frequency 3 x week (alternate days) • Intensity 4–7/10 • Slower repetition speed
• Rest periods 30–60 seconds

| Aerobic training: choose from stationary cycle, step machine, rowing machine, treadmill (avoid elliptical machine) | Month 1 5–15 minutes | Month 2 15–30 minutes | Month 3 30–40 minutes |
|---|---|---|---|
| 1. Body-weight Modified Push-ups | 2 x 12 | 2 x 15 | 3 x 12 |
| 2. Free-standing Barbell Plié Squats | 2 x 12 | 2 x 15 | 3 x 12 |
| 3. Bench Step | 2 x 12 | 2 x 15 | 3 x 12 |
| 4. Hip Adductor Machine | 2 x 12 | 2 x 15 | 3 x 12 |
| 5. Machine-lying Leg Curl | 2 x 12 | 2 x 15 | 3 x 12 |
| 6. Machine Cable Front Lateral Pull-down | 2 x 12 | 2 x 15 | 3 x 12 |
| 7. Supported Bent-over Row Machine | 2 x 12 | 2 x 15 | 3 x 12 |
| 8. Machine Shoulder Press | 2 x 8 | 2 x 12 | 3 x 8 |
| 9. Standing Barbell Curl | 2 x 8 | 2 x 12 | 3 x 8 |
| 10. Cable Tricep Push-down | 2 x 8 | 2 x 12 | 2 x 8 |
| 11. Hip Flexor Apparatus | 2 x 8 | 2 x 12 | 3 x 8 |
| 12. Shell Prone Ball Roll-up | 2 x 6 | 2 x 8 | 3 x 6 |

## Endomorph Program

Gym program • Frequency: weights 2 x week, aerobics 3 x week (alternate days) • Intensity 5–8/10 • Moderate repetition speed • Rest periods 1–2 minutes

| Aerobic training: choose from stationary cycle, rowing machine, treadmill, elliptical machine, swimming (moderate step machine) | Month 1 8–15 minutes | Month 2 12–20 minutes | Month 3 15–30 minutes |
|---|---|---|---|
| 1. Dumb-bell Flat Bench Flyes | 2 x 15 | 3 x 12 | 3 x 15 |
| 2. Barbell Reverse Lunge | 2 x 15 | 3 x 12 | 3 x 15 |
| 3. Free-standing Lateral Lunge | 2 x 15 | 3 x 12 | 3 x 15 |
| 4. Supine Abductor Stabilization with Ball | 2 x 15 | 3 x 12 | 3 x 15 |
| 5. Chin-up Assist Machine | 2 x 12 | 2 x 15 | 3 x 12 |
| 6. Seated Low Cable Pulley Rows | 2 x 15 | 3 x 12 | 3 x 15 |
| 7. Dumb-bell Seated Shoulder Press | 2 x 12 | 2 x 15 | 3 x 12 |
| 8. Seated Bent-over Raises on Ball | 2 x 15 | 3 x 12 | 3 x 15 |
| 9. Seated Overhead Tricep Extension on Ball with Theraband | 2 x 12 | 2 x 15 | 3 x 12 |
| 10. Dumb-bell Concentration Curl | 2 x 15 | 3 x 12 | 3 x 15 |
| 11. Hip Flexor Apparatus | 2 x max | 3 x max | 4 x max |
| 12. Body-weight Oblique Crunch—Ball between Legs | 2 x max | 3 x max | 4 x max |

## Mesomorph Program

Gym program • Frequency 3 x week (alternate days) • Intensity 5–8/10 • Rest periods 1–2 minutes

| Aerobic training: choose from stationary cycle, rowing machine, treadmill (incline), swimming, step machine | Month 1 8–10 minutes | Month 2 10–15 minutes | Month 3 10–25 minutes |
|---|---|---|---|
| 1. Cable Cross-over | 2 x 12 | 3 x 8–10 | 3 x 12 |
| 2. Shell Prone Ball Roll-up | 2 x 10 | 3 x 8 | 3 x 12 |
| 3. Free-standing Barbell Squats | 2 x 12 | 3 x 8–10 | 3 x 12 |
| 4. Free-standing Lateral Lunge | 2 x 12 | 3 x 8–10 | 3 x 12 |
| 5. Seated Calf Raise Machine | 2 x 12 | 3 x 8–10 | 3 x 12 |
| 6. Chin-up Assist Machine | 2 x 12 | 3 x 8–10 | 3 x 12 |
| 7. Seated Low Cable Pulley Rows | 2 x 12 | 3 x 8–10 | 3 x 12 |
| 8. Rear Deltoid Machine | 2 x 10 | 2 x 15 | 3 x 10 |
| 9. Dumb-bell Seated Shoulder Press | 2 x 10 | 2 x 15 | 3 x 10 |
| 10. Standing Barbell Curl | 2 x 10 | 2 x 15 | 3 x 10 |
| 11. Supine Barbell French Curl | 2 x 10 | 2 x 15 | 3 x 10 |
| 12. Seated Bent-over Raises on Ball | 2 x 10 | 2 x 15 | 3 x 10 |
| 13. Reverse Incline Bench Sit-up | 3 x max | 4 x max | 4 x max |
| 14. Body-weight Oblique Crunch—Ball between Legs | 3 x max | 4 x max | 4 x max |

## Ectomorph Program

Gym program • Frequency: aerobics 2 x week, weights, day A 2 x week, day B 2 x week (alternate days: A B rest A B rest) • Intensity 5–8/10 • Slower repetition speed • Rest periods 1–3 minutes

| Aerobic training: choose from stationary cycle, step, rowing machine, treadmill on incline (avoid elliptical machine) | Month 1 5–10 minutes | Month 2 6–12 minutes | Month 3 6–15 minutes |
|---|---|---|---|
| Day A 1. Incline Pec Deck Machine | 2 x 8 | 2 x 12 | 3 x 8 |
| Day A 2. Incline Dumb-bell Bench Press | 2 x 8 | 2 x 12 | 3 x 8 |
| Day A 3. Free-standing Barbell Squats | 2 x 8 | 2 x 12 | 3 x 8 |
| Day A 4. Modified Barbell Bent-leg Deadlift | 2 x 8 | 2 x 12 | 3 x 8 |
| Day A 5. Free-standing Lateral Lunge | 2 x 8 | 2 x 12 | 3 x 8 |
| Day A 6. Seated Calf Raise Machine | 2 x 8 | 2 x 12 | 3 x 8 |
| Day A 7. Supine Barbell French Curl | 2 x 8 | 3 x 6 | 4 x 6 |
| Day A 8. Tricep Rope Pull-down | 2 x 8 | 3 x 6 | 4 x 6 |
| Day B 1. Chin-up Assist Machine | 2 x 8 | 2 x 12 | 3 x 8 |
| Day B 2. Seated Low Cable Pulley Rows | 2 x 8 | 2 x 12 | 3 x 8 |
| Day B 3. Machine Shoulder Press | 2 x 8 | 2 x 12 | 3 x 8 |
| Day B 4. Rear Deltoid Machine | 2 x 8 | 3 x 6 | 4 x 6 |
| Day B 5. Standing Barbell Curl | 2 x 8 | 3 x 6 | 4 x 6 |
| Day B 6. Supine Barbell French Curl | 2 x 8 | 3 x 6 | 4 x 6 |
| Day B 7. Combination Crunch | 3 x max | 4 x max | 4 x max |
| Day B 8. Body-weight Oblique Crunch—Ball between Legs | 3 x max | 4 x max | 4 x max |

# PROGRAM 4: POSTURAL/FUNCTIONAL STRENGTH AND FLEXIBILITY

## Endomorph Program

Gym program • Frequency: aerobics 4 x week, weights 2 x week (alternate days) • Intensity 4–7/10
• Rest periods 30–60 seconds

| Aerobic training: choose from stationary cycle, rowing machine, treadmill, elliptical machine, swimming (avoid step machine) | Month 1 15–25 minutes | Month 2 20–30 minutes | Month 3 25–40 minutes |
|---|---|---|---|
| 1. Transverse Activation in Four-point Kneeling | 2 x 15 | 2 x 18 | 2 x 22 |
| 2. Abdominal Stabilization Program | 2 x max | 2 x max | 3 x max |
| 3. Mid-back Prone Scapula Stabilization on Bench | 2 x 12–15 | 2 x 15 | 2 x 18 |
| 4. Standing Cable Pull-over | 2 x 15 | 2 x 18 | 2 x 22 |
| 5. Standing Reverse Grip Cable Rows | 2 x 15 | 2 x 18 | 2 x 22 |
| 6. Body-weight Modified Push-ups | 2 x 12–15 | 2 x 15 | 2 x 18 |
| 7. Barbell Reverse Lunge | 2 x 15 | 2 x 18 | 2 x 18 |
| 8. Double Leg Bridge with Shoulder Flexion | 2 x 12–15 | 2 x 15 | 2 x 18 |
| 9. Supine Abductor Stabilization with Ball | 2 x 15 | 2 x 18 | 2 x 22 |
| 10. Seesaw with Ball | 2 x 10 | 2 x 12 | 2 x 12 |

STRETCHES 2 x 30 seconds each: Neck and Shoulder Stretch, Full-body Stretch, Standing Chest and Anterior Shoulder Stretch, Side-to-side Hip Rolls, Ball Shoulder Stretch, Supine Lying Single Leg Hamstring Stretch, Seated Side Stretch on Ball, Spine Roll, Standing Iliopsoas Stretch, Gastrocnemius Stretch

## Mesomorph Program

Gym program • Frequency: 3 x week (alternate days) • Intensity 4–7/10
• Rest periods 30–60 seconds

| Aerobic training: choose from stationary cycle, rowing machine, treadmill, elliptical machine, swimming, step machine | Month 1 8–12 minutes | Month 2 12–15 minutes | Month 3 10–25 minutes |
|---|---|---|---|
| 1. Plank Pose Stabilization on Ball | 2 x 20 secs | 2 x 30 secs | 2 x 40 secs |
| 2. Progressive Abdominal Stabilization Program | 2 x max | 2 x max | 3 x max |
| 3. Mid-back Prone Scapula Stabilization on Bench | 2 x 12–15 | 2 x 18 | 2 x 22 |
| 4. Standing Cable Pull-over | 2 x 12–15 | 2 x 18 | 2 x 22 |
| 5. Standing Reverse Grip Cable Rows | 2 x 12–15 | 2 x 18 | 2 x 22 |
| 6. Body-weight Modified Push-ups | 2 x 12–15 | 2 x 18 | 2 x 22 |
| 7. Free-standing Lateral Lunge | 2 x 12–15 | 2 x 18 | 2 x 22 |
| 8. Supine Abductor Stabilization with Ball | 2 x 12–15 | 2 x 18 | 2 x 22 |
| 9. Seesaw with Ball | 2 x 12–15 | 2 x 18 | 2 x 22 |
| 10. Double Leg Bridge with Shoulder Flexion | 2 x 12–15 | 2 x 18 | 2 x 22 |

STRETCHES 2 x 30 seconds each: Neck and Shoulder Stretch, Full-body Stretch, Standing Chest and Anterior Shoulder Stretch, Side-to-side Hip Rolls, Ball Shoulder Stretch, Supine Lying Single Leg Hamstring Stretch, Seated Side Stretch on Ball, Spine Roll, Standing Iliopsoas Stretch, Gastrocnemius Stretch

## Ectomorph Program

Gym program • Frequency 3 x week (alternate days) • Intensity 4–7/10 • Slower repetition speed
• Rest periods 1–2 minutes

| Aerobic training: choose from stationary cycle, step machine, rowing machine, treadmill (avoid elliptical machine) | Month 1 5–10 minutes | Month 2 6–12 minutes | Month 3 6–15 minutes |
|---|---|---|---|
| 1. Shell Prone Ball Roll-up | 2 x 12 | 2 x 15 | 3 x 12 |
| 2. Abdominal Stabilization Program | 2 x max | 3 x max | 3 x max |
| 3. Body-weight Oblique Crunch—Ball between legs | 2 x max | 3 x max | 3 x max |
| 4. Chin-up Assist Machine | 2 x 12 | 2 x 15 | 3 x 12 |
| 5. Mid-back Prone Scapula Stabilization on Bench | 2 x 12 | 2 x 15 | 3 x 12 |
| 6. Standing Cable Pull-over | 2 x 12 | 2 x 15 | 3 x 12 |
| 7. Standing Reverse Grip Cable Rows | 2 x 12 | 2 x 15 | 3 x 12 |
| 8. Body-weight Modified Push-ups | 2 x 12 | 2 x 15 | 3 x 12 |
| 9. Free-standing Lateral Lunge | 2 x 12 | 2 x 15 | 3 x 12 |
| 10. Modified Barbell Bent-leg Deadlift | 2 x 12 | 2 x 15 | 3 x 12 |
| 11. Supine Abductor Stabilization with Ball | 2 x 12 | 2 x 15 | 3 x 12 |

STRETCHES 2 x 30 seconds each: Neck and Shoulder Stretch, Full-body Stretch, Standing Chest and Anterior Shoulder Stretch, Side-to-side Hip Rolls, Ball Shoulder Stretch, Supine Lying Single Leg Hamstring Stretch, Seated Side Stretch on Ball, Spine Roll, Standing Iliopsoas Stretch, Gastrocnemius Stretch

## Endomorph Program

Home/home gym program • Frequency: aerobics 4 x week, weights 3 x week (alternate days) • Intensity 4–6/10
• Rest periods 30–60 seconds

| Aerobic training: choose from stationary cycle, rowing machine, treadmill, elliptical machine, swimming, walking outdoors (avoid step machine) | Month 1 5–20 minutes | Month 2 15–30 minutes | Month 3 30–45 minutes |
|---|---|---|---|
| 1.  Wall Push-ups on Bar | 2 x 8 | 2 x 12 | 2 x 15 |
| 2.  Squats with Ball between Legs | 2 x 8 | 2 x 12 | 2 x 15 |
| 3.  Prone Hip Extensions | 2 x 8 | 2 x 12 | 2 x 15 |
| 4.  Alternate Arm and Leg Raises on Ball | 2 x 6 each side | 2 x 8 each side | 2 x 10 each side |
| 5.  Double Leg Bridge with Shoulder Flexion | 2 x 8 | 2 x 12 | 2 x 15 |
| 6.  Free-standing Calf Raise | 2 x 8 | 2 x 12 | 2 x 15 |
| 7.  Dumb-bell Standing Lateral Raise | 2 x 6 | 2 x 10 | 2 x 12 |
| 8.  Dumb-bell Bent-over Rows | 2 x 6 | 2 x 10 | 2 x 12 |
| 9.  Dumb-bell Seated Shoulder Press | 2 x 6 | 2 x 10 | 2 x 12 |
| 10. Two-stage Crunch | 2 x max | 2 x max | 2 x max |
| 11. Abdominal Stabilization Program | 1 x max | 2 x max | 3 x max |
| 12. Body-weight Oblique Crunch—Ball between Legs | 1 x max | 2 x max | 2 x max |

## Mesomorph Program

Gym program • Frequency: aerobics 4 x week, weights 3 x week (alternate days) • Intensity 4–7/10
• Rest periods 30–60 seconds

| Aerobic training: choose from stationary cycle, rowing machine, treadmill, elliptical machine, swimming, step machine, walking/jogging outdoors | Month 1 8–20 minutes | Month 2 12–25 minutes | Month 3 15–35 minutes |
|---|---|---|---|
| 1.  Body-weight Modified Push-ups | 2 x 10 | 2 x 12 | 3 x 10 |
| 2.  Squats with Ball between Legs | 2 x 10 | 2 x 12 | 3 x 10 |
| 3.  Free-standing Calf Raise | 2 x 10 | 2 x 12 | 3 x 10 |
| 4.  Double Leg Bridge with Shoulder Flexion | 2 x 10 | 2 x 12 | 3 x 10 |
| 5.  Alternate Arm and Leg Raises on Ball | 2 x 6 each side | 2 x 8 each side | 2 x 10 each side |
| 6.  Dumb-bell Bent-over Rows | 2 x 10 | 2 x 12 | 3 x 10 |
| 7.  Dumb-bell Standing Lateral Raise | 2 x 8 | 2 x 10 | 2 x 12 |
| 8.  Dumb-bell Seated Shoulder Press | 2 x 8 | 2 x 10 | 2 x 12 |
| 9.  Two-stage Crunch | 1 x max | 2 x max | 2 x max |
| 10. Abdominal Stabilization Program | 1 x max | 2 x max | 2 x max |

## Ectomorph Program

Gym program • Frequency 3 x week (alternate days) • Intensity 4–7/10 • Slower repetition speed
• Rest periods 30–60 seconds

| Aerobic training: choose from stationary cycle, treadmill (avoid elliptical machine), walking/jogging outdoors | Month 1 8–15 minutes | Month 2 10–18 minutes | Month 3 12–20 minutes |
|---|---|---|---|
| 1.  Body-weight Modified Push-ups | 2 x 8 | 2 x 10 | 3 x 8 |
| 2.  Squats with Ball between Legs | 2 x 8 | 2 x 10 | 3 x 8 |
| 3.  Bench Step (short height) | 2 x 8 | 2 x 10 | 3 x 8 |
| 4.  Free-standing Lateral Lunge | 2 x 8 | 2 x 10 | 3 x 8 |
| 5.  Dumb-bell Bent-over Rows | 2 x 8 | 2 x 10 | 3 x 8 |
| 6.  Double Leg Bridge with Shoulder Flexion | 2 x 8 | 2 x 10 | 3 x 8 |
| 7.  Alternate Arm and Leg Raises on Ball | 2 x 6 each side | 2 x 8 each side | 3 x 6 each side |
| 8.  Dumb-bell Seated Shoulder Press | 2 x 6 | 2 x 10 | 2 x 12 |
| 9.  Body-weight Oblique Crunches—Ball between Legs | 2 x max | 2 x max | 3 x max |
| 10. Two-stage Crunch | 2 x max | 2 x max | 2 x max |
| 11. Abdominal Stabilization Program | 2 x max | 2 x max | 3 x max |

# AEROBIC TRAINING

The term "cardiovascular exercise" or "aerobic exercise" refers to exercise that is long in duration, works a combination of muscles and systems, and is performed continuously at an elevated heart rate. Examples include walking, running, cycling, swimming, and skiing. "Aerobic" literally means "with oxygen," and refers to oxygen's role in oxidizing ("burning") carbohydrates and fats to produce adenosine triphosphate, the basic form of energy used in the cellular reactions that give power to the exercise effort. The benefits of aerobic training include better heart and lung function and capacity, lower blood pressure, improved metabolism, improved immunity, reduced stress and tension, and enhanced self-esteem and self-image. This type of exercise is one of the most important components of a health-related fitness program. Apply the following basic principles and concepts to help you choose the right type and level of aerobic exercise for you, and to make the exercise as safe, effective, and rewarding as possible.

| BORG CR10 SCALE | |
|---|---|
| • 0 | Rest |
| • 1 | Very easy |
| • 2 | Easy |
| • 3 | Moderate |
| • 4 | Somewhat hard |
| • 5 | Hard |
| • 6 | |
| • 7 | Very hard |
| • 8 | |
| • 9 | Very, very hard |
| • 10 | Maximal |

## Frequency of Exercise

This refers to the number of aerobic sessions per week. For improvements in cardiovascular fitness, the American College of Sports Medicine (ACSM) recommends three to five days per week of aerobic training for most aerobic programs. For beginners and the unfit, the recommended starting level is training three days a week with no more than two days' rest in between; for example, aerobic training on Mondays, Wednesdays, and Fridays. Over time, this can be increased to up to five sessions a week.

As your fitness improves and the intensity of your training increases, the frequency of the sessions will be influenced by the intensity of the exercise. Relatively hard sessions require more rest than moderate, low-intensity ones, and high-impact exercise needs more recovery time than low-impact exercise, especially in the untrained. Once you have progressed to advanced fitness, it is best to vary your program with some shorter, harder sessions, and some longer, more moderate ones. To reduce injury risk you can alternate high-impact sessions with low-impact ones.

## Intensity of Exercise

Typical questions posed by beginners include "How hard should I train?" and "How do I know what level to train at to achieve the best benefits?" There are several methods of assessing your training needs. The simplest method involves using the Rated Perceived Exertion (RPE) scale, in which you match the level you feel you are working at to the values nominated on the scale. Most gyms use scales of 1–10 or 6–20. On the original Borg scale (6–20), you would aim for a rating of 12–16. On the newer 1–10 category ratio (CR10) scale (see above), this would correlate to approximately 4–6 out of 10.

Another accurate and even simpler method is the Talk Test. It basically says, as the name suggests, that while you perform aerobic exercise you should be warm and sweating, but still able to talk without gasping for breath.

A more technical and specific method involves setting the intensity by using heart-rate measurement during exercise as a guide. There is a degree of correlation between the amount of oxygen consumed at a given workload, the heart rate, and the aerobic benefit of training at that heart rate. Evidence confirms that greater cardiovascular benefits occur when training takes place at a certain heart-rate range. Training below this level delivers diminished benefits, and training above it prematurely fatigues and over-trains you, reducing aerobic benefits.

Various formulae exist to calculate the correct level of training heart rate. The most common method is the percent of Maximal Heart Rate (MHR) calculation, or Training Heart Rate method (THR). You start by calculating your Predicted Maximal Heart Rate (PMHR). For women, this is found by subtracting your age from 226. You then calculate a THR range somewhere between 60 and 90 percent of your PMHR. For lower levels of fitness or longer sessions, use 60 to 75 percent of your PMHR; for higher fitness levels and shorter sessions, use 75 to 90 percent of your PMHR.

The percent of MHR is a conservative formula, and those who are very fit may be able to increase the prescribed heart rate for aerobic training by 10–12 beats per minute. For this, you can use the Karvonen formula. Although this is not used as commonly as the above method, it has a more accurate correlation to the oxygen consumption for a given exercise workload. In this method your resting heart rate is subtracted from your PMHR, your THR is calculated according to the 60–90 percent, and finally your resting heart rate is added back to give your actual THR.

Get an instructor to show you how to monitor your pulse rate while exercising. At first just find the pulse (the neck or wrist is best for this), and learn how to count the beats. Then you can apply this to your exercise program. Alternatively, many aerobic machines in gyms have built-in heart-rate monitors. Personal heart-rate monitors are also very reasonably priced and readily available these days.

The ACSM recommends training at a range of 60–90 percent of MHR or 50–85 percent of the Karvonen formula for cardiovascular fitness benefits. Lower intensities of 50–60 percent of MHR may be necessary for individuals with low levels of cardiovascular fitness. For the very unfit, benefits can even be derived from as little as 40–50 percent of MHR.

**Note** If you take any medication that affects your resting and exercising heart rate, for example, certain blood pressure and heart drugs, consult your doctor for advice to suit your needs.

### Types of Aerobic Exercise

The types of aerobic exercise you choose will largely depend on the facilities and environments available to you, your fitness level, your likes and dislikes, and your confidence and experience, especially in outdoor situations.

Some aerobic exercises, such as walking, running, and cycling, tend to be purely aerobic and constant in nature (Type 1), while others, including swimming, aerobics, and tennis, require higher levels of skill and complexity (Type 2). A third group, which includes activities such as basketball and mountain biking, can be categorized as being variable in intensity and involves a higher percentage of strength and flexibility (Type 3).

If you are a beginner and/or unfit, it may be best to begin with exercises in the Type 1 group. If you are younger, fitter, and seek more variety and cross-training benefits, Types 2 or 3 are going to be more challenging for you.

In weight-bearing activities the body's weight acts directly against gravity (e.g. walking). In non-weight-bearing exercise the body's weight against gravity is reduced (e.g. swimming). The terms "high impact" and "low impact" refer to the amount of impact on the joints and skeletal system that is produced by specific activities. A clear example is the difference between walking (low impact) and running (high impact). In high-impact training there is greater injury risk, with the result that your program's progression must be more conservative. These differences in exercise types will determine the best exercises for you. For example, if you are susceptibile to knee injuries, high-impact running would not be an ideal choice for you, and walking or swimming would be a better option. If you are unfit or a beginner, including no-impact or low-impact and non-weight-bearing exercise can reduce your injury risk, while allowing training loads to be maintained until your body is ready for more weight-bearing and impact.

### Duration of Exercise

Overall, the ACSM recommends 20–60 minutes of continuous aerobic activity, not including warm-ups and cool-downs. However, unfit individuals can start with as little as 5 minutes and build from there up to 20 minutes. Very unfit or infirm individuals, for whom even this is too much, can start with short, 5–10 minute sessions, repeated at more regular intervals. Women with intermediate fitness levels should perform aerobic exercise for 15–45 minutes per session, while those who are very fit can exercise for 30–60 minutes in a session. In general, exercise duration can increase as adaptation to training occurs, while training at a safe and effective intensity. It is best if the warm-up and cool-down are specific to the activity—for example, if you are going running, start with some walking or light jogging.

### Exercises

1. Walking, page 30
2. Jogging/Running, page 32
3. Aerobics, page 34
4. Swimming and Aqua-aerobics, page 35
5. Aerobic Machines, page 36

# WALKING

Whole-body exercise • Compound/
multi-joint • Close chain • Weight-
bearing • Low impact • Constant type
• Low skill • Beginner to advanced

Walking is probably the most widely recommended low-injury risk aerobic activity, with tremendous fitness and health rewards. Using up to 200 of the muscles in your body, it is an easy exercise to start with and offers wide variety as you progress. It is most suitable for those who are physically unfit, have a sedentary lifestyle, are overweight, or older, or are unable to do high-impact exercise. Walking is less intense and lower in impact than running, and therefore carries a much lower injury risk.

*Analysis of movement: lower body*

Walking may be divided into the swing and stance phases, with the stance phase being divided further into heel-strike, mid-stance, and toe-off. In the normal pattern of walking, during the swing phase the leg leaves the ground and moves forward to the next point, with the leg in slight hip external rotation. Into the stance phases, the foot lands in heel-strike, with the heel landing with the foot in ankle supination. Mid-stance follows as the body moves forward and the leg moves back. Here the foot is in full contact with the ground and is pronated at the ankle. In the final stance phase, toe-off, the foot returns to ankle supination, and then leaves the ground into the next swing phase, and the cycle is repeated. During the stance phases, the leg is in slight hip internal rotation.

In the stance phase the leg moves backward, powering the body forward and adding momentum to the opposite leg, which is swinging forward. The concentric phase (shortening under load) for the quadriceps is when the leg moves forward; for the hamstring and calf muscles it is when the leg moves back. When the leg moves forward, the hamstrings and calf muscles are mostly passive. When the leg moves back, the Iliopsoas and quadriceps are mostly passive. The adductors, deep external rotators of the hips and Popliteus also contribute to hip or knee flexion and extension, as well as to the subtle movements of the knees and hips during walking.

Movement at the ankle is a complex interaction of three subtler movements, and has been simplified here for easier understanding. For simplicity's sake, the hip rotators and ankle supinators and pronators have been omitted from the analyses on the opposite page.

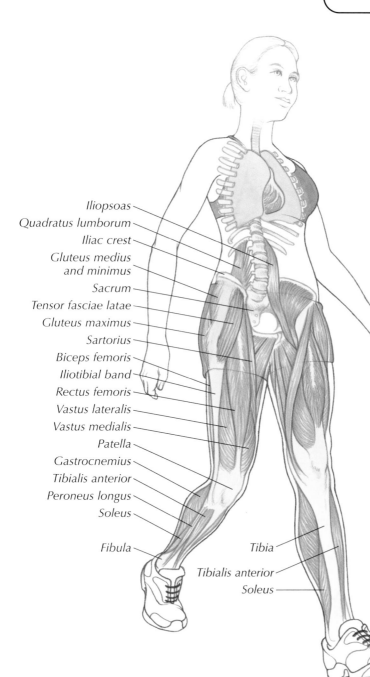

Iliopsoas
Quadratus lumborum
Iliac crest
Gluteus medius
and minimus
Sacrum
Tensor fasciae latae
Gluteus maximus
Sartorius
Biceps femoris
Iliotibial band
Rectus femoris
Vastus lateralis
Vastus medialis
Patella
Gastrocnemius
Tibialis anterior
Peroneus longus
Soleus
Fibula
Tibia
Tibialis anterior
Soleus

| ANALYSIS OF MOVEMENT | JOINT 1 | JOINT 2 | JOINT 3 |
|---|---|---|---|
| Main joints | Hips | Knees | Ankles |
| Joint movement | Swing phase (forward movement of leg): flexion<br>Stance phases (backward movement of leg): extension | Swing phase (forward movement of leg): extension<br>Stance phases (backward movement of leg): flexion | Swing phase (forward movement): dorsiflexion<br>Stance phases (backward movement of leg): plantarflexion |
| Main mobilizing muscles | Swing phase:<br>Iliopsoas<br>Rectus femoris of Quadriceps<br>Pectineus<br>Sartorius<br>Stance phases:<br>Gluteus maximus<br>Hamstring group<br>Deep external hip rotators | Swing phase:<br>Quadricep group<br>Stance phases:<br>Hamstring group<br>Popliteus<br>Gastrocnemius<br>Gracilis<br>Sartorius | Swing phase:<br>Tibialis anterior<br>Extensor digitorum longus<br>Extensor hallucis longus<br>Stance phases:<br>Gastrocnemius<br>Soleus<br>Flexor digitirum longus<br>Flexor hallucis longus<br>Peroneus brevis<br>Peroneus longus<br>Plantaris<br>Tibialis posterior |

**Main stabilizing muscles**

Abdominal group, Erector spinae, and Quadratus lumborum at the trunk
Gluteus medius and minimus, Deep lateral rotators, and Adductor group at the hips
Ankle stabilizers and Gastrocnemius in the lower legs

**Exercise progression**

Walking longer, faster, more frequently, and uphill.

## Sample Walking Program

| | Week 1 | Week 2 | Week 3 | Week 4 | Week 5 | Week 6 | Week 7 | Week 8 | Week 9 | Week 10 |
|---|---|---|---|---|---|---|---|---|---|---|
| **Beginner** | Suitable for those who are very unfit, under a doctor's care, overweight, smokers or over 35 | | | | | | | | | |
| Frequency | 2–3 | 2–3 | 3 | 3 | 3–4 | 3–4 | 4 | 4 | 4 | 4 |
| Time | 10 | 12 | 15 | 18 | 20 | 22 | 25 | 30 | 32 | 35 |
| **Intermediate** | Suitable for regular exercisers or those with moderately active lifestyles or who find the beginner's program too easy | | | | | | | | | |
| Frequency | 3 | 3 | 3 | 3–4 | 4 | 4 | 4–5 | 4–5 | 4–5 | 4–5 |
| Time | 20 | 22 | 25 | 30 | 32 | 35 | 38 | 40 | 42 | 45 |
| **Advanced** | Suitable for regular walkers and those with higher fitness levels. Slowly bring in uphill walking a couple of days a week | | | | | | | | | |
| Frequency | 4 | 4 | 4–5 | 4–5 | 4–6 | 4–6 | 4–6 | 4–6 | 4–6 | 4–6 |
| Time | 30 | 35 | 35 | 40 | 30–40 | 30–45 | 35–45 | 35–50 | 35–55 | 35–60 |

## Tips for walking programs

If you are a beginner, start walking two to three times week for as little as 10 minutes depending on your age, weight, and fitness. Keep to a brisk, consistent pace. Monitor and set your intensity by using the RPE scale or Talk Test, or by monitoring your heart rate (see page 29). Initially, walk on flat ground wearing suitable footwear. Increase the time and frequency as your training progresses. Slowly add uphill and off-road walking. Also vary the pace and distance. You can use a treadmill if the weather is bad or if time is an issue, but do walk outside whenever possible.

# JOGGING AND RUNNING

Whole-body exercise • Compound/multi-joint • Open chain • Weight-bearing • High impact • Constant type • Low skill • Beginner to advanced

➡ In 1972 at the summer Olympics in Munich, American Frank Shorter won the Olympic marathon, capturing the imagination of the American public and giving birth to the popular modern phenomenon of running as a form of exercise and sport. Although running is not as popular as it was in the 1980s, it is a common and important aspect of gym cross-training programs.

*Analysis of movement: lower body*

Walking and running are virtually identical from an exercise analysis point of view. The major difference is that in running there is a point between stance and swing phases where both legs are momentarily off the ground.

*Injury risks in running*

Although running burns more calories per minute than walking, it carries one of the highest risks of the aerobic exercises. It requires consistent training and appropriate rest planning.

• Running is high impact and the forces through the joints are between five and ten times higher in running than in walking, hence the higher risk of injury. The required stabilization effort of the muscles is also greater in running. Both these factors can increase the risk of knee and lower back problems in running. Common running injuries also occur when the ankle remains in pronation in the toe-off of the stance phase. This is usually accompanied by increased external hip rotation, often due to underlying posture and/or genetic predisposition.

• Women, in particular, have a greater injury risk than men, due to their wider pelvises. This means that the "carriage angle," the angle of the femur bone to the knee joint, is more acute. The increased impact forces through the knee are displaced, giving women more risk of injury on the medial knee (inside), and the underside of the patella (knee cap).

• In running there is an increased injury risk if you are overweight, unfit and sedentary, older, or have a history of knee or lower back problems.

| ANALYSIS OF MOVEMENT | JOINT 1 | JOINT 2 | JOINT 3 |
|---|---|---|---|
| Main joints | Hips | Knees | Ankles |
| Joint movement | Swing phase (forward movement of leg): flexion<br>Stance phases (backward movement of leg): extension | Swing phase (forward movement of leg): extension<br>Stance phases (backward movement of leg): flexion | Swing phase (forward movement): dorsiflexion<br>Stance phases (backward movement of leg): plantarflexion |
| Main mobilizing muscles | Swing phase:<br>Iliopsoas<br>Rectus femoris of quadriceps<br>Pectineus<br>Sartorius<br>Stance phases:<br>Gluteus maximus<br>Hamstring group<br>Deep external hip rotators | Swing phase:<br>Quadricep group<br>Stance phases:<br>Hamstring group<br>Popliteus<br>Gastrocnemius<br>Gracilis<br>Sartorius | Swing phase:<br>Tibialis anterior<br>Extensor digitorum longus<br>Extensor hallucis longus<br>Stance phases:<br>Gastrocnemius<br>Soleus<br>Flexor digitorum longus<br>Flexor hallucis longus<br>Peroneus brevis<br>Peroneus longus<br>Plantaris<br>Tibialis posterior |

**Main stabilizing muscles**

Abdominal group, Erector spinae, and Quadratus lumborum at the trunk
Gluteus medius and minimus, Deep lateral rotators, and Adductor group at the hips
Ankle stabilizers and Gastrocnemius in the lower leg

**Exercise progression**

Running longer, faster, more frequently, and uphill.

## Sample Running/Walking Program

| Beginner | Suitable for walkers looking for a new challenge and those who have never run before, but are medically fit to do so. | | | | | | | | | |
|---|---|---|---|---|---|---|---|---|---|---|
| | Week 1 | Week 2 | Week 3 | Week 4 | Week 5 | Week 6 | Week 7 | Week 8 | Week 9 | Week 10 |
| Frequency | 3 | 3 | 3 | 3 | 3 | 3 | 3 | 3 | 3 | 3 |
| Run/walk intervals | 30 sec/ 90 sec | 60 sec/ 90 sec | 90 sec/ 90 sec | 1 min/ 1 min | 2 min/ 1 min | 4 min/ 1 min | 6 min/ 1 min | 8 min/ 1 min | 10 min/ 1 min | 12 min/ 1 min |
| Total time | 25 | 25 | 25 | 25 | 25 | 25 | 25 | 25 | 25 | 25 |

### Tips for running/walking programs

Starting with walking, or a walking/running program, rather than with running straight off, reduces the risk of stress fractures and should be done if you are unfit, overweight, or have not run for a while. Do it three times a week for a minimum of four weeks and a maximum of ten. Use intervals of jogging and walking on the flat, with the jogging intervals getting longer and the walking intervals getting shorter. The walking should be done at a brisk pace. Proper running footwear is essential. Jogging implies a slower, more leisurely pace compared with running: in jogging the emphasis is on distance, in running the emphasis is on speed.

## Sample Running Program: 6-mile Run

| Intermediate to advanced | Suitable for anyone who wants to start running and is medically fit to do so. The program assumes you are jogging at a 9.5-minute/mile pace. | | | | | | | | | |
|---|---|---|---|---|---|---|---|---|---|---|
| | Week 1 | Week 2 | Week 3 | Week 4 | Week 5 | Week 6 | Week 7 | Week 8 | Week 9 | Week 10 |
| Monday | 10 W/J | 10 W/J | 10 J | 12 J | 15 J | 18 J | 20 J | 20 J | 20 J | 20 J |
| Tuesday | Rest | Rest | Rest | Rest | Rest | Rest | Rest | Rest | Rest | Rest |
| Wednesday | 10 J | 12 J | 15 J | 18 J | 22 J | 26 J | 32 J | 38 J | 42 J | 35 J |
| Thursday | Rest | Rest | Rest | Rest | Rest | Rest | Rest | Rest | Rest | Rest |
| Friday | 15 W/J | 20 W/J | 10 J | 12 J | 15 J | 18 J | 22 J | 25 J | 25 J | 20 J |
| Saturday | Rest | Rest | Rest | Rest | Rest | Rest | Rest | Rest | Rest | Rest |
| Sunday | 20 J | 25 J | 30 J | 30 J | 35 J | 40 J | 45 J | 50 J | 55 J | 60 J |
| Key to chart abbreviations: J = Jogging, W/J = Walking/Jogging intervals, numbers represent minutes. | | | | | | | | | | |

### Tips for running programs

Running requires consistent training, especially if you started out sedentary or overweight. The initial aim should be to increase time on the feet, not speed. For racing distances of less than 7 miles (10 km), a training frequency of three times a week is the minimum. For up to a half-marathon (14 miles/21.1 km), a training frequency of four times a week is the minimum and five is preferable. Long runs are done once a week, usually on weekends. Include hills or interval training once a week as appropriate to the goal. Allow one or two weeks of taper—the longer the race, the harder the training, and the longer the taper. Initially, with the build-up in training, use 3-, 7-, and 10-mile (5-, 10-, and 15-km) races as part of the training for a first half-marathon. In all of these, emphasize running to the finish as comfortably as possible, not racing against the clock. Only after running the distance several times is it advisable to start racing against your personal best time. If you want to progress to a full marathon, run three to four half-marathons before building up to a full one. The jump from half- to full marathon is quite drastic.

# AEROBICS

Whole-body exercise • Compound/multi-joint • Variable according to type of class: choose one appropriate to your fitness level and taste • Constant to variable type • Low to high skill • Beginner to advanced

→ Exercise physiologist Dr Kenneth Cooper is regarded as the original pioneer of the aerobics movement, both coining the term "aerobics" and developing the exercise form. His 1970 book *The New Aerobics* reported the benefits of this type of exercise. It included scientific exercise programs for running, walking, swimming, and bicycling.

The intense popularity of aerobics developed in the 1980s and 90s. Jane Fonda released her first exercise video, *Jane Fonda's Workout*, in 1982, which sold 17 million copies, more than any home video ever. Gin Miller's innovation of step aerobics in 1989 was distinguished from other forms of aerobic exercise by the use of an elevated platform (the step), which enabled a more vigorous workout than could be achieved with "regular" aerobics.

Although aerobics have decreased in popularity since the late 1980s, they now have greater variety with more individual challenge. A variety of classes offers a thorough workout, with the major component being cardio-vascular. Look for aerobics boxing classes (Tae Bo, Katabox) and indoor cycling classes (Johnny G Spinning). Aerobics dance is a type of aerobics exercise usually done as a group class, involving stepping and movement patterns performed to music and led by an instructor. Many aerobics classes have moved away from the "no pain, no gain," "go-for-the-burn" emphasis of the 1970s and 80s, and now incorporate core stabilization principles, strength-conditioning work, and the use of accessories such as weights and stability balls.

If you are a beginner or unfit, start with beginner level and low-impact classes, and progress to more advanced, complicated, and higher-impact classes over at least several months. In the bigger classes, poor form and over- or under-training are common problems, as there is less supervision and contact with the instructor. If you have any physical limitations that would be affected by exercise, you should inform the class leader so that he or she may offer options that are safe and effective for you to perform.

# SWIMMING AND AQUA-AEROBICS

Whole-body exercise • Compound/multi-joint • Open chain • Non-weight bearing • Non-impact • Constant type • Medium to high skill • Beginner to advanced

➡️ The first swimming instruction book was written in 1538 by Nikolaus Wynmann. Around 1800, competitive swimming commenced in Europe, mostly using the breaststroke, and swimming was part of the first modern Olympic Games in 1896.

## The Benefits of Swimming Exercise

Because the density of the mammalian body is similar to that of water, swimming places minimal impact and less stress on the joints and bones than other forms of exercise. Swimming and aqua-aerobics are therefore often favored for rehabilitation, the infirm, and those with disabilities. Swimming trains most of the muscles in the body. Excessive kick and leg work in most strokes, especially in the front crawl and butterfly, is seen as a disadvantage as the larger leg muscles consume more oxygen than the upper body, depriving it of oxygen.

A lower heart-rate response for similar effort level is involved in swimming compared with cycling or jogging, due to the swimmer's prone position and immersion in a cooler environment. Swimming requires a higher level of skill than other forms of exercise, and fatigue sets in earlier with unskilled swimmers.

While breaststroke generates the most significant movement with the legs of the four swimming styles, the front crawl (see ilustration below) propels the body mainly with the arms. More of the back muscles are used in backstroke than in the front crawl. Butterfly stroke is technically the hardest stroke to master, requiring a strong upper body and abdominal strength and power.

## Training tips for swimming training

Beginners should begin with interval training, i.e. swimming laps with rest periods in between. Start with as little as five to ten laps in total, and progress by increasing the duration of lap sets and slightly reducing the rest periods. You can use swimming aids such as kick-boards, pool-buoys, or paddle flippers to enhance buoyancy, vary the workout and enhance strength benefits. Maintain a relaxed, constant pace. Develop constant rhythmic technique and pacing, and avoiding excessive rocking of the body.

## Aqua-aerobics

Resistance in water is about 12 times greater than on land, so aqua-aerobics can deliver an ideal low-impact, moderate resistance workout with cardiovascular benefits. Easy access, adequate water temperature, and water depth are all considerations when planning an aqua routine. Aqua-aerobics is also good for injury rehabilitation, and for those with orthopedic conditions such as knee problems, although it is recommended that such classes are done in a warmed pool where people can stand. This improves postural stabilization, especially of the lower body, which is harder to maintain in deep-water workouts. A range of accessories, such as water dumb-bells, webbed gloves, "noodles," and water belts, is available to offer variety and greater intensity to water exercises.

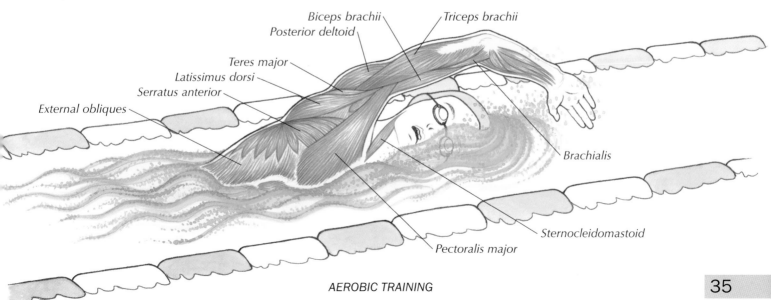

Biceps brachii
Triceps brachii
Posterior deltoid
Teres major
Latissimus dorsi
Serratus anterior
External obliques
Brachialis
Sternocleidomastoid
Pectoralis major

# AEROBIC MACHINES

Whole-body exercise • Mostly compound/multi-joint • Mostly constant type • Low to medium skill • Beginner to advanced

Aerobic machines such as stationary cycles, treadmills, rowing machines, and step machines provide viable and practical options to outside exercise. The effects on the body of using a rowing machine—which combines both upper and lower body workouts—are analyzed on these pages.

## General tips for using aerobic machines

· Correct use and body positions are important for safe and effective use of aerobic machines. Get instruction from a professional when using a machine for the first time.
· Use aerobic machines as part of an overall routine. Once past the beginner phase, vary your workouts to minimize training plateaus, where the results are beginning to diminish due to the body adapting to the overload.
· Aerobic machines are ideal for exercise warm-ups. Choose a rowing machine or stationary cycle for this.

## Using a Rowing Machine
### Description

Using your legs, propel your body backward by pushing through your feet. Using the momentum generated by your legs, as your hands approach your knees transfer the pulling force to your arms and flex your elbows to bring the bar toward your chest. Return and repeat.

> **STARTING POSITION**
> · Sitting on the machine's moveable seat, adjust and fasten the foot straps.
> · Reach forward to grasp the bar with an overhand grip.

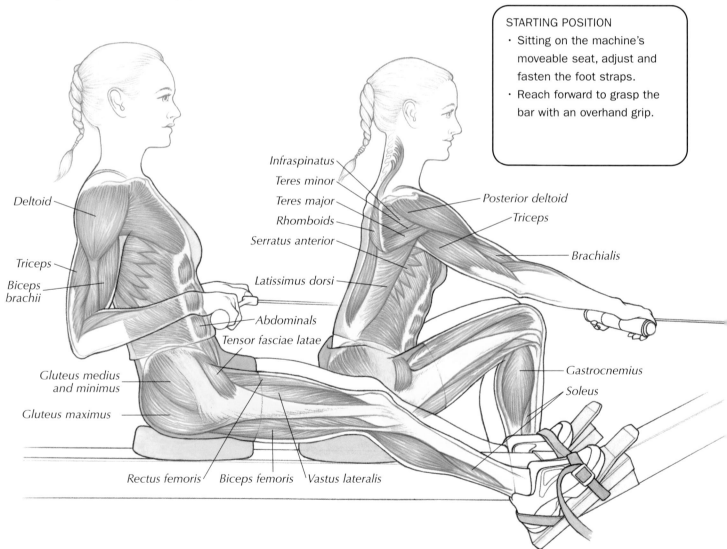

Deltoid
Triceps
Biceps brachii
Gluteus medius and minimus
Gluteus maximus
Rectus femoris
Biceps femoris
Vastus lateralis

Infraspinatus
Teres minor
Teres major
Rhomboids
Serratus anterior
Latissimus dorsi
Abdominals
Tensor fasciae latae
Posterior deltoid
Triceps
Brachialis
Gastrocnemius
Soleus

## Tips for good form

- Start with a slow, controlled motion and good form.
- Avoid hunching or rounding your shoulders during the exercise. Keep your chest open and your shoulder blades depressed.
- Avoid rounding your mid- and lower back. Instead, pivot your upper body from the hips. Keep your pelvis neutral and your spine aligned.
- Inhale on the backward phase.
- Let your hips move only in a range of 20° or so. On the forward motion you should move 10° forward of vertical, while on the backward motion you need to move 10° past vertical.

| Main stabilizing muscles |
| --- |
| Hips and legs: Hamstrings, Gluteal muscles, and Adductors<br>Trunk: Abdominal group, Quadratus lumborum, and Erector spinae<br>Shoulder joints: Rotator cuff muscles<br>Shoulder blades: Serratus anterior, Rhomboids, and Lower trapezius |

| ANALYSIS OF MOVEMENT | JOINT 1 | JOINT 2 | JOINT 3 |
| --- | --- | --- | --- |
| Main joints | Knees | Hips | Trunk |
| Joint movement | Arm pull/leg push phase: extension<br>Return phase: flexion | Arm pull/leg push phase: extension<br>Return phase: flexion | Arm pull/leg push phase: partial extension<br>Return phase: partial flexion |
| Main mobilizing muscles | Arm pull/leg push phase: Quadricep group<br>Return phase: Hamstring group | Arm pull/leg push phase: Gluteus maximus Hamstring group<br>Return phase: Iliopsoas Rectus femoris Pectineus | Arm pull/leg push phase: Erector spinae<br>Return phase: Abdominal group |
| | JOINT 4 | JOINT 5 | JOINT 6 |
| Main joints | Scapula | Shoulders | Elbows |
| Joint movement | Arm pull/leg push phase: adduction (retraction), downward rotation, and controlled depression<br>Return phase: abduction (protraction), upward rotation, and controlled elevation | Arm pull/leg push phase: extension, horizontal abduction<br>Return phase: flexion, horizontal adduction | Arm pull/leg push phase: flexion<br>Return phase: extension |
| Main mobilizing muscles | Arm pull/leg push phase (concentric phase): Lower trapezius Lower rhomboids<br>Return phase (eccentric phase): Lower trapezius Upper rhomboids Also Serratus anterior | Arm pull/leg push phase (concentric phase): Latissimus dorsi Teres major Posterior deltoid Teres minor Infraspinatus<br>Return phase (eccentric phase): Latissimus dorsi Teres major Posterior deltoid Teres minor Infraspinatus Also Pectoralis major and Anterior deltoid | Arm pull/leg push phase (concentric phase): Biceps brachii Brachialis Brachoradialis<br>Return phase (eccentric phase): Biceps brachii Brachialis Brachoradialis Also Triceps brachii |

In functional fitness training (fitness training geared toward the requirements of day-to-day living), you want to train the muscles in the manner in which they were naturally intended to function.

Maintaining overall postural strength as well as relative strength/flexibility balance between opposing muscle groups (for example, the abdominals and lower back muscles) is key in functional fitness. Poor postural control affects the quality, safety, and effectiveness of your movements and exercises. It is likely to promote compensatory patterns, with the result that joints and muscles will not work in the manner they were intended to function. This increases the risk of injury and premature aging, as well as musculoskeletal problems that are typical of Western living.

Stabilizers are muscles whose prime purpose is to maintain the stability and alignment of the rest of the body, anchoring it effectively while other muscles perform the exercise or movement. For example, when doing barbell bicep curls, the rotator cuff muscles stabilize and align the shoulder area, the abdominal and lower back groups maintain the alignment of the spine, and the bicep muscles help lift the weight by flexing the elbow joints.

The abdominal group is one of several important stabilizers highlighted throughout this book. Other muscles that perform important stabilizing functions, and are discussed in more depth elsewhere in this book include:

### Section 4. Legs and Hips
Gluteal group
Tensor fasciae latae
Rectus femoris of the quadriceps
Hamstring group
Iliopsoas
Adductor group
Tibialis posterior in the legs and hips

### Section 5. Back and Shoulders
Erector spinae
Quadratus lumborum
Lower and Mid-trapezius
Serratus anterior
Rhomboids
Rotator cuff group in the back and shoulders.

Stabilizers are prone to weakness and laxity over time. They are best trained using slow, controlled work done against body weight over longer duration. The exercises in this section are focused on improving this aspect of fitness.

---

## Exercise Balls

Used several times in this chapter, exercise balls are useful aids in certain types of exercise.

### Stability Ball
Known as Swiss balls, Pezzi balls, or stability balls, these heavy-duty exercise balls are made of high-quality vinyl varying in size between 18 and 33 in (45 and 85 cm). They were first used in physical therapy with children afflicted with cerebral palsy to develop balance and maintain reflex response.

When used in an exercise, a stability ball creates an unstable base position, which necessitates greater activation of the body's natural postural stabilizers during the completion of the exercise. While this helps to make an exercise more functional, the overuse of stability balls and their application to contrived exercises has met with some criticism.

### BOSU Ball
"BOSU" is an acronym for "Both Sides Up," and the BOSU Ball Balance Trainer is the brainchild of David Weck. He created the ball in 1999 to help him rehabilitate a back injury, and later that year the US ski team employed a crude version to use in preparing for the Olympics. The use of the BOSU ball spread, and coaches found it to be useful for improving functional movement and balance at the same time.

*Major Muscles of the Lower Anterior Trunk*

| Name | Joints Crossed | Origin | Insertion | Action |
|------|---------------|--------|-----------|--------|
| **Rectus abdominis** | Anterior spine | Crest of the pubis | Xiphoid process and the cartilage of the 5th to 7th ribs | Lumbar flexion (both sides); lateral flexion to right (right side); lateral flexion to left (left side). Controls the posterior tilt of the pelvis (together with external obliques) |
| **External obliques** | Anterior spine | Lateral borders of the lower 8 ribs | Four aspects: anterior side of the iliac crest; inguinal ligament; crest of the pubis; lower anterior fascia of the Rectus abdominus | Lumbar flexion (both sides); lumbar lateral flexion to the right and rotation to the left (right side); lumbar lateral flexion to the left and rotation to right (left side). Controls the posterior tilt of the pelvis (together with the Rectus abdominus) |
| **Internal obliques** | Anterior spine | Three aspects: upper section of the inguinal ligament; anterior two-thirds of the crest of the ilium; lumbar fascia | Costal cartilages of the 7th to 10th ribs and linea alba (imagine a V-shape from hips to ribs) | Lumbar flexion (both sides); lumbar lateral flexion and rotation to right (right side); lumbar lateral flexion and rotation to left (left side) |
| **Transverse abdominus** | Anterior spine | Four aspects: inguinal ligament; medial rim of iliac crest; medial surface of lower 6 rib cartilages; lumbar fascia | Three aspects: crest of the pubis; iliopectineal line; linea alba. It joins here with the transverse abdominus from the other side | The best type of contraction for this muscle is isometric, drawing the abdomen in toward the spine |

**Notes** These muscles are listed in order from the most superficial to the deepest.
In rotating the trunk, the external and internal obliques combine (for example, when the left elbow moves to the right knee, the left external obliques and the right internal obliques work together to rotate the trunk).
For other stabilizing muscles, see relevant sections.

*Exercises*

1. Posture Basics, page 40
2. Seated Ball Balance, page 42
3. Transverse Activation in 4-point Kneeling, page 43
4. Plank Pose Stabilization on Ball, page 44
5. Shell Prone Ball Roll-up, page 45
6. Abdominal Stabilization Program, page 46
7. Two-stage Crunch, page 48
8. Reverse Incline Bench Sit-up, page 49
9. Body-weight Oblique Crunch—Ball Between Legs, page 50
10. Combination Crunch, page 51
11. Hip Flexor Apparatus, page 52
12. Mid-back Scapular Stabilization on Bench, page 53
13. Kneeling Heel Touch, page 54

The stabilizing muscles such as the abdominals help to maintain a posture balanced against the force of gravity. It is also important to learn how to stabilize the shoulder blades before doing strength work with the upper limbs to prevent the shoulders from hunching and rounding forward, promoting neck pain. Relaxation breathing helps to relax the muscles and joints, and ensures a more stable postural base for exercise.

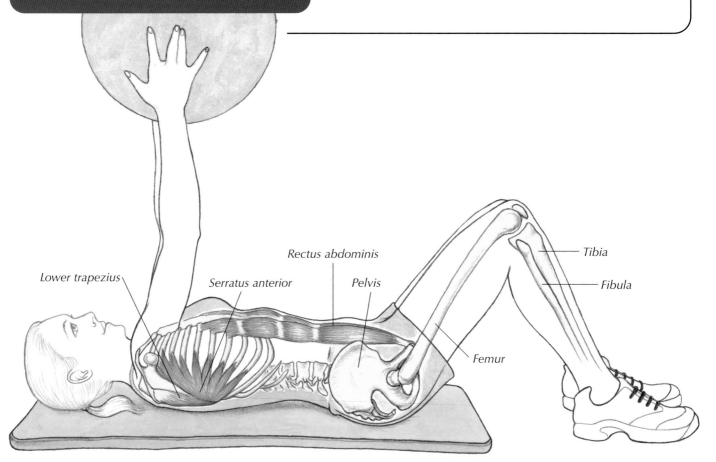

*Lower trapezius*

*Serratus anterior*

*Rectus abdominis*

*Pelvis*

*Tibia*

*Fibula*

*Femur*

*Supine Lying: Neutral Spine with Scapula Release*
- Lie supine with a neutral spine and your legs either straight or bent (as shown above).
- Hold a stability ball above your chest with your arms extended and your elbows soft.
- As you inhale, extend your arms toward the ceiling, gently rounding your shoulder blades forward, but keeping your elbows soft.
- Relax your shoulder blades and let them settle into the mat.
- As your arms come down, gently depress them and wrap them forward against the ribs, activating the Serratus anterior and Lower trapezius.

- You should be able to feel a little widening under your armpit at the side.
- Return and repeat.

*Serratus anterior and Lower trapezius*
These two muscles stabilize the shoulder blades against the ribs. Learning to actively release and use them in your posture, as in this exercise, will counteract typical neck and shoulder tension.

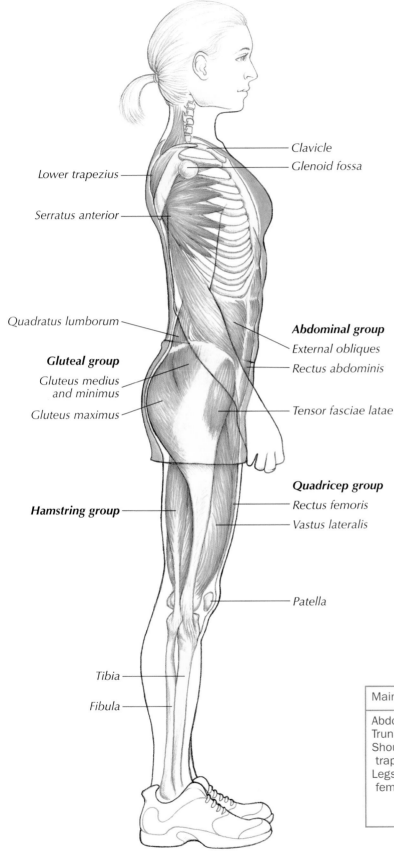

Clavicle

Glenoid fossa

Lower trapezius

Serratus anterior

Quadratus lumborum

**Gluteal group**

Gluteus medius
and minimus

Gluteus maximus

**Hamstring group**

**Abdominal group**

External obliques

Rectus abdominis

Tensor fasciae latae

**Quadricep group**

Rectus femoris

Vastus lateralis

Patella

Tibia

Fibula

### Neutral Spine: Stand and Breathe

- Keep your weight balanced through the middle of your feet.
- Breathe in deeply through your nose, feeling your ribcage open under your arms.
- Keep your heels down and imagine lifting your ankles and shin bones while you exhale naturally through your mouth.
- Soften your knees.
- Breathe in deeply again, this time "pulling" your quadriceps up from your knee. As you do so, rotate the upper thigh gently inward. Feel it open space in your lower back as you let your breath out.
- Breathe in deeply again, gently lengthening your spine up from your pelvis. Gradually draw in your abdominal muscles, but let the coccyx down as you exhale the next breath.
- Breathe in deeply again, while lifting and opening your chest without sticking the lower border of your ribs forward. Release your shoulder blades down, and wrap forward against your ribs as you let your breath out. You will feel the expansion under your arms.
- Relax your arms and shoulders.
- Breathing in again, gently lengthen your neck from the shoulders while balancing your head over your feet. Your eyes should look up slightly to the horizon as you exhale this breath.

Main stabilizing muscles

Abdominals, mainly the obliques and transverse
Trunk: Quadratus lumborum and Erector spinae
Shoulder blades: Serratus anterior, Rhomboids, and Lower trapezius
Legs and hips: Adductor group, Hamstring group, Rectus femoris, and Gluteal group

# SEATED BALL BALANCE

Core exercise • Whole-body stabilization • Intermediate to advanced

To ascertain the size of stability ball you should be using, sit correctly on a ball: your knees should be level or slightly below your hips and bent at 90°, and your feet should be flat. If you are older, not fully fit or overweight, use a larger ball that is slightly under-inflated. Decrease the ball size as you progress.

## Description
Raise one foot off the ground by extending your knee, and raise your opposite arm at the same time. Return and alternate.

## Tips for good form
· Avoid compromising posture alignment.
· Avoid momentum—use a slow, controlled movement.
· Relax your shoulders, and avoid dropping your head.

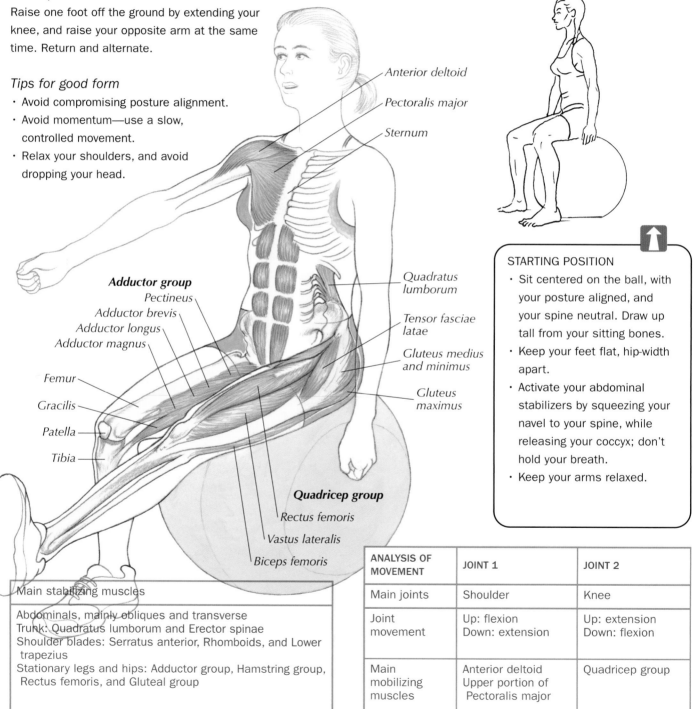

Anterior deltoid
Pectoralis major
Sternum
Quadratus lumborum
Tensor fasciae latae
Gluteus medius and minimus
Gluteus maximus

**Adductor group**
Pectineus
Adductor brevis
Adductor longus
Adductor magnus
Femur
Gracilis
Patella
Tibia

**Quadricep group**
Rectus femoris
Vastus lateralis
Biceps femoris

### STARTING POSITION
· Sit centered on the ball, with your posture aligned, and your spine neutral. Draw up tall from your sitting bones.
· Keep your feet flat, hip-width apart.
· Activate your abdominal stabilizers by squeezing your navel to your spine, while releasing your coccyx; don't hold your breath.
· Keep your arms relaxed.

### Main stabilizing muscles
Abdominals, mainly obliques and transverse
Trunk: Quadratus lumborum and Erector spinae
Shoulder blades: Serratus anterior, Rhomboids, and Lower trapezius
Stationary legs and hips: Adductor group, Hamstring group, Rectus femoris, and Gluteal group

| ANALYSIS OF MOVEMENT | JOINT 1 | JOINT 2 |
| --- | --- | --- |
| Main joints | Shoulder | Knee |
| Joint movement | Up: flexion Down: extension | Up: extension Down: flexion |
| Main mobilizing muscles | Anterior deltoid Upper portion of Pectoralis major | Quadricep group |

*ABDOMINALS, STABILIZATION, AND BALANCE*

# TRANSVERSE ACTIVATION IN 4-POINT KNEELING

Whole-body stabilization • Isolation focus on abdominals • Closed chain • Body-weight • Beginner to advanced

This exercise helps to create awareness of and strengthens the deepest abdominal muscle, the Transverse abdominus; this helps to keep the abdomen flat, and activates expulsion and expiration of the abdominal cavity.

## Tips for good form

- Use a slow, controlled full range of movement.
- Avoid rounding or arching your mid- and lower back. Keep your pelvis neutral and your spine aligned.
- Keep your chest open and shoulder blades depressed.
- As the Transverse abdominus moves toward your spine, your waist just above the crest of the hip (the "love handles") should seem to get smaller.

## Description

Inhale deeply. As you breathe out, draw your navel to your spine, so that you see the abdominals moving toward the spine while the spine remains neutral. Return and repeat.

### STARTING POSITION

- Kneel on all fours, with your knees and hands directly under your hips and shoulders.
- Maintain a neutral spine.
- Keep your chest open. Aim to depress and widen your shoulder blades against your back.

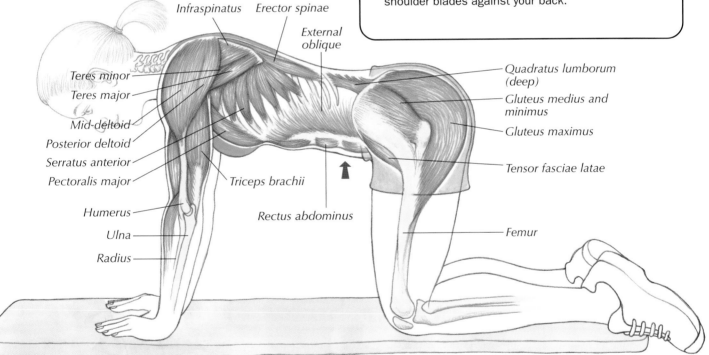

| ANALYSIS OF MOVEMENT | JOINT 1 |
|---|---|
| Main joints | Trunk |
| Joint movement | None |
| Main mobilizing muscles | Transverse abdominus |

Main stabilizing muscles

Abdominals, mainly the Rectus, External and Internal oblique
Trunk: Quadratus lumborum, Erector spinae, Adductor group, and Gluteus medius and minimus
Shoulder joints: Anterior deltoid, Pectoralis major, and Rotator cuff muscles
Shoulder blades: Serratus anterior, Rhomboids, and Lower trapezius
Arms: Triceps

# PLANK POSE STABILIZATION ON BALL

Whole-body stabilization • Focus on abdominals and mid-back stabilizers • Close chain • Body-weight • Intermediate to advanced

→ Exercises such as this help to strength the stabilizing endurance of the abdominal muscles. This can, in turn, help to reduce typical lower back pain associated with weak functional stability of the trunk muscles. The addition of the stability ball enhances the core stabilization work.

## Description

The primary aim is to maintain the stabilization and alignment for a period of time. Progress from 10 to 60 seconds in maintaining the pose. Placing the ball curved side up under the feet emphasizes lower body stabilization. Placing the ball curved side down under the hands increases upper body stability work.

## Tips for good form

· Lengthen your body through the crown of your head, keeping your chin tucked in slightly.
· Avoid rounding or arching your back. Keep your pelvis neutral and your spine aligned.
· Avoid hanging on or hunching your shoulder blades. Keep your chest open and your shoulder blades depressed.
· Do not hold your breath—breathe in a relaxed manner.

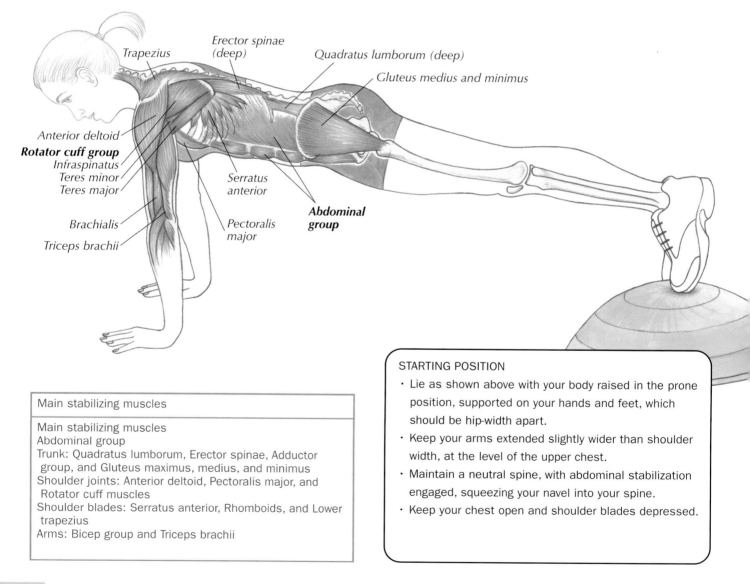

Trapezius
Erector spinae (deep)
Quadratus lumborum (deep)
Gluteus medius and minimus
Anterior deltoid
**Rotator cuff group**
Infraspinatus
Teres minor
Teres major
Serratus anterior
**Abdominal group**
Brachialis
Pectoralis major
Triceps brachii

### STARTING POSITION
· Lie as shown above with your body raised in the prone position, supported on your hands and feet, which should be hip-width apart.
· Keep your arms extended slightly wider than shoulder width, at the level of the upper chest.
· Maintain a neutral spine, with abdominal stabilization engaged, squeezing your navel into your spine.
· Keep your chest open and shoulder blades depressed.

| Main stabilizing muscles |
| --- |
| Main stabilizing muscles |
| Abdominal group |
| Trunk: Quadratus lumborum, Erector spinae, Adductor group, and Gluteus maximus, medius, and minimus |
| Shoulder joints: Anterior deltoid, Pectoralis major, and Rotator cuff muscles |
| Shoulder blades: Serratus anterior, Rhomboids, and Lower trapezius |
| Arms: Bicep group and Triceps brachii |

ABDOMINALS, STABILIZATION, AND BALANCE

# SHELL PRONE BALL ROLL-UP

Core exercise • Compound/multi-joint exercise • Whole-body stabilization • Close chain • Body-weight • Intermediate to advanced

➡ This exercise provides a unique integration of spinal mobilization, lower back stretching, and whole body stabilization.

## Description

Draw your knees in toward your chest, so that the ball rolls forward to your hands. Keep your arms stabilized. Return, maintaining postural stability by using the abdominal and upper body stabilizers. Repeat.

**STARTING POSITION**

· Kneel and slowly lean over until your hands touch the floor (see left). Let the ball support your body weight. Avoid looking up.
· Walk your hands forward until the ball is under your thighs and you are in the plank position.
· Keep your arms extended slightly wider than shoulder width, with your hands underneath your shoulders.
· Maintain a neutral spine.

*Quadratus lumborum*

*Erector spinae*

*Serratus anterior*

**Rotator cuff group**
*Infraspinatus*
*Teres major*
*Teres minor*

*Gluteus medius and minimus*

*Gluteus maximus*

*Hamstring group*

**Quadricep group**

*Posterior deltoid*
*Triceps brachii*
*Biceps brachii*
*Brachioradialis*

*Pectoralis major*

*Brachialis*

### Main stabilizing muscles

Abdominal group
Trunk: Quadratus lumborum, Erector spinae, Adductor group, and Gluteus medius and minimus
Shoulders: Anterior deltoid, Pectoralis major, and Rotator cuff muscles
Shoulder blades: Serratus anterior, Rhomboids, and Lower trapezius
Arms: Bicep group and Triceps brachii

## Tips for good form

· Use slow, controlled movements.
· Avoid looking up, and keep your chin slightly tucked in.
· Try to keep your spine lengthened.
· Avoid hunching your shoulder blades and keep your chest open.
· Breathe in a relaxed manner.

| ANALYSIS OF MOVEMENT | JOINT 1 | JOINT 2 | JOINT 3 |
|---|---|---|---|
| Main joints | Knee | Hip | Spine |
| Joint movement | Roll up: flexion Roll out: extension | Roll up: flexion Roll out: extension | Roll up: flexion Roll out: extension |
| Main mobilizing muscles | Hamstring group Gastrocnemius | Iliopsoas Rectus femoris | Abdominal group |

# ABDOMINAL STABILIZATION PROGRAM

Core exercise • Isolated • Stabilization focus on abdominals • Open chain • Body-weight • Beginner to advanced

Adapted from the work of Shirley Sahrmann, a physical therapist who specializes in abdominal rehabilitation, this is a series of progressive exercises aimed at strengthening the stabilization strength of the abdominals and pelvic floor. The exercises are also ideal for restoring diastasis recti, a separation of the abdominal muscles that can occur during pregnancy. Most other abdominal work is unsuitable for pregnant and postpartum mothers, as it tends to create too much intra-abdominal pressure and back strain.

## Tips for good form

- Move to the next level when you can perform 20 repetitions on each side without discomfort or moving the back.
- Avoid momentum—use a slow, controlled movement.
- Avoid hunching your shoulders. Keep your chest open, head and spine neutral, and shoulder blades depressed.
- Avoid tensing the buttocks or forcing the lower back down into the mat. Concentrate on using the abdominals.

## Description

It is important to master each level of this exercise before moving to the next.

1. **Starting position—abdominal isolation** Lie supine with your hips and knees bent, and your feet flat on the floor, hip-width apart. Keep your arms relaxed at your sides. Maintain a neutral spine, with abdominal stabilization engaged, mildly squeezing your navel into your spine without moving the spine. Make sure that you breathe easily as you squeeze, building up the time you hold the contraction.

2. **Leg slide** In the starting position, and while maintaining a neutral spine and engaging abdominal stabilization, slowly slide one leg out until it is flat on the floor. Return, and relax the abdominals. Engage and repeat with the opposite leg.

| ANALYSIS OF MOVEMENT | JOINT 1 |
|---|---|
| Main joints | Hip |
| Joint movement | Away from body: extension<br>Return: flexion |
| Main mobilizing muscles | Iliopsoas<br>Rectus femoris |

| Main stabilizing muscles |
|---|
| Abdominal group<br>Neck: Sternocleidomastoid<br>Shoulder blades: Serratus anterior, Rhomboids, and Lower trapezius<br>Hips: Iliopsoas, Rectus femoris |

**Note** Most of the work in this exercise is performed by the stabilizing muscles.

CAUTION If you have had a Caesarean section you can commence the exercise once the incision has healed—you should, however, obtain clearance from your obstetrician, gynecologist, or general practitioner before recommencing any exercise.

3. **Knee raises** From the starting position, and while maintaining a neutral spine and engaging abdominal stabilization, raise one leg so that the knee is vertically above the hip and the lower leg is parallel with the ground. Return, and repeat with the opposite leg.

5. **Leg extensions** Starting from the same position, with your hips and knees bent at 90° so that your knees are vertically above the hips and your lower leg is parallel with the ground, extend the leg straight out, keeping the foot 12–24 in (30–60 cm) off the ground. In the beginning you can extend the leg a shorter distance. As you master the exercise, extend farther until the leg is fully extended.

4. **Heel touch** Now start from a similar position, but with your hips and knees bent at 90°, so that your knees are vertically above the hips and the lower leg is parallel with the ground. While maintaining a neutral spine and engaging abdominal stabilization, lower the heel of one leg to the ground. Maintain the 90° bend at the knee. Return, and repeat with the opposite leg.

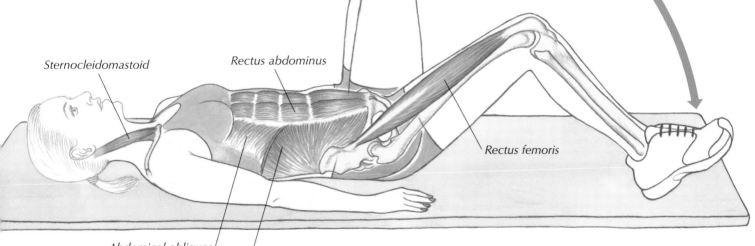

*Sternocleidomastoid*

*Rectus abdominus*

*Rectus femoris*

*Abdominal obliques*

*Transverse obliques (deepest)*

*Exercise variation and progression*
Try using a stability ball for variety: for example, in Step 2 use a ball underfoot when you slide your leg out. To progress you can add shoulder flexions: as the legs move away from the body, the arms move in the opposite direction.

# TWO-STAGE CRUNCH

Auxiliary exercise • Isolated • Pull • Open chain • Body-weight/stability ball • Beginner to advanced

➡️ This version of the crunch helps to slow the exercise down, and to remove cheating with regard to the momentum, which is often generated by doing the exercise too fast.

## Description

**Phase 1** As you exhale, slowly curl your head and neck. Keep your chin slightly tucked in and your shoulder blades still on the mat. Pause.

**Phase 2** Continue curling up your upper body by flexing your trunk. Your scapula should lift off the mat while your lower back remains on the mat, stable and neutral. Pause, return, and repeat.

## Tips for good form

· Avoid momentum. Use a slow, full range of movement.
· Keep your tailbone on the mat.
· Avoid forcing your neck or forcing your chin forward to lift the body. Keep your chin tucked in slightly and neutral with your cervical spine as you curl up.
· Avoid pulling your trunk up from your hands—activate and isolate the abdominals.
· Avoid hunching your shoulders. Keep your chest open and your shoulder blades depressed, and avoid pulling.
· Exhale on the up-phase.

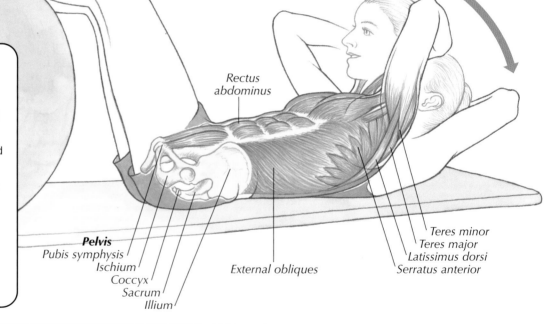

**STARTING POSITION**
· Lie supine with your hips and knees bent at 90° and your lower legs resting on a stability ball.
· Keep your hands unclasped behind your head.
· Maintain neutral alignment in the cervical spine.
· Keep abdominal stabilization active.

*Rectus abdominus*

*Teres minor*
*Teres major*
*Latissimus dorsi*
*Serratus anterior*

*External obliques*

**Pelvis**
*Pubis symphysis*
*Ischium*
*Coccyx*
*Sacrum*
*Illium*

| ANALYSIS OF MOVEMENT | PHASE 1 | PHASE 2 |
|---|---|---|
| Main joints | Cervical spine | Cervical and thoracic spine |
| Joint movement | Up: flexion Down: extension | Up: flexion Down: extension |
| Main mobilizing muscles | Sternocleidomastoid | Rectus abdominus Obliques |

| Main stabilizing muscles | |
|---|---|
| PHASE 1 | PHASE 2 |
| Abdominal group Shoulder blades: Serratus anterior, Rhomboids, and Lower trapezius | Sternocleidomastoid at the neck Shoulder blades: Serratus anterior, Rhomboids, and Lower trapezius |

*ABDOMINALS, STABILIZATION, AND BALANCE*

# REVERSE INCLINE BENCH SIT-UP

Auxiliary exercise • Compound/multi-joint • Pull • Open chain • Body-weight • Intermediate to advanced

This modified version of the sit-up is safer for the lower back and offers more control. It also tends to place more concentration on the lower rectii of the abdominals.

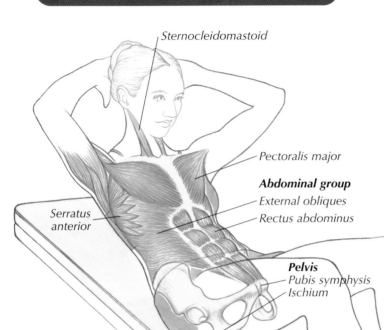

Sternocleidomastoid

Serratus anterior

Pectoralis major

**Abdominal group**
External obliques
Rectus abdominus

**Pelvis**
Pubis symphysis
Ischium

## Description

As you exhale, slowly curl up your upper body by flexing your trunk. Complete the movement by transferring into hip flexion, bringing your upper body toward your knees. Pause, return slowly, and repeat.

## Tips for good form

· Avoid momentum, which puts your lower back at risk and reduces the exercise's benefits. Use a slow, controlled, full range of movement.
· Keep your tailbone on the mat.
· Avoid forcing your neck or forcing your chin forward as you lift up. Keep your chin tucked in slightly and neutral with the cervical spine.
· Do not pull your trunk up from your hands—activate and isolate the abdominals.
· Avoid hunching your shoulders, and keep your chest open and shoulder blades depressed.
· Exhale on the up-phase, inhale on the down-phase.

| Main stabilizing muscles | |
| --- | --- |
| **PHASE 1** | **PHASE 2** |
| Neck: Sternocleidomastoid Shoulder blades: Serratus anterior, Rhomboids, and Lower trapezius | Trunk: Rectus abdominus and Obliques Neck: Sternocleidomastoid Shoulder blades: Serratus anterior, Rhomboids, and Lower trapezius |

| ANALYSIS OF MOVEMENT | PHASE 1 First phase same as crunch range of movement | PHASE 2 Remainder of movement to raise shoulder blades and lower back |
| --- | --- | --- |
| Main joints | Spine | Hip |
| Joint movement | Up: flexion Down: extension | Up: flexion Down: extension |
| Main mobilizing muscles | Rectus abdominus Obliques | Iliopsoas Rectus femoris |

STARTING POSITION
· On a 15°–30° incline bench, lie supine with your knees bent and your feet flat.
· Keep your hands unclasped behind your head.
· Maintain neutral alignment in the cervical spine.
· Keep abdominal stabilization active.

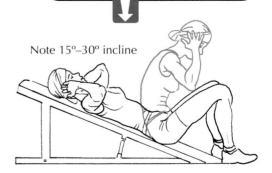

Note 15°–30° incline

# BODY-WEIGHT OBLIQUE CRUNCH— BALL BETWEEN LEGS

Auxiliary exercise • Isolated • Pull
• Open chain • Body-weight
• Beginner to advanced

➡ The oblique crunch is a simple variation of the crunch that focuses on the external and internal obliques. In this version, the use of the ball between the legs further isolates the abdominals, and creates additional core stability work in the hip area.

## Description

As you exhale, slowly curl up and rotate your upper body, bringing your elbow in to the opposite knee. Keep the ball stable between your legs, but do not force the squeeze. Your scapula should lift off the mat, while your lower back remains stable and neutral on it. Pause, return, and repeat. Finish the set, then change direction.

## Tips for good form

· Avoid momentum. Use a slow, full range of movement.
· Keep your chin tucked in and neutral.
· Avoid pulling your trunk up from your hand, and cheating with shoulder movement to bring your elbow to your knee.
· Exhale on the up-phase, inhale on the down-phase.

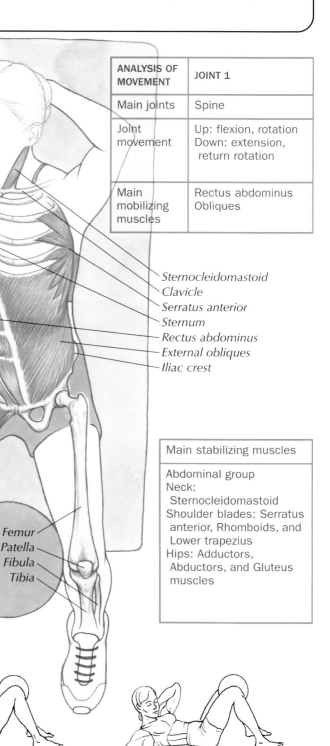

| ANALYSIS OF MOVEMENT | JOINT 1 |
|---|---|
| Main joints | Spine |
| Joint movement | Up: flexion, rotation Down: extension, return rotation |
| Main mobilizing muscles | Rectus abdominus Obliques |

Sternocleidomastoid
Clavicle
Serratus anterior
Sternum
Rectus abdominus
External obliques
Iliac crest

Gluteus medius
Gluteus minimus

**Adductor group**
Pectineus
Adductor brevis (underneath)
Adductor longus
Adductor magnus
Gracilis

Femur
Patella
Fibula
Tibia

### Main stabilizing muscles

Abdominal group
Neck:
 Sternocleidomastoid
Shoulder blades: Serratus anterior, Rhomboids, and Lower trapezius
Hips: Adductors, Abductors, and Gluteus muscles

## STARTING POSITION

· Lie supine with your knees bent and feet flat, hip-width apart.
· Place a small (9 in/23 cm) stability ball between your legs.
· Put one hand out to the side, and the other under your head.
· Maintain neutral alignment in the cervical spine.
· Keep abdominal stabilization active.

*ABDOMINALS, STABILIZATION, AND BALANCE*

# COMBINATION CRUNCH

Auxiliary exercise • Isolated • Pull
• Open chain • Body-weight
• Intermediate to advanced

This exercise promotes a full-peak contraction of the abdominals. Note that tight back extensor muscles such as the Erector spinae will inhibit peak contraction and range of motion.

Ulna
Radius
Humerus
Rectus abdominus
Sternocleidomastoid
Scapula
Lower trapezius
Serratus anterior
External obliques
Femur
Pelvis
Ischium
Coccyx
Sacrum
Ilium

### STARTING POSITION
· Lie supine with your knees bent, hip-width apart, and vertically above the hips.
· Keep your hands unclasped behind your head.
· Maintain neutral alignment in the cervical spine.
· Keep abdominal stabilization active.

## Description

As you exhale, slowly curl up your upper body by flexing your trunk. At the same time, reverse curl your hips off the floor to meet at a mid-point. Pause, return, and repeat.

## Tips for good form

· As you crunch, let the spine form a consistent C-curve. Keep your abdominal muscles in.
· Avoid momentum, and use a slow, full range of movement.
· Curl the tailbone down to the mat slowly.
· Keep your chin tucked in slightly as you curl up.
· Avoid pulling your trunk up from your hands—activate and isolate the abdominals.
· Keep your chest open and shoulder blades depressed.
· Exhale on the up-phase, inhale on the down-phase.

| ANALYSIS OF MOVEMENT | JOINT 1 | JOINT 2 |
|---|---|---|
| Main joints | Neck | Spine |
| Joint movement | Up: flexion<br>Down: extension | Up: flexion<br>Down: extension |
| Main mobilizing muscles | Sternocleidomastoid | Rectus abdominus<br>Obliques |

| Main stabilizing muscles |
|---|
| Abdominal group<br>Neck: Sternocleidomastoid<br>Shoulder blades: Serratus anterior, Rhomboids, and Lower trapezius<br>Hips: Iliopsoas and Rectus femoris |

# HIP FLEXOR APPARATUS

Auxiliary exercise • Whole-body stabilization • Focus on abdominals, mid- and lower back, and shoulder stabilizers • Open chain • Body-weight • Intermediate to advanced

➡️ The Hip Flexor Apparatus is often reported to be useful for working the lower abdominals. This is misleading. While local muscle fatigue is felt in the lower abdominal area, the abdominals work as a whole, contracting isometrically to stabilize and maintain a neutral spine.

## Tips for good form

- Avoid momentum—use a slow, controlled motion.
- Avoid collapsing at the scapula so that the shoulders look hunched. Lift up your body by depressing the scapula through the action of the Lower trapezius and Serratus anterior.
- Keep your chest open.
- Inhale on the up-phase.
- Note that those with weak abdominal stabilization are unlikely to be able to perform this exercise without acute lower back pain or discomfort.

## Description

Raise your knees to hip height, while maintaining a stabilized trunk. Return, and repeat.

Sternocleidomastoid
Deltoid
Pectoralis major
Biceps brachii

**Abdominal group**
*External oblique*
*Rectus abdominis*

Serratus anterior

Pelvis

Iliopsoas     Rectus femoris

| ANALYSIS OF MOVEMENT | JOINT 1 |
|---|---|
| Main joints | Hip |
| Joint movement | Up: flexion<br>Down: extension |
| Main mobilizing muscles | Iliopsoas<br>Rectus femoris<br>Tensor fasciae latae |

| Main stabilizing muscles |
|---|
| Abdominal group<br>Neck: Sternocleidomastoid<br>Shoulder blades: Serratus anterior, Rhomboids, and Lower trapezius<br>Shoulder joints: Rotator cuff group |

**Note** Most of the work in this exercise is performed by the stabilizing muscles.

### STARTING POSITION

- Support yourself in the apparatus with your weight on your forearms, chest open, spine neutral, and back and buttocks leaning against the backrest.
- Your legs should be dangling, and your abdominals stabilizing the pelvis.

➡️

# MID-BACK SCAPULAR STABILIZATION ON BENCH

Upper-body stabilization • Focus on mid-back stabilizers • Open chain • Body-weight • Intermediate to advanced

The scapular stabilizers keep the shoulder blades flat against the back and depressed during upper body exercises. If the shoulders are weak they tend to hunch, the chest closes, and the scapulae 'wing', causing neck pain and shoulder tension.

## Description

Lying prone on a bench, slowly raise your arms forward and outward with your elbows flexed. Your palms should face your head, your thumbs point to the ceiling. Keep the scapula depressed and shoulders relaxed throughout. Hold for 5 seconds, and return. Repeat.

## Tips for good form

· Avoid momentum—use a slow, controlled movement.
· Avoid hunching your shoulders. Keep your chest open and shoulder blades depressed.
· Avoid dropping your elbows.

Trapezius

Posterior deltoid
Mid-deltoid
Biceps brachii
Brachialis

Triceps brachii

**Rotator cuff group**
Teres minor
Infraspinatus

Rhomboids

Latissimus dorsi

Illiac crest
Pelvis
Sacrum

### STARTING POSITION

· Lie prone on a bench, with your head higher than your feet.
· Stabilize your feet on the ground, keeping your knees soft.
· Keep your posture aligned and stabilized.
· Keep your arms at your sides.

| Main stabilizing muscles | Abdominal group<br>Neck: Sternocleidomastoid<br>Shoulder blades: Serratus anterior, Rhomboids, and Mid- and Lower trapezius<br>Shoulder joints: Rotator cuff group |
|---|---|

| ANALYSIS OF MOVEMENT | JOINT 1 |
|---|---|
| Main joints | Shoulder |
| Joint movement | Up: horizontal abduction, flexion<br>Down: horizontal abduction, extension |
| Main mobilizing muscles | Posterior deltoid<br>Latissimus dorsi<br>Teres major |

# KNEELING HEEL TOUCH

Whole-body stabilization • Focus on abdominal and lower back stabilizers • Close chain • Body-weight • Advanced

This unique exercise, which is derived from Yoga back bends, offers a novel challenge to the abdominal and other postural muscles.

## Description

Lean and rotate your torso, and bring one hand to the opposite heel. Rotate from the trunk to look back at your foot and increase the rotation. Return, and repeat on the opposite side. For a slightly easier start, you can place Yoga blocks next to each ankle, and aim to touch them instead of your ankles. Due to the increased height, less lean and rotation will be required.

## Tips for good form

· Use a slow, controlled movement.
· When you lean and rotate, spread the movements evenly throughout the whole of your trunk to avoid straining your lower back.
· Avoid tensing your buttocks or hunching your shoulders, which will hinder your movement.
· Exhale as you reach back.

### STARTING POSITION

· Kneel on a folded exercise mat.
· Position your knees under your hips, and maintain a neutral spine.
· Engage abdominal stabilization, drawing your navel toward your spine. This is essential in this exercise in order to protect the back.
· Extend your arms in front of you at shoulder height, with your palms down and shoulder blades drawn down and wide.

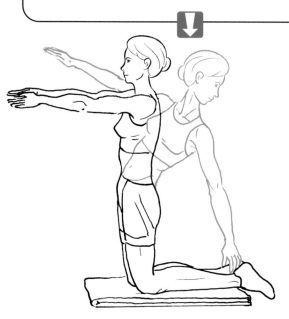

| ANALYSIS OF MOVEMENT | JOINT 1 | JOINT 2 | JOINT 3 |
|---|---|---|---|
| Main joints | Spine | Scapula | Shoulder |
| Joint movement | Backward movement: rotation and extension<br>Return: return rotation and flexion | Backward movement: adduction (retraction)<br>Return: abduction (protraction) | Backward movement: extension<br>Return: flexion |
| Main mobilizing muscles | Erector spinae<br>Quadratus lumborum<br>Abdominal obliques | Rhomboids<br>Trapezius | Latissimus dorsi<br>Teres major<br>Lower aspect of Pectoralis major<br>Posterior deltoid |

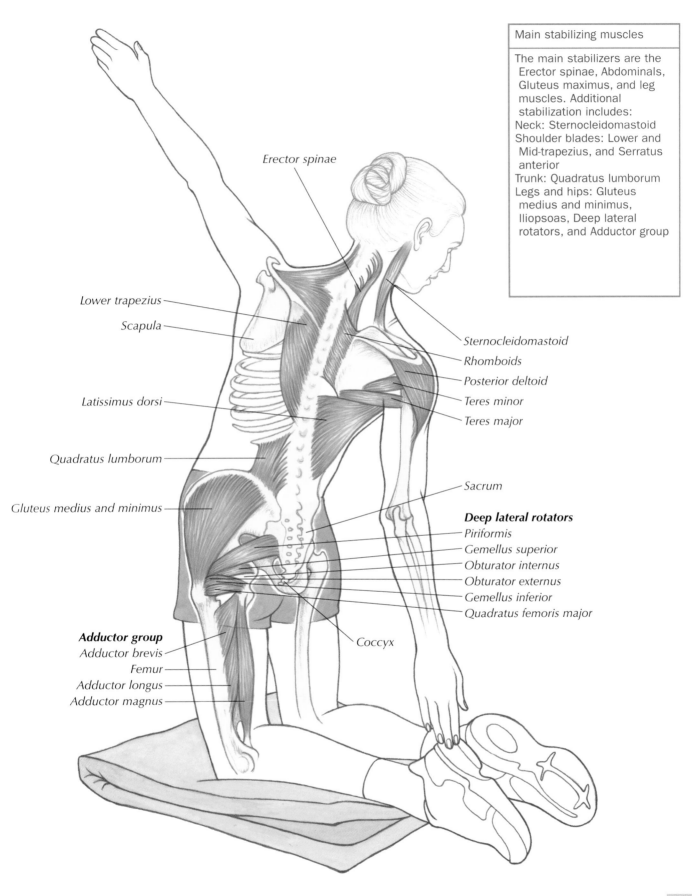

Erector spinae

Main stabilizing muscles

The main stabilizers are the Erector spinae, Abdominals, Gluteus maximus, and leg muscles. Additional stabilization includes:
Neck: Sternocleidomastoid
Shoulder blades: Lower and Mid-trapezius, and Serratus anterior
Trunk: Quadratus lumborum
Legs and hips: Gluteus medius and minimus, Iliopsoas, Deep lateral rotators, and Adductor group

Lower trapezius

Scapula

Latissimus dorsi

Quadratus lumborum

Gluteus medius and minimus

Sternocleidomastoid

Rhomboids

Posterior deltoid

Teres minor

Teres major

Sacrum

**Deep lateral rotators**
Piriformis
Gemellus superior
Obturator internus
Obturator externus
Gemellus inferior
Quadratus femoris major

Coccyx

**Adductor group**
Adductor brevis
Femur
Adductor longus
Adductor magnus

*ABDOMINALS, STABILIZATION, AND BALANCE*

# CHEST

The breast is a structure consisting mostly of fat tissue, which is supported by the pectoral muscle. It is impossible to strengthen, firm, or enlarge the actual breast with exercise due to the lack of muscle fibres in the tissue, but chest exercises will assist in the support of breasts that are either large or sagging. Training will not reverse the natural ageing of the breast, especially if you have breast-fed, but it will result in a moderate and pleasant toning effect. While surgery can yield more dramatic effects, whether you have breast surgery or not, your exercise program should include the chest exercises recommended in this section.

Strengthening the pectoral muscles underlying the breast can moderately increase your chest size, but not your cup size. However, in the course of the "normal" aging process, after the age of 20 women tend to lose 1 lb (500 g) of muscle and gain 2–4½ lb (1–2 kg) of fat per year. Therefore, as you tone the pectoral muscles and lose some fat, there may be no change in your chest size. In fact, the breasts may even get smaller because of the reduction in fat tissue.

A simple tip: if you are looking for a fuller bust, proper upper body posture will enhance this. Conversely, rounding your shoulders will make your chest look flatter. Include a balance of mid- and upper-back exercises (see section on back and shoulders starting on page 92), and some time on a rowing machine to enhance the strength of the postural muscles that keep the chest open and the shoulders relaxed.

The Serratus anterior acts as a dynamic stabilizer by depressing the shoulder blades and keeping them flat against the back. "Hanging" from the shoulder blades while doing chest exercises such as push-ups is a sign of a weak/inactive Serratus anterior and should be avoided. Instead, aim to depress and widen the shoulder blades against your back, thereby activating the Serratus anterior and Lower trapezius. This stabilization principle applies to all chest exercises.

## Major Muscles of the Chest

| Name | Joints crossed | Origin | Insertion | Action |
|------|----------------|--------|-----------|--------|
| **Pectoralis major** | Shouder | Clavicular (upper portion): medial half of the anterior surface of the clavicle. Sternal (mid-portion) and abdominal (lower) portion: anterior surface of the costal cartilages of the first 6 ribs and the adjoining portion of the sternum | Flat tendon of the inter-tubercular groove of the humerus | Shoulder: adduction, horizontal adduction, medial rotation, flexion |
| **Pectoralis minor** | Scapula to ribs | Anterior surface of the 3rd to the 5th ribs | Coracoid process of the scapula | Scapula: abduction (protraction), downward rotation, depression |
| **Anterior deltoid** | Shoulder | Anterior lateral third of the clavicle | Lateral side of the humerus | Shoulder: flexion, medial rotation |
| **Coracobrahialis** | Shoulder | Coracoid process of the scapula | Middle medial border of humeral shaft | Shoulder: horizontal adduction |

**Notes** The Triceps brachii and Anconeus are detailed in Section 6, Arms. The Rotator cuff group, Serratus anterior, Rhomboids, Trapezius, Latissimus dorsi, and Teres major are detailed in Section 5, Back and Shoulders.

## Exercises

| | | |
|---|---|---|
| 1. Body-weight Modified Push-ups, page 57 | 4. Incline Dumb-bell Bench Press, page 60 | 7. Incline Pec Deck Machine, page 65 |
| 2. Wall Push-ups on Bar, page 58 | 5. Barbell Bench Press, page 62 | 8. Dumb-bell Flat Bench Flyes, page 66 |
| 3. Bench Press Machine, page 59 | 6. Body-weight Dips, page 64 | 9. Cable Crossover, page 67 |

# BODY-WEIGHT MODIFIED PUSH-UPS

Core exercise • Compound/multi-joint
• Push • Close chain • Body-weight
• Functional • Beginner to advanced

Renata Hamplová from the Czech Republic holds the women's world record for the most push-ups over three and ten minutes, both set in 1995. She managed to do 190 and 426 push-ups respectively.

## Description
Maintaining your postural alignment, lower your body to the floor by bending at the elbows. Return by pushing up until your arms are straight. Repeat.

## Tips for good form
· Use a slow, controlled movement.
· Maintain alignment, keeping your ears, shoulders, hips, and knees in line.
· Avoid compensating with momentum.
· Avoid "hanging" from your shoulder blades. Aim to depress and widen your shoulder blades by keeping them flat against your back.

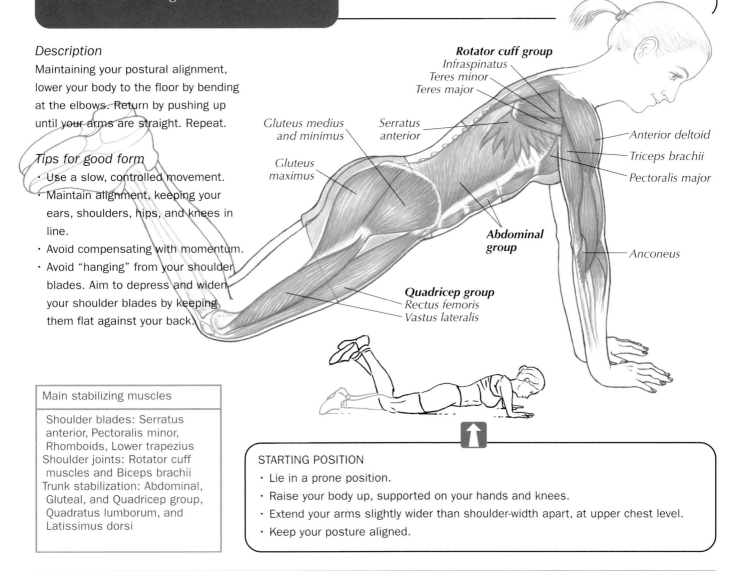

Rotator cuff group
Infraspinatus
Teres minor
Teres major
Serratus anterior
Gluteus medius and minimus
Gluteus maximus
Anterior deltoid
Triceps brachii
Pectoralis major
Abdominal group
Anconeus
Quadricep group
Rectus femoris
Vastus lateralis

### Main stabilizing muscles
Shoulder blades: Serratus anterior, Pectoralis minor, Rhomboids, Lower trapezius
Shoulder joints: Rotator cuff muscles and Biceps brachii
Trunk stabilization: Abdominal, Gluteal, and Quadricep group, Quadratus lumborum, and Latissimus dorsi

### STARTING POSITION
· Lie in a prone position.
· Raise your body up, supported on your hands and knees.
· Extend your arms slightly wider than shoulder-width apart, at upper chest level.
· Keep your posture aligned.

| ANALYSIS OF MOVEMENT | JOINT 1 | JOINT 2 | JOINT 3 |
|---|---|---|---|
| Main joints | Elbow | Shoulder | Scapulothoracic |
| Joint movement | Up: extension<br>Down: flexion | Up: horizontal adduction, flexion<br>Down: horizontal abduction, extension | Up: partial upward rotation, abduction (protraction)<br>Down: partial downward rotation, adduction (retraction) |
| Main mobilizing muscles | Triceps brachii<br>Anconeus | Pectoralis major, emphasis on the sternal and clavicular aspects<br>Coracobrachialis<br>Anterior deltoid | Serratus anterior |

# WALL PUSH-UPS ON BAR

Core exercise • Compound/multi-joint
• Push • Close chain • Body-weight
• Functional • Beginner to advanced

Women often avoid upper body strength training for fear of developing bulky muscles. In fact, upper body training is most likely to give a woman better posture, poise, and confidence. This version of the push-up is an easy start to modified push-ups (page 57).

## Description

Maintaining your postural alignment, lower your body to the bar at upper chest level by bending at the elbows. Return, by pushing your body up until your arms are straight. Repeat.

## Tips for good form

- Use a slow, controlled movement.
- Maintain alignment. Keep your ears, shoulders, hips, knees, and ankles in line.
- Avoid compensating with momentum.
- Avoid "hanging" from your shoulder blades. Aim to depress and widen your shoulder blades by keeping them flat against your back.

### STARTING POSITION

- Lean on a hip-height bar with your arms extended slightly wider than shoulder-width apart at upper chest level.
- Support your body-weight through your extended arms.
- Keep your posture aligned.

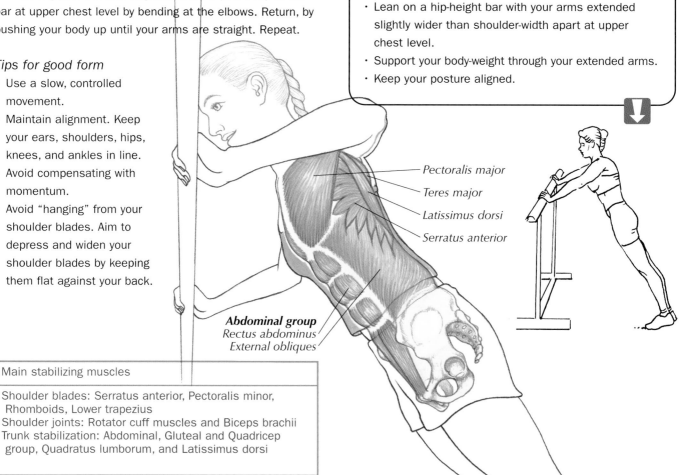

Pectoralis major
Teres major
Latissimus dorsi
Serratus anterior

**Abdominal group**
Rectus abdominus
External obliques

### Main stabilizing muscles

Shoulder blades: Serratus anterior, Pectoralis minor, Rhomboids, Lower trapezius
Shoulder joints: Rotator cuff muscles and Biceps brachii
Trunk stabilization: Abdominal, Gluteal and Quadricep group, Quadratus lumborum, and Latissimus dorsi

| ANALYSIS OF MOVEMENT | JOINT 1 | JOINT 2 | JOINT 3 |
|---|---|---|---|
| Main joints | Elbow | Shoulder | Scapulothoracic |
| Joint movement | Up: extension<br>Down: flexion | Up: horizontal adduction, flexion<br>Down: horizontal abduction, extension | Up: partial upward rotation, abduction (protraction)<br>Down: partial downward rotation, adduction (retraction) |
| Main mobilizing muscles | Triceps brachii<br>Anconeus | Pectoralis major, emphasis on the sternal and clavicular aspects<br>Coracobrachialis<br>Anterior deltoid | Serratus anterior |

# BENCH PRESS MACHINE

Core exercise • Compound/multi-joint
• Push • Open chain • Barbell
• Intermediate to advanced

This exercise offers the safety of a machine with the feel of a free-weight exercise. It is an ideal preparation for the Dumbbell and Barbell Bench Presses.

## Description

Raise the bar by pressing up and extending your elbows. Return, stopping just before the rest position and keeping the bar under tension. Repeat.

## Tips for good form

· Get good form before increasing weight.
· Avoid momentum—use a slow, controlled movement.
· Breathe out when raising the bar.
· Avoid "hanging" from the shoulder blades (see final tip, opposite).

### STARTING POSITION

· Adjust the bar starting position to just below chest level.
· Lie supine with your feet on a bench or shoulder-width apart on the ground for stability. Keep your spine aligned.
· Take hold of the bar at upper chest level.

### FINISHING POSITION

Pectoralis major

Anterior deltoid

Biceps brachii

Brachialis

Triceps brachii

Coracobrachialis

**Abdominal group**
Rectus abdominus
External obliques

Serratus anterior

Latissimus dorsi

Main stabilizing muscles

Shoulder blades: Serratus anterior, Pectoralis minor, and Lower trapezius
Shoulder joints: Rotator cuff muscles and Biceps brachii
Mild trunk stabilization: Abdominal and Gluteal group, Rhomboids, Trapezius, and Latissimus dorsi

| ANALYSIS OF MOVEMENT | JOINT 1 | JOINT 2 | JOINT 3 |
|---|---|---|---|
| Main joints | Elbow | Shoulder | Scapulothoracic |
| Joint movement | Up: extension<br>Down: flexion | Up: horizontal adduction, flexion<br>Down: horizontal abduction, extension | Up: partial upward rotation, abduction (protraction)<br>Down: partial downward rotation, adduction (retraction) |
| Main mobilizing muscles | Triceps brachii<br>Anconeus | Pectoralis major, emphasis on the sternal and clavicular aspects<br>Coracobrachialis<br>Anterior deltoid | Serratus anterior |

# INCLINE DUMB-BELL BENCH PRESS

Core exercise • Compound/multi-joint
• Push • Open chain • Barbell
• Intermediate to advanced

➡ A greater range of motion is possible in this exercise than in the Barbell Bench Press, allowing you to work your muscles through a greater range of contraction. In addition, more postural stabilization is needed because the weights need to be controlled independently.

## Description

Bending your elbows, lower the dumb-bells in line with your upper chest, and return by pressing until your arms are extended. Repeat.

## Exercise variation and progression

As a variation, you can try doing this exercise on a flat bench rather than an inclined one. The Bench Press Machine exercise on the previous page, which uses a fixed weight rather than a free one, offers the safety of a machine with the feel of this exercise.

## Tips for good form

· The incline angle of this exercise shifts the work toward the upper chest. Note that most gym incline benches are set at too high an angle.
· Get good form before increasing the weight.
· Avoid momentum—use a slow, controlled movement.
· Keep your chest open, and avoid tensing and rolling your shoulders inward. As you work, depress and widen your shoulder blades, keeping them flat against your back and thereby activating the Serratus anterior and Lower trapezius.
· Do not bring the dumb-bells together completely on the upward motion: keep them about 6 in (15 cm) apart.
· Breathe out when raising the dumb-bells.

| Main stabilizing muscles |
|---|
| Shoulder blades: Serratus anterior, Pectoralis minor, and Lower trapezius<br>Shoulder joints: Rotator cuff muscles and Biceps brachii<br>Mild trunk stabilization: Abdominal and Gluteal group, Rhomboids, Trapezius, and Latissimus dorsi |

| ANALYSIS OF MOVEMENT | JOINT 1 | JOINT 2 | JOINT 3 |
|---|---|---|---|
| Main joints | Elbow | Shoulder | Scapulothoracic |
| Joint movement | Up: extension<br>Down: flexion | Up: horizontal adduction, flexion<br>Down: horizontal abduction, extension | Up: upward rotation, partial abduction (protraction)<br>Down: downward rotation, partial adduction (retraction) |
| Main mobilizing muscles | Triceps brachii<br>Anconeus | Pectoralis major, emphasis on the sternal and clavicular aspects<br>Coracobrachialis<br>Anterior deltoid | Serratus anterior |

*Women-specific training tip—progressing through
bench press exercises*

Men generally progress straight from the Bench Press
Machine (page 59) to the Barbell Bench Press (page 62).
Women may find it best to go from the Bench Press Machine
to the Incline Dumb-bell Bench Press in order to gain greater
range, stability, and balance with controllable dumb-bells
before going on to the free-weight barbell version.

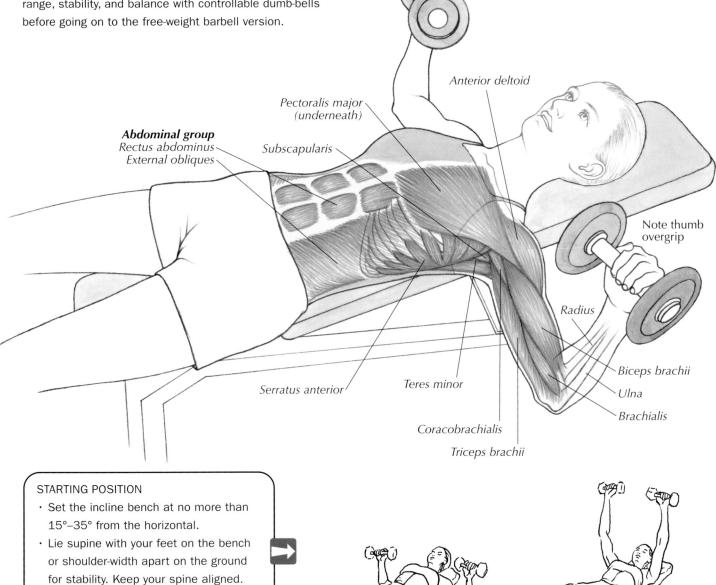

Anterior deltoid

Pectoralis major
(underneath)

**Abdominal group**
Rectus abdominus
External obliques

Subscapularis

Note thumb
overgrip

Radius

Biceps brachii

Ulna

Brachialis

Serratus anterior

Teres minor

Coracobrachialis

Triceps brachii

STARTING POSITION
· Set the incline bench at no more than
  15°–35° from the horizontal.
· Lie supine with your feet on the bench
  or shoulder-width apart on the ground
  for stability. Keep your spine aligned.
· Lift the dumb-bells to your knees, using
  momentum.
· Lie back, lifting the weights above chest
  level, supported vertically above your
  elbows.

# BARBELL BENCH PRESS

Core exercise • Compound/multi-joint
• Push • Open chain • Barbell
• Intermediate to advanced

According to *Wikipedia*, the online encyclopedia, Becca Swanson holds the world record for the women's bench press. She pressed 551 lb (250 kg) on August 26, 2006 at the APF/WPO Debbie Kruck Bench Press Contest in Daytona Beach, USA.

## Description

Remove the bar from the rack. Bending your elbows, lower the bar in line with your upper chest. Return by pressing until your arms are extended. Repeat.

## Tips for good form

· Get good form before increasing weight.
· Avoid momentum—use a slow, controlled movement.
· Breathe out when raising the bar.
· As you work, depress and widen your shoulder blades, keeping them flat against your back, thereby activating the Serratus anterior and Lower trapezius.

### STARTING POSITION

· Lie down in a supine position.
· Maintain a medium grip on the barbell, slightly wider than shoulder-width.
· Keep your spine aligned. If possible, raise your feet onto the bench to reduce arching in the lower back.

**Note** A wider grip places more emphasis on the outer pectoral muscles, while a closer grip places more emphasis on the triceps, Anterior deltoid, and inner pectoral muscles.

| ANALYSIS OF MOVEMENT | JOINT 1 | JOINT 2 | JOINT 3 |
|---|---|---|---|
| Main joints | Elbow | Shoulder | Scapulothoracic |
| Joint movement | Up: extension<br>Down: flexion | Up: horizontal adduction, flexion<br>Down: horizontal abduction, extension | Up: partial upward rotation, abduction (protraction)<br>Down: partial downward rotation, adduction (retraction) |
| Main mobilizing muscles | Triceps brachii<br>Anconeus | Pectoralis major, emphasis on the sternal and clavicular aspects, Coracobrachialis<br>Anterior deltoid | Serratus anterior |

*Learning to Bench Press*

· Develop your initial strength with Modified Push-ups.
· Then progress to the Bench Press Machine, which offers the safety of a machine with the feel of the free-weight version of the exercise.
· From here go on to the Barbell Bench Press, using lighter weight bars and enlisting the aid of an instructor/spotter until you gain confidence.

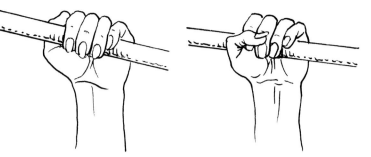

*There are two types of grip that can be used with this exercise. The one shown on the left, above, is the easiest and suitable for the beginner. The thumb overgrip shown on the right is more advanced but it does enhance the quality of the exercise.*

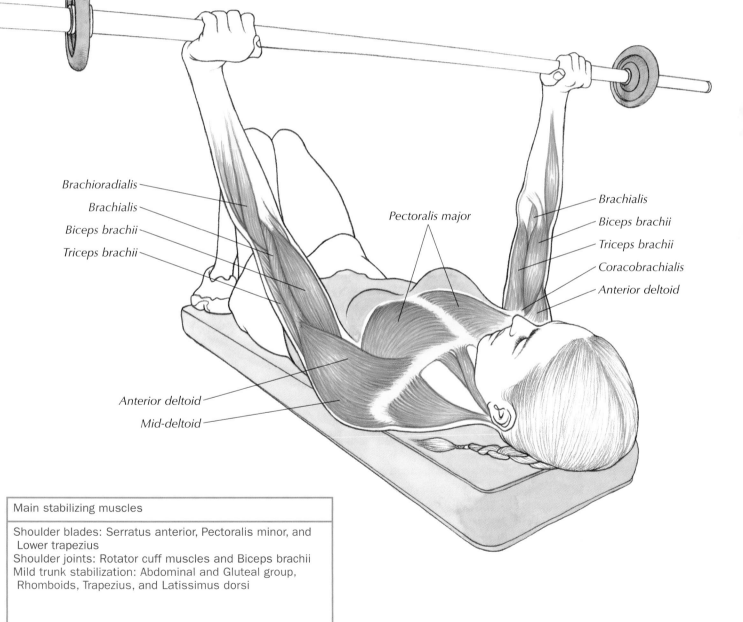

Brachioradialis
Brachialis
Biceps brachii
Triceps brachii

Pectoralis major

Brachialis
Biceps brachii
Triceps brachii
Coracobrachialis
Anterior deltoid

Anterior deltoid
Mid-deltoid

Main stabilizing muscles

Shoulder blades: Serratus anterior, Pectoralis minor, and Lower trapezius
Shoulder joints: Rotator cuff muscles and Biceps brachii
Mild trunk stabilization: Abdominal and Gluteal group, Rhomboids, Trapezius, and Latissimus dorsi

# BODY-WEIGHT DIPS

- Core exercise • Compound/multi-joint
- Push • Open chain • Body-weight
- Intermediate to advanced

➡️ Although this is one of the most common and versatile exercises, postural compensation and cheating are common. For the best results, start with only as many repetitions as you can do using the correct technique.

## Description

Lower your body until you feel a stretch in your chest, controlling your movement with the strength of your chest and arms. Push your body up in the same posture. Repeat.

## Tips for good form

- Avoid momentum—use a slow, controlled movement.
- Avoid hunching and rounding your shoulders. Keep your chest open and your shoulder blades depressed.
- Concentrate on squeezing from the chest and triceps.
- Breathe out on the upward motion.

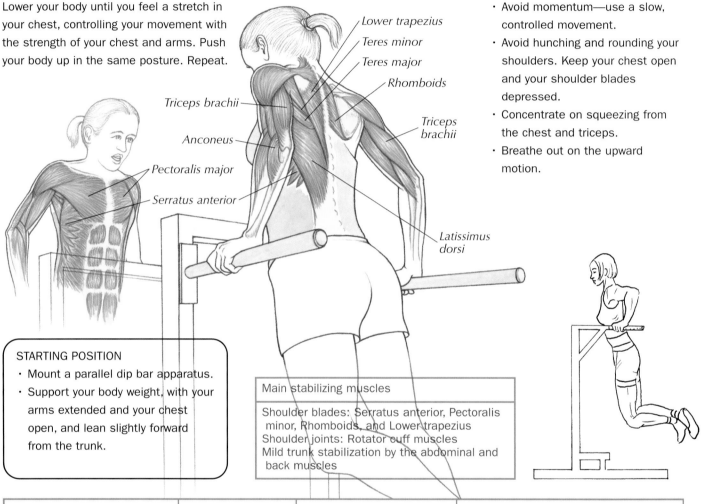

Lower trapezius
Teres minor
Teres major
Rhomboids
Triceps brachii
Triceps brachii
Anconeus
Pectoralis major
Serratus anterior
Latissimus dorsi

### STARTING POSITION
- Mount a parallel dip bar apparatus.
- Support your body weight, with your arms extended and your chest open, and lean slightly forward from the trunk.

### Main stabilizing muscles

Shoulder blades: Serratus anterior, Pectoralis minor, Rhomboids, and Lower trapezius
Shoulder joints: Rotator cuff muscles
Mild trunk stabilization by the abdominal and back muscles

| ANALYSIS OF MOVEMENT | JOINT 1 | JOINT 2 | JOINT 3 |
|---|---|---|---|
| Main joints | Elbow | Shoulder | Scapulothoracic |
| Joint movement | Up: extension<br>Down: flexion | Up: adduction, flexion<br>Down: abduction, extension | Up: adduction (retraction), partial elevation, and upward rotation<br>Down: abduction (protraction), partial depression, and downward rotation |
| Main mobilizing muscles | Triceps brachii<br>Anconeus | Pectoralis major<br>Pectoralis minor<br>Coracobrachialis<br>Latissimus dorsi<br>Teres major | Serratus anterior<br>Lower trapezius<br>Rhomboids |

CHEST

# INCLINE PEC DECK MACHINE

Auxiliary exercise • Isolated/single joint
• Push • Open chain • Machine
• Beginner to advanced

→ This machine is known by a variety of names, including Butterfly Machine and Chest Fly Machine. Using the incline version focuses the attention on the lower pectoral muscles, enhancing their ability to support and firm the breasts.

## Description
Push the pads together in front of your chest. Pause, then move them in a controlled way back to the sides. Repeat.

## Tips for good form
· Get good form before increasing weight.
· Sit tall on your sitting bones, with spine aligned.
· Avoid momentum—use a slow, controlled movement.
· Avoid hunching or rounding your shoulders. Keep your chest open and your shoulder blades depressed.
· Breathe out when squeezing the pads together.
· Keep your feet wide for the best stability.

Sternocleidomastoid

Pectoralis major

Anterior deltoid

Brachialis

Biceps brachii

Triceps brachii

Coracobrachialis

Teres major

Latissimus dorsi

Serratus anterior

**Abdominal group**
Rectus abdominus
External obliques

### Main stabilizing muscles
Shoulder blades: Serratus anterior, Pectoralis minor, Rhomboids, Trapezius, especially Lower trapezius
Shoulder joints: Rotator cuff muscles, and Biceps brachii
Trunk stabilization: Abdominal and Gluteal group, and Latissimus dorsi

### STARTING POSITION
· Sit in the machine.
· Place your forearms on the pads, so that your elbows are at shoulder height.
· Keep your shoulders relaxed and your chest open.
· Keep your spine aligned, with your feet raised onto the foot rests.

| ANALYSIS OF MOVEMENT | JOINT 1 | JOINT 2 |
|---|---|---|
| Main joints | Shoulder | Scapulothoracic |
| Joint movement | Inward: horizontal adduction, partial adduction<br>Return: horizontal abduction, partial abduction | Inward: partial abduction<br>Return: partial adduction |
| Main mobilizing muscles | Pectoralis major, emphasis on the sternal and abdominal aspect (lower)<br>Coracobrachialis<br>Anterior deltoid | Serratus anterior |

FINISHING POSITION

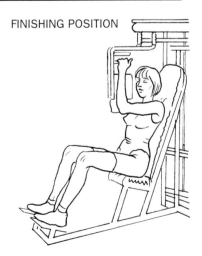

# DUMB-BELL FLAT BENCH FLYES

Auxiliary exercise • Isolation/single joint • Push • Open chain • Dumb-bell • Beginner to advanced

➡ The dumb-bells used in this exercise originated in India in the 11th century, when stone weights known as *nals* were used in "gyms" by those performing strength-training exercises.

## Description
Lower the dumb-bells to your sides until your chest muscles are stretched. Return and repeat.

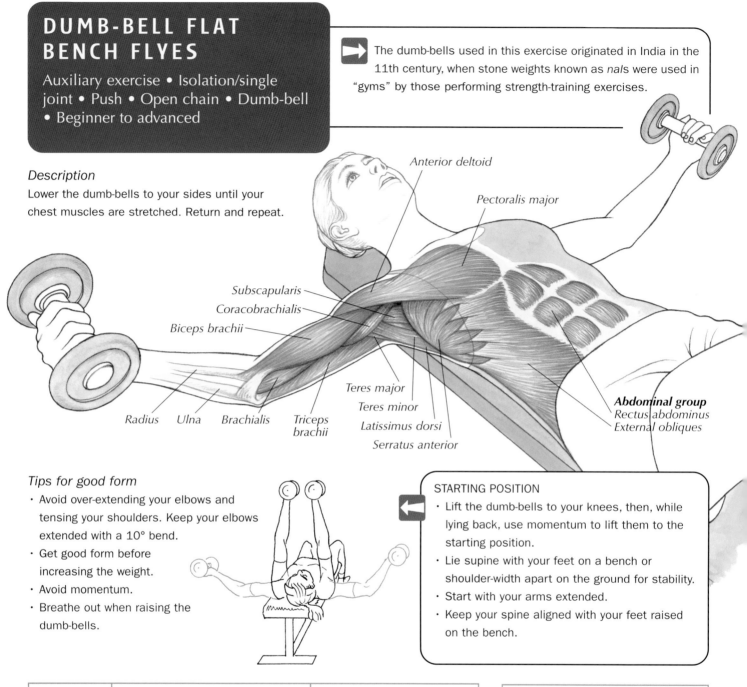

*Anterior deltoid*

*Pectoralis major*

*Subscapularis*
*Coracobrachialis*
*Biceps brachii*

*Radius*  *Ulna*  *Brachialis*  *Triceps brachii*

*Teres major*
*Teres minor*
*Latissimus dorsi*
*Serratus anterior*

***Abdominal group***
*Rectus abdominus*
*External obliques*

## Tips for good form
· Avoid over-extending your elbows and tensing your shoulders. Keep your elbows extended with a 10° bend.
· Get good form before increasing the weight.
· Avoid momentum.
· Breathe out when raising the dumb-bells.

### STARTING POSITION
· Lift the dumb-bells to your knees, then, while lying back, use momentum to lift them to the starting position.
· Lie supine with your feet on a bench or shoulder-width apart on the ground for stability.
· Start with your arms extended.
· Keep your spine aligned with your feet raised on the bench.

| ANALYSIS OF MOVEMENT | JOINT 1 | JOINT 2 |
|---|---|---|
| Main joints | Shoulder | Scapulothoracic |
| Joint movement | Up: horizontal adduction<br>Down: horizontal abduction | Inward: partial abduction (protraction)<br>Return: partial adduction (retraction) |
| Main mobilizing muscles | Pectoralis major, emphasis on the sternal and clavicular aspect<br>Coracobrachialis<br>Anterior deltoid<br>Biceps brachii (short head) | Serratus anterior |

Main stabilizing muscles

Shoulder blades: Serratus anterior, Pectoralis minor, Rhomboids, and Lower trapezius
Shoulder joints: Rotator cuff muscles and Biceps brachii
Elbow joints: Triceps brachii and Brachialis
Wrists: Wrist flexors
Mild trunk stabilization by the Abdominal and Gluteal group, and Latissimus dorsi

# CABLE CROSSOVER

Auxiliary exercise • Isolation/single joint • Push • Open chain • Cable machine • Intermediate to advanced

→ The Cable Crossover is done on a bilateral cable-pulley machine. The first commercial gym cable-pulley version of this machine was developed in the 1950s by American fitness pioneer Jack LaLanne.

## Description

Bring the cable attachments together in front of your body, keeping your elbows in a fixed position. Return to the starting position, and repeat. Rotate your shoulders inward on the forward motion, and outward on the return.

### STARTING POSITION

· Stand positioned equidistant between the cables.
· Place one foot in front of the other, shoulder-width apart.
· Keep your knees gently bent, body leaning forward slightly.

FINISHING POSITION

## Tips for good form

· Avoid momentum.
· Avoid over-extending your elbows.
· Keep your chest and shoulders open.
· Squeeze from the chest.
· Exhale when bringing cables together.

**Superficial Layer**
Anterior deltoid
Biceps brachii
Wrist flexors
Brachialis
Triceps brachii
Coracobrachialis
Latissimus dorsi
**Pectoralis major**
Sternal aspect
Abdominal aspect
Serratus anterior
**Abdominal group**
External obliques
Rectus abdominus
Gluteus medius and minimus
Tensor fascia latae
Sartorius
**Quadricep group**
Rectus femoris
Vastus lateralis

**Deep Layer**
Pectoralis minor

| ANALYSIS OF MOVEMENT | JOINT 1 | JOINT 2 |
|---|---|---|
| Main joints | Shoulder | Scapulothoracic |
| Joint movement | Inward: adduction, partial horizontal adduction, medial rotation<br>Return: abduction, partial horizontal abduction, lateral rotation | Inward: abduction (protraction), partial downward rotation<br>Return: abduction (retraction), partial upward rotation |
| Main mobilizing muscles | Pectoralis major, emphasis on the sternal and abdominal aspect (lower)<br>Pectoralis minor<br>Anterior deltoid<br>Coracobrachialis<br>Biceps brachii (short head)<br>Latissimus dorsi | Serratus anterior |

Main stabilizing muscles

Shoulder blades: Serratus anterior, Pectoralis minor, Rhomboids, and Lower trapezius
Shoulder joints: Rotator cuff muscles and Biceps brachii
Elbow joints: Triceps brachii and Brachialis
Wrists: Wrist flexors
Mild trunk stabilization by the Abdominal and Gluteal group, and Latissimus dorsi
General leg muscles maintaining the standing position

# LEGS AND HIPS

One of the things that differentiates humans from most other mammals is that we have two legs and they have four. This means that we have greater mobility but less stability than other mammals. Conditioned legs are essential to good stability because if the legs are weak, the back and upper body will compensate. In women, two areas are of specific focus—the knees and the hip region.

Female athletes have a four to six times greater chance of serious knee injury than their male counterparts. There are various predisposing factors to this. Studies show that women are more likely to begin exercising from a knock-kneed position (valgus), and when going into knee flexion this position is increased. Women also have wider pelvises, which results in a more acute angle from the femur to the knee joint. They also have softer ligaments and tendons due to hormonal effects, which are pronounced during ovulation and pregnancy.

Many women are concerned that leg exercises such as squats will cause their buttocks to become bigger, but the opposite is generally true. A combination of aerobic exercise and strength conditioning, together with nutritional changes, is likely to result in reasonable fat loss. Among leg exercises, squats are thought to strengthen gluteus muscles more than lunges, although lunges actually take the glutes through a greater range of motion than squats. If less strengthening emphasis on the glutes is desired when doing squats, a wider stance should be used. This will reduce the involvement of the glutes and quads and increase the activation of the adductors.

The natural tilt of a woman's pelvis is more likely to be slightly anterior than in men, creating an increased lordosis and emphasizing the buttocks. Poor posture and atrophied hamstring muscles can also make the buttocks look disproportionate. Wearing high heels tends to weaken the hamstrings and glutes, and causes them to lose tone.

Addressing all these factors should create an accentuated curve of the hamstrings and improve the shape of the buttocks as fat is reduced and the thigh and buttock muscles increase tone. As the buttocks tighten and lift, the legs will also appear slightly longer and more shapely.

## Muscles of the Legs and Hips

| Name | Joints crossed | Origin | Insertion | Action |
|---|---|---|---|---|
| Gastrocnemius | Ankle and knee | Condyles at the base of the femur | Posterior surface of the calcaneus at the back of the heel | Ankle plantarflexion (strong); knee flexion (weak) |
| Soleus | Ankle | Upper two-thirds of the posterior surface of the tibia and fibula | Posterior surface of the calcaneus at the back of the heel | Ankle plantarflexion |
| Quadriceps: Rectus femoris | Hip and knee | Anterior, inferior iliac spine of the pelvis | Patella (knee cap) and the patella ligament to the tibial tuberosity | Hip flexion; knee extension |
| Quadriceps: Vastus lateralis; Vastus intermedius; Vastus medialis | Knee | Lateral, anterior, and medial surface of the femur | Into the patella border | Knee extension |
| Hamstrings: Short and long Biceps femoris (lateral aspect); Semitendinosus and Semimembranosus (medial aspect) (generally work as one muscle) | Hip and knee | Biceps femoris short head on the posterior femur, on the lower Linea aspera, and the Lateral condyloid ridge. The other heads originate on the ischial tuberosity of the pelvis | Biceps femoris inserts onto the head of the fibula and the lateral condyle of the tibia. Semitendinosus/ Semimembranosus insert onto medial condyle of the tibia | Hip: extension Knee: flexion Biceps femoris also actions lateral rotation of the hip and knee. Semitendinosus/ Semimembranosus also medially rotate the hip and knee |

| Name | Joints crossed | Origin | Insertion | Action |
|------|----------------|--------|-----------|--------|
| **Adductor Group:** Pectineus, Adductor brevis, Adductor longus, Adductor magnus, Gracilis (generally act as one muscle) | Hip (Gracilis also crosses the knee) | Pubis and ischium of the pelvis | Along the medial femur, on the lesser trochanter, linea aspera, and medial condyloid ridge. The Gracilis inserts on the medial superior tibia | Main action is hip adduction |
| **Tensor fasciae latae** | Hip | Anterior superior iliac spine | Iliotibial band (ITB) | Hip: abduction, flexion, assists in medial rotation |
| **Gluteus maximus** | Hip | Posterior crest of the ilium, the sacrum, and fascia of the lumbar vertebrae | Iliotibial band of the fasciae latae | Hip: extension, lateral rotation |
| **Gluteus medius** and **minimus** (together known as abductors) | Hip | Outer surface of the ilium (both) | Greater trochanter of the femur (both) | Hip: abduction, lateral rotation (medius), medial rotation (medius and minimus) |
| **Iliopsoas** | Hip | Inner surface of the ilium, base of the sacrum, sides of the last thoracic, and five lumbar vertebrae | Lesser trochanter of the femur | Hip flexion |
| **Deep lateral rotators of the hip:** Piriformis, Gemellus superior and inferior, Obturator externus and internus, Quadratus femoris (found deep to the gluteus maximus) | Hip | Anterior sacrum, the posterior ischium, and the obturator foramen | Superior and inferior aspects of the greater trochanter | Hip lateral rotation |

**Notes** Other significant leg muscles that are not detailed here for purposes of simplicity include the Tibialis anterior and posterior, Peroneals and Sartorius. The Latissimus dorsi, Trapezius, Rhomboids, Erector spinae and Quadratus lumborum are detailed further in Section 5, Back and Shoulders.

## *Exercises*

1. Squats with Ball between Legs, page 70
2. Free-standing Barbell Plié Squats, page 71
3. Free-standing Barbell Squats, page 72
4. Machine Incline Leg Press, page 74
5. Barbell Reverse Lunge, page 75
6. Free-standing Lateral Lunge, page 76
7. Bench Step, page 77
8. Modified Barbell Bent Leg Deadlift, page 78
9. Double Leg Bridge with Shoulder Flexion, page 79
10. Ball Bridge, page 80
11. Side-lying Ball Lift, page 81
12. Hip Abductor Machine, page 82
13. Hip Adductor Machine, page 83
14. Supine Adductor Stabilization with Ball, page 84
15. Cable Hip Abductions, page 85
16. Prone Hip Extensions, page 86
17. Machine-lying Leg Curl, page 87
18. Seesaw with Ball, page 88
19. Yoga Quad Stretch with Forward Lean, page 89
20. Free-standing Calf Raise, page 90
21. Seated Calf Raise Machine, page 91

# SQUATS WITH BALL BETWEEN LEGS

Core exercise • Compound/multi-joint • Push • Close chain • Body-weight • Beginner to Intermediate

➡️ The squat is one of the most basic core movements. This exercise focuses on the mechanical basics of posture and alignment for the squat. It is essential that these are correct before proceeding to all similar leg exercises.

## Description

Slowly lower your body, moving your hips back as if sitting into a chair. Keep the ball between your knees, with your big toe vertically in line with your inside knee. Lower to approximately 90° of knee flexion—stop before your upper leg becomes parallel with the floor. Return, and repeat.

### STARTING POSITION
· Stand with your feet shoulder-width apart.
· Keep your posture aligned, maintaining a neutral spine.
· Keep your knees soft. Support a 9 in (22 cm) soft ball between your knees.
· Keep your arms crossed in front of your body.

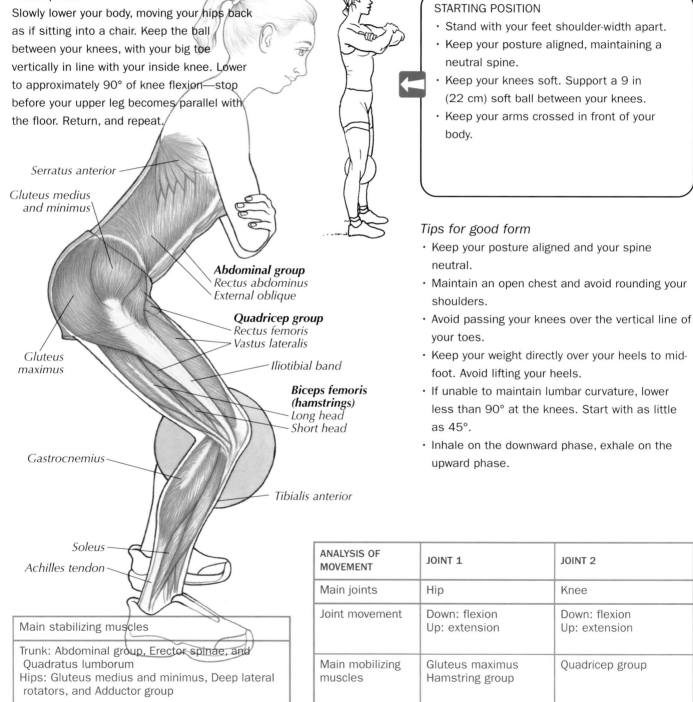

Serratus anterior

Gluteus medius and minimus

**Abdominal group**
Rectus abdominus
External oblique

**Quadricep group**
Rectus femoris
Vastus lateralis

Gluteus maximus

Iliotibial band

**Biceps femoris (hamstrings)**
Long head
Short head

Gastrocnemius

Tibialis anterior

Soleus

Achilles tendon

### Tips for good form
· Keep your posture aligned and your spine neutral.
· Maintain an open chest and avoid rounding your shoulders.
· Avoid passing your knees over the vertical line of your toes.
· Keep your weight directly over your heels to mid-foot. Avoid lifting your heels.
· If unable to maintain lumbar curvature, lower less than 90° at the knees. Start with as little as 45°.
· Inhale on the downward phase, exhale on the upward phase.

## Main stabilizing muscles

Trunk: Abdominal group, Erector spinae, and Quadratus lumborum
Hips: Gluteus medius and minimus, Deep lateral rotators, and Adductor group

| ANALYSIS OF MOVEMENT | JOINT 1 | JOINT 2 |
|---|---|---|
| Main joints | Hip | Knee |
| Joint movement | Down: flexion<br>Up: extension | Down: flexion<br>Up: extension |
| Main mobilizing muscles | Gluteus maximus<br>Hamstring group | Quadricep group |

# FREE-STANDING BARBELL PLIÉ SQUATS

Core exercise • Compound/multi-joint
• Push • Close chain • Barbell
• Intermediate to advanced

There are countless variations possible to the plié squat, which takes it name from the French term meaning "bent." This word refers to the ballet movement of knee bends done with the legs turned out.

## Description

Slowly lower your body, moving your hips back as if sitting into a chair. Lower to approximately 90° of knee flexion, stopping before your upper leg becomes parallel with the floor. Return, and repeat.

### STARTING POSITION

• If using the squat rack, take the bar off the squat rack as described on page 73.
• Stand with your feet double shoulder-width apart and up to 45° outwardly rotated.
• Keep your knees soft.

*Quadratus lumborum*
*Gluteus medius and minimus*
*Iliopsoas*
*Tensor faciae latae*
*Gluteus maximus*
*Sartorius*

**Quadricep group**
*Rectus femoris*
*Vastus medialis*

**Quadricep group**
*Rectus femoris*
*Vastus lateralis*
*Vastus medialis*

*Tibia*

*1*
*2*
*3*
*4*

*Patella*

**Adductor group**
*1. Adductor longus*
*2. Gracilis*
*3. Adductor magnus*
*4. Gracilis insertion*

*Soleus*

*Gastrocnemius*
*Tibialis anterior*
*Peroneus longus*

*Soleus*

## Tips for good form

• Follow the tips provided for Free-standing Barbell Squats on the next page.

| ANALYSIS OF MOVEMENT | JOINT 1 | JOINT 2 |
|---|---|---|
| Main joints | Hip | Knee |
| Joint movement | Down: flexion, abduction<br>Up: extension, adduction | Down: flexion<br>Up: extension |
| Main mobilizing muscles | Gluteus maximus<br>Hamstring group<br>Adductor group | Quadricep group (emphasis is on lateral aspects) |

| Main stabilizing muscles |
|---|
| Trunk: Abdominal group, Erector spinae, and Quadratus lumborum<br>Hips: Deep lateral rotators, Gluteus medius and minimus, and Adductor group<br>Lower legs: Ankle stabilizers and Gastrocnemius |

# FREE-STANDING BARBELL SQUATS

Core exercise • Compound/multi-joint
• Push • Close chain • Barbell
• Intermediate to advanced

Done correctly, barbell squats are a valuable basic component of any woman's strength conditioning and toning routine.

## Description
Slowly lower your body, moving your hips back as if sitting into a chair. Lower to approximately 90° of knee flexion, stopping before your upper leg is parallel with the floor. Return and repeat.

## Tips for good form
· Get good form before increasing the weight.
· Avoid momentum; use a slow, controlled movement.
· Keep your posture aligned and your spine neutral.
· Maintain an open chest, and avoid rounding your shoulders.
· Keep your knees from passing over the vertical line of your toes.
· Keep your weight directly over your heels to mid-foot, and avoid lifting your heels.
· If you cannot maintain lumbar curvature, lower to less than 90°. Start with as little as 45° of movement at your knees.
· Inhalation on the downward phase helps to increase intra-abdominal pressure: keep your shoulders open, and avoid spinal flexion. Exhale on the upward movement.

### STARTING POSITION
· Take the bar off the squat rack and move back into a safe space for squatting.
· Stand with your feet shoulder-width apart, and with soft knees.
· Keep your posture aligned, maintaining a neutral spine.
· Hold the bar wider than your shoulders, according to what feels comfortable.

### Women-specific training tip—positioning the bar
Women commonly experience more discomfort than men with the bar placement across the Upper trapezius, having less soft tissue and a smaller area to place the bar onto. One recommendation is to emphasize opening the shoulders and chest. This will relax the tissues of the Upper trapezius, providing a better cushion for the bar. In some gyms, padded bar rolls are also available.

CAUTION If you experience any form of knee pain, do not proceed with this exercise. Beginners should get advice on weight to begin with.

| ANALYSIS OF MOVEMENT | JOINT 1 | JOINT 2 |
|---|---|---|
| Main joints | Hip | Knee |
| Joint movement | Down: flexion Up: extension | Down: flexion Up: extension |
| Main mobilizing muscles | Gluteus maximus Hamstring group | Quadricep group |

| Main stabilizing muscles |
|---|
| Trunk: Abdominal group, Erector spinae, and Quadratus lumborum |
| Hips: Gluteus medius and minimus, Deep lateral rotators and Adductor group |
| Lower legs: Ankle stabilizers and Gastrocnemius |

## Training tip—posture and alignment

Note the angle of the head and eyes, the maintenance of a neutral spine through alignment of the ears, shoulders, and hips, the alignment of the pelvis and the retention of the lumbar curvature, the maintenance of the neutral knee angle, and the position of the knees in relation to the feet.

## Training tip—weight distribution over the feet

Keep your weight distributed between the three points of the soles of your feet. Do not let your knees collapse inward, or force the weight through your big toes and forefeet. Keep your feet flat, and avoid lifting your heels.

## Training tip—learning to squat

· Start free-standing squats with a broomstick on your shoulders and a chair behind you as you squat. The broomstick will give you a sense of carrying the weight on your shoulders, and the chair will get you to bring your hips back to the right depth, while offering some security.

· Then learn how to take a bar from the squat rack. On the rack, the bar should be at upper-chest height, so that at the pick-up your knees are bent. Dip your upper body underneath the bar. Position the bar on the "meat" of your shoulders on the Upper trapezius.

· Inhale, keeping your eyes looking slightly above the horizon, then pick up the bar by standing up into the weight. When ready, walk back into the starting position.

· Follow the reverse procedure for taking the bar off your shoulders.

## Women-specific training tip—women and knee injury risk

Statistics show that women are more prone to knee injury than men. This may be due to the wider pelvis of women and the more angled femur to the knee joint that renders women's knee joints less stable during exercise movements. Adapting the squat to suit a woman's body is therefore important to obtain safe and effective results. If you feel unstable in the squat, or if there is too much pressure on your knees, place your feet wider than shoulder-width apart in the starting position.

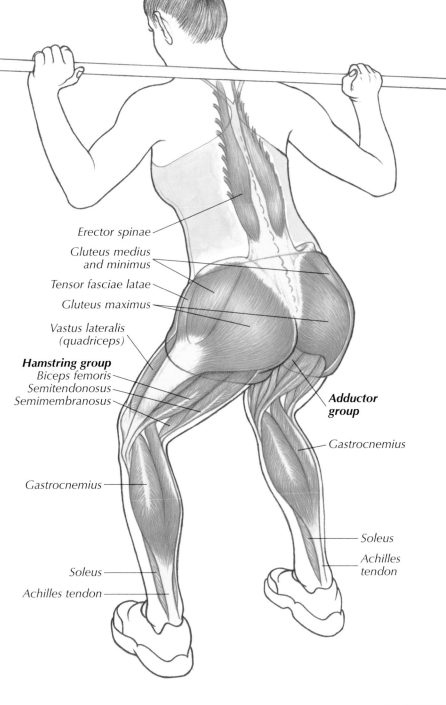

Erector spinae

Gluteus medius and minimus

Tensor fasciae latae

Gluteus maximus

Vastus lateralis (quadriceps)

**Hamstring group**
Biceps femoris
Semitendonosus
Semimembranosus

**Adductor group**

Gastrocnemius

Gastrocnemius

Soleus

Achilles tendon

Soleus

Achilles tendon

# MACHINE INCLINE LEG PRESS

Core exercise • Compound/multi-joint
• Push • Open chain • Machine
• Intermediate to advanced

Leg press machines have been around since 1943, when Clancy Ross and Leo Stern developed the first one.

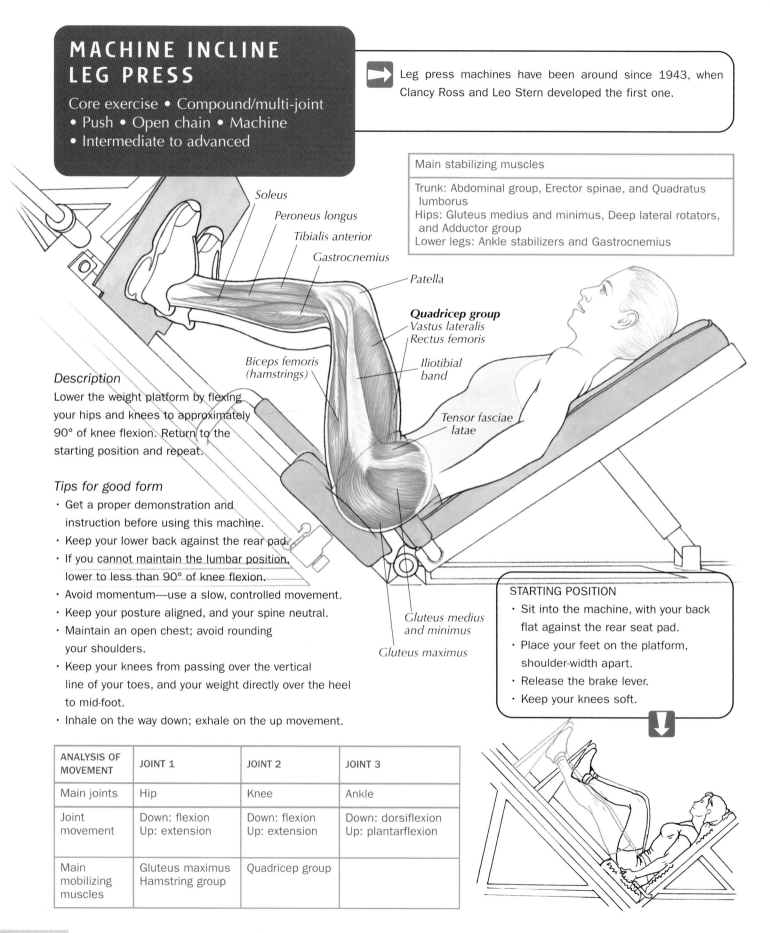

Soleus

Peroneus longus

Tibialis anterior

Gastrocnemius

Patella

*Quadricep group*
Vastus lateralis
Rectus femoris

Iliotibial band

Biceps femoris (hamstrings)

Tensor fasciae latae

Gluteus medius and minimus

Gluteus maximus

Main stabilizing muscles

Trunk: Abdominal group, Erector spinae, and Quadratus lumborus
Hips: Gluteus medius and minimus, Deep lateral rotators, and Adductor group
Lower legs: Ankle stabilizers and Gastrocnemius

## Description

Lower the weight platform by flexing your hips and knees to approximately 90° of knee flexion. Return to the starting position and repeat.

## Tips for good form

· Get a proper demonstration and instruction before using this machine.
· Keep your lower back against the rear pad.
· If you cannot maintain the lumbar position, lower to less than 90° of knee flexion.
· Avoid momentum—use a slow, controlled movement.
· Keep your posture aligned, and your spine neutral.
· Maintain an open chest; avoid rounding your shoulders.
· Keep your knees from passing over the vertical line of your toes, and your weight directly over the heel to mid-foot.
· Inhale on the way down; exhale on the up movement.

## STARTING POSITION

· Sit into the machine, with your back flat against the rear seat pad.
· Place your feet on the platform, shoulder-width apart.
· Release the brake lever.
· Keep your knees soft.

| ANALYSIS OF MOVEMENT | JOINT 1 | JOINT 2 | JOINT 3 |
|---|---|---|---|
| Main joints | Hip | Knee | Ankle |
| Joint movement | Down: flexion<br>Up: extension | Down: flexion<br>Up: extension | Down: dorsiflexion<br>Up: plantarflexion |
| Main mobilizing muscles | Gluteus maximus<br>Hamstring group | Quadricep group | |

# BARBELL REVERSE LUNGE

Core exercise • Compound/multi-joint
• Push • Open chain • Barbell
• Intermediate to advanced

Lunges are to women what squats are to men. Most trainers prefer lunges for women, naming reduced knee stress and increased buttock conditioning compared with the squat as reasons. The reverse lunge, specifically, is regarded as safer and more suitable for women than the forward lunge.

## Description

Slowly step backward with one leg into the lunge position, bending both knees and lowering your hips so that the forward thigh is parallel with the floor. The front knee should be vertically above the foot and ankle. Return to the starting position by contracting off the front foot through the mid-foot and heel. Do not push off your back leg.

## Tips for good form

· Keep your trunk upright and your weight centered between both your legs during the exercise.
· Avoid lifting your front heel; keep your front knee from passing over the vertical line of your toes.
· To avoid cheating by leaning too far forward from the trunk and putting pressure on the fronts of the knees, use a slow, controlled movement rather than a shorter step.
· Keep your posture aligned, and your spine neutral.
· Keep your chest open, and avoid rounding your shoulders.

**Abdominal group**
External obliques
Rectus abdominus

Semitendonosus (hamstrings)

Tensor fasciae latae

Gluteus medius and minimus

**Adductor group**
Pectineus
Adductor brevis
Adductor longus
Adductor magnus

**Quadricep group**
Rectus femoris
Vastus lateralis
Vastus medialis

Sartorius

Gastrocnemius

Soleus

| Main stabilizing muscles |
| --- |
| Trunk: Abdominal group, Erector spinae, and Quadratus lumborum<br>Hips: Gluteus medius and minimus, Deep lateral rotators, and Adductor group<br>Lower leg: Ankle stabilizers and Gastrocnemius |

### STARTING POSITION
· Stand with your feet shoulder-width apart.
· Support the bar comfortably on the Upper trapezius.
· Keep your posture aligned, maintaining a neutral spine.

| ANALYSIS OF MOVEMENT | JOINT 1 | JOINT 2 |
| --- | --- | --- |
| Main joints | Hip (front leg) | Knee (front leg) |
| Joint movement | Down: flexion<br>Up: extension | Down: flexion<br>Up: extension |
| Main mobilizing muscles | Gluteus maximus<br>Hamstring group | Quadricep group |

# FREE-STANDING LATERAL LUNGE

Core exercise • Compound/multi-joint
• Push • Close chain • Body-weight
• Beginner to intermediate

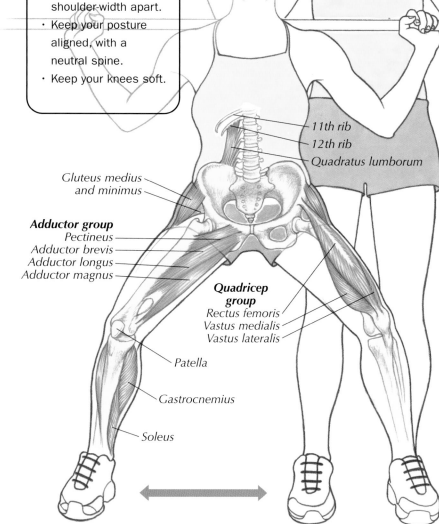

This is a variation on the squat and lunge that brings in more activation of the lateral and medial hip and thigh muscles.

## Description

Step one leg sideways double shoulder-width apart and slowly lower your body into the squat position, moving your hips back as if sitting into a chair. Lower to approximately 90° of knee flexion, stopping before your upper leg is parallel with the floor. Return, change legs, and repeat.

### STARTING POSITION
- Stand with your feet shoulder-width apart.
- Keep your posture aligned, with a neutral spine.
- Keep your knees soft.

## Tips for good form

- Keep your posture aligned, and your spine neutral.
- Maintain an open chest; avoid rounding your shoulders.
- Keep your knees from passing over the vertical line of your toes, your big toe vertically in line with your inside knee.
- Keep your weight directly over your heels to mid-foot. Avoid lifting your heels.
- If unable to maintain lumbar curvature, lower less than 90° at the knees—start with as little as 45°.
- Inhale on the downward phase; exhale on the upward motion.

**Labels on illustration:**
11th rib
12th rib
Quadratus lumborum
Gluteus medius and minimus
**Adductor group**
Pectineus
Adductor brevis
Adductor longus
Adductor magnus
**Quadricep group**
Rectus femoris
Vastus medialis
Vastus lateralis
Patella
Gastrocnemius
Soleus

| ANALYSIS OF MOVEMENT | JOINT 1 | JOINT 2 |
|---|---|---|
| Main joints | Hip | Knee |
| Joint movement | Down: abduction, then flexion Up: extension, then adduction | Down: flexion Up: extension |
| Main mobilizing muscles | Hip abduction: Gluteus medius and minimus Hip flexion and extension: Gluteus maximus, Hamstring group Hip adduction: Adductor group | Quadricep group |

| Main stabilizing muscles |
|---|
| Trunk: Abdominal group, Erector spinae, and Quadratus lumborum Hips: Gluteus medius and minimus, and Adductor group (when not mobilizing), and Deep lateral rotators |

# BENCH STEP

Core exercise • Compound/multi-joint
• Push • Open chain • Body-weight
• Intermediate to advanced

Using a platform creates an effective workout for the buttock muscles due to the increased range of hip movement.

## Description

With control, step forward up on to the platform. Return to the starting position, controlling the lowering of your body from the leg on the platform.

### STARTING POSITION

· Stand with your feet shoulder-width apart, just behind a stable platform at a height of 12–16 in (30–40 cm).
· Fold your arms in front of your chest with your shoulders relaxed.
· Keep your posture aligned, and maintain a neutral spine.

Erector spinae
(superficial to
Quadratus lumborum)

11th rib
12th rib

Quadratus
lumborum (deep)

Gluteus medius
and minimus

Tensor fasciae latae

Gluteus maximus

Iliotibial band

Vastus lateralis
(Quadricep group)

**Hamstring group**
Biceps femoris
Semitendonosus
Semimembranosus

Gastrocnemius

Soleus

Achilles tendon

| ANALYSIS OF MOVEMENT | JOINT 1 | JOINT 2 |
|---|---|---|
| Main joints | Hip (leg stepping up) | Knee (leg stepping up) |
| Joint movement | Up: flexion, then extension Down: flexion, then extension | Up: flexion, then extension Down: flexion, then extension |
| Main mobilizing muscles | Hip flexion (up): Iliopsoas (Iliopsoas down is passive) Hip extension (up and down): Gluteus maximus, Hamstring group | Knee extension (up) and flexion (down): Quadricep group Knee extension (down): Hamstring group |

| Main stabilizing muscles |
|---|
| Trunk: Abdominal group, Erector spinae, and Quadratus lumborum Hips: Gluteus medius and minimus, Deep lateral rotators, and Adductor group Lower leg: Ankle stabilizers and Gastrocnemius |

### Tips for good form

· Keep your trunk upright and your weight centered.
· Generate the upward movement by pushing down into the middle and rear of the foot.
· Prevent your front knee from passing over the vertical line of your toes.
· Use a slow, controlled movement. Use a shorter step if you find yourself cheating.
· Keep your posture aligned and your spine neutral.
· Keep your chest open; avoid rounding your shoulders.
· Inhale on the way up.

# MODIFIED BARBELL BENT LEG DEADLIFT

Core exercise • Compound/multi-joint
• Pull • Close chain • Barbell
• Intermediate to advanced

→ The original deadlift represents the three lifts in the competitive sport of power lifting, but it is also one of the most complete and functional exercises. This modified version represents an important exercise for a woman's conditioning program.

## Description

Squat by flexing forward at the hips and bend the knees slightly until you feel the tension in your hamstrings. Squat no lower than 90° flexion of the knees. Return, lifting the bar, by extending the knees and hips, using the strength of your back, hips, and thighs. Specifically, contract from your glutes and hamstrings.

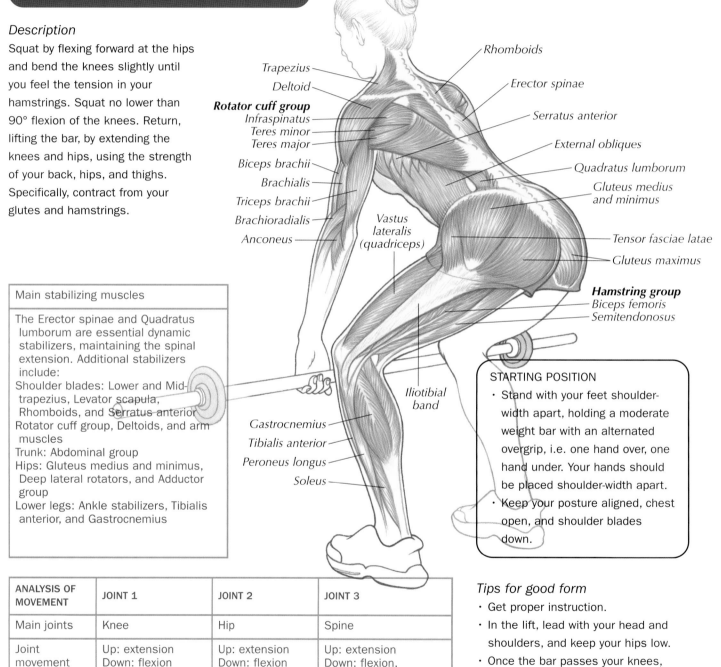

Trapezius
Deltoid
**Rotator cuff group**
Infraspinatus
Teres minor
Teres major
Biceps brachii
Brachialis
Triceps brachii
Brachioradialis
Anconeus
Vastus lateralis (quadriceps)
Gastrocnemius
Tibialis anterior
Peroneus longus
Soleus
Iliotibial band

Rhomboids
Erector spinae
Serratus anterior
External obliques
Quadratus lumborum
Gluteus medius and minimus
Tensor fasciae latae
Gluteus maximus
**Hamstring group**
Biceps femoris
Semitendonosus

### Main stabilizing muscles

The Erector spinae and Quadratus lumborum are essential dynamic stabilizers, maintaining the spinal extension. Additional stabilizers include:
Shoulder blades: Lower and Mid-trapezius, Levator scapula, Rhomboids, and Serratus anterior
Rotator cuff group, Deltoids, and arm muscles
Trunk: Abdominal group
Hips: Gluteus medius and minimus, Deep lateral rotators, and Adductor group
Lower legs: Ankle stabilizers, Tibialis anterior, and Gastrocnemius

### STARTING POSITION

· Stand with your feet shoulder-width apart, holding a moderate weight bar with an alternated overgrip, i.e. one hand over, one hand under. Your hands should be placed shoulder-width apart.
· Keep your posture aligned, chest open, and shoulder blades down.

| ANALYSIS OF MOVEMENT | JOINT 1 | JOINT 2 | JOINT 3 |
|---|---|---|---|
| Main joints | Knee | Hip | Spine |
| Joint movement | Up: extension Down: flexion | Up: extension Down: flexion | Up: extension Down: flexion, back to neutral |
| Main mobilizing muscles | Quadricep group | Gluteus maximus Hamstring group | Erector spinae |

## Tips for good form

· Get proper instruction.
· In the lift, lead with your head and shoulders, and keep your hips low.
· Once the bar passes your knees, push your hips forwards.
· Keep the bar close to your body.
· Inhale on the upward phase; exhale on the downward movement.

# DOUBLE LEG BRIDGE WITH SHOULDER FLEXION

Auxiliary exercise • Isolated/single joint • Push • Close chain • Body-weight • Beginner to advanced

➡️ Bridge work was originally used in back rehabilitation and physical therapy. This adaptation is one of several core stability exercises that have made their way into gym routines.

## Description
Slowly raise your trunk and lower back by extending your hips, keeping the arms relaxed. Pause, return, and repeat.

## Tips for good form
· Lead from the hips.
· Keep your knees hip-width apart.
· Keep your shoulders relaxed, and your chest open.

STARTING POSITION
· Lie supine with your knees bent and your feet flat.
· Raise your arms vertically toward the ceiling.
· Keep your shoulders relaxed and release your shoulder blades down.

**Hamstring group**
Semimembranosus
Semitendonosus

**Biceps femoris**
Short head
Long head

**Quadricep group**
Vastus lateralis
Rectus femoris

Tensor fascia latae

Gluteus medius and minimus

Tibia

Tibialis anterior

Peroneus longus

Gracilis (adductors)

Gluteus maximus

Erector spinae

| ANALYSIS OF MOVEMENT | JOINT 1 |
| --- | --- |
| Main joints | Hips |
| Joint movement | Up: extension<br>Down: flexion |
| Main mobilizing muscles | Gluteus maximus<br>Hamstring group |

| Main stabilizing muscles |
| --- |
| The main stabilizers are the Erector spinae, Abdominals, and Quadricep group.<br>Additional stabilization:<br>Shoulders: Rotator cuff group and Anterior deltoid<br>Shoulder blades: Lower and Mid-trapezius and Serratus anterior<br>Trunk: Quadratus lumborum<br>Hips: Gluteus medius and minimus, Deep lateral rotators and Adductor group |

# BALL BRIDGE

Whole-body stabilization • Push
• Close chain • Body-weight
• Beginner to advanced

➡️ This exercise progresses bridging with the use of a stability ball under the lower legs.

## Description

As you exhale, slowly raise your trunk and lower back by extending your hips, keeping your arm position relaxed. Pause, return, and repeat.

### STARTING POSITION

· Lie supine with your knees bent, and your calf muscles on a stability ball.
· Keep your feet and knees hip-width apart.
· Keep your arms relaxed at your sides.
· Maintain a neutral spine, keep abdominal stabilization engaged, and mildly squeeze your navel to your spine without moving the spine.

### Tips for good form

· Work slowly and with control.
· Lead from the hips.
· Keep your knees hip-width apart.
· Keep your shoulders relaxed, your chest open, and the feeling of expansion under your arms.

Soleus

Peroneus longus

**Hamstring group
Biceps femoris**
Long head
Short head

Iliotibial band

**Quadricep group**
Vastus lateralis
Rectus femoris

Tensor fasciae latae

Gluteus medius and minimus

Rectus abdominus

External obliques

**Hamstring group**
Semimembranosus
Semitendonosus

Gluteus maximus

Iliac crest

Erector spinae    Serratus anterior

| ANALYSIS OF MOVEMENT | JOINT 1 |
|---|---|
| Main joints | Hips |
| Joint movement | Up: extension Down: flexion |
| Main mobilizing muscles | Gluteus maximus Hamstring group |

Main stabilizing muscles

The main stabilizers are the Erector spinae, Abdominals, and Quadricep group.
Additional stabilization:
Shoulder blades: Lower and Mid-trapezius, and Serratus anterior
Trunk: Quadratus lumborum
Hips: Gluteus medius and minimus, Deep lateral rotators, and Adductor group

# SIDE-LYING BALL LIFT

Auxiliary exercise with significant stabilization emphasis • Isolation/single joint • Pull/push • Open chain • Body-weight • Intermediate to Advanced

 This unique exercise isolates the legs and hips, and allows both adductors and abductors to work at the same time.

## Description
Slowly side-lift the ball only 1–2 in (2–5 cm), pause, return, and repeat. Change over and repeat on the other side.

| ANALYSIS OF MOVEMENT | JOINT 1 | JOINT 2 |
| --- | --- | --- |
| Main joints | Top hip | Bottom hip |
| Joint movement | Up: abduction Down: adduction | Up: adduction Down: abduction |
| Main mobilizing muscles | Gluteus medius and minimus Tensor fasciae latae | Adductor group |

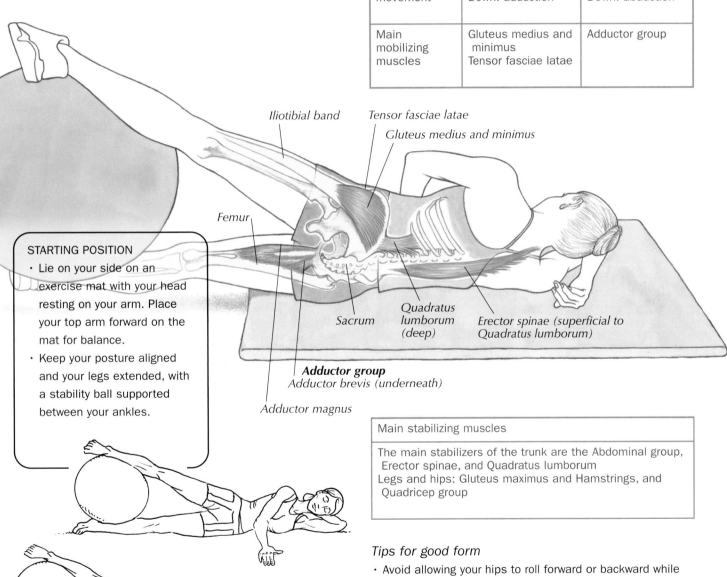

Iliotibial band

Tensor fasciae latae

Gluteus medius and minimus

Femur

Quadratus lumborum (deep)

Sacrum

Erector spinae (superficial to Quadratus lumborum)

**Adductor group**
Adductor brevis (underneath)

Adductor magnus

### STARTING POSITION
· Lie on your side on an exercise mat with your head resting on your arm. Place your top arm forward on the mat for balance.
· Keep your posture aligned and your legs extended, with a stability ball supported between your ankles.

Main stabilizing muscles

The main stabilizers of the trunk are the Abdominal group, Erector spinae, and Quadratus lumborum
Legs and hips: Gluteus maximus and Hamstrings, and Quadricep group

## Tips for good form
· Avoid allowing your hips to roll forward or backward while performing the exercise; engage the abdominals to stabilize the spine and pelvis.
· Work slowly and avoid momentum.
· Avoid lifting more than 2 in (5 cm ).

# HIP ABDUCTOR MACHINE

Auxiliary exercise • Isolation/single joint
• Push • Open chain •Machine
• Beginner to advanced

The adductor and abductor machines are easily confused, but the muscles they train work together as postural stabilizers (side-to-side). As a result, it is beneficial to train on both machines in the same session.

## Description
Squeeze your legs apart. Pause, return, and repeat.

## Tips for good form
- Work slowly against moderate resistance. Avoid momentum.
- Avoid arching your back as you abduct the hips.
- Concentrate on squeezing from the Gluteus medius and minimus. Avoid working from your feet or knees.

Erector spinae

Quadratus lumborum

Tensor fasciae latae

Iliotibial band

Gluteus medius and minimus

Gluteus maximus

Vastus medialis

Sartorius

Gracilis

**Hamstring group**

| ANALYSIS OF MOVEMENT | JOINT 1 |
|---|---|
| Main joints | Hips |
| Joint movement | Outward: abduction Inward: adduction |
| Main mobilizing muscles | Gluteus medius and minimus |

| Main stabilizing muscles |
|---|
| Main stabilizers: Abdominal group, Erector spinae, and Quadratus lumborum |

### STARTING POSITION
- Sit in the machine, with your legs against the pads.
- Sit on your sitting bones, keeping your chest open and your spine aligned.
- Some machines need a lever release to position the legs properly.

# HIP ADDUCTOR MACHINE

Auxiliary exercise • Isolated/single joint
• Pull • Open chain • Machine
• Beginner to advanced

→ "Spot reduction," the invalid concept that training an area repeatedly can shape and tone it through local weight loss, led to the popularity of the adductor and abductor machines. Used correctly, these machines can benefit the adductors' role as postural stabilizers and safeguard against medial knee injuries.

*Description*
Squeeze your legs together. Pause, return, and repeat.

*Tips for good form*
· Work slowly against moderate resistance. Avoid momentum.
· Concentrate on squeezing from the adductors, as opposed to working from the feet.

| ANALYSIS OF MOVEMENT | JOINT 1 |
| --- | --- |
| Main joints | Hips |
| Joint movement | Inward: adduction<br>Outward: abduction |
| Main mobilizing muscles | Adductor group, namely Pectineus, Adductor brevis, Adductor longus, Adductor magnus, Gracilis |

| Main stabilizing muscles |
| --- |
| Abdominal group, Erector spinae, and Quadratus lumborum |

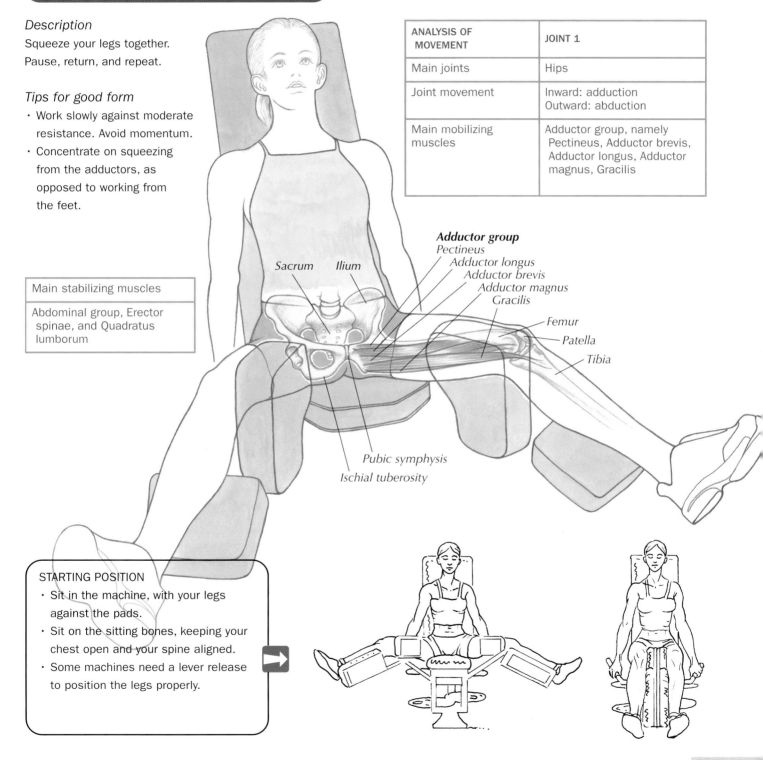

Sacrum   Ilium

**Adductor group**
Pectineus
Adductor longus
Adductor brevis
Adductor magnus
Gracilis

Femur
Patella
Tibia

Pubic symphysis
Ischial tuberosity

STARTING POSITION
· Sit in the machine, with your legs against the pads.
· Sit on the sitting bones, keeping your chest open and your spine aligned.
· Some machines need a lever release to position the legs properly.

→

# SUPINE ADDUCTOR STABILIZATION WITH BALL

Auxiliary exercise with significant stabilization emphasis • Isolation/single joint • Pull/push • Open chain • Body-weight • Beginner to advanced

→ This unique exercise uses a stability ball to integrate the adductors with whole-body stabilization. It is more functional and advanced than traditional hip exercises.

### Description

Maintain abdominal stabilization, exhale, and extend your leg at the knees. As you advance you can extend the leg so that it is 45° from the floor or higher. This will engage more stabilization effort from the abdominals, but should only be done if no back condition is present. Return, and repeat.

Patella

**Quadricep group**
Vastus lateralis

Rectus femoris

Tensor fasciae latae

Sternocleidomastoid

**Abdominal group**
Rectus abdominus
External obliques

Gluteus medius and minimus

Serratus anterior

Iliac crest

### STARTING POSITION

- Lie supine with your hips and knees bent, and the stability ball held between your lower leg and ankles.
- Keep your arms relaxed at your sides.
- Maintain a neutral spine, with abdominal stabilization engaged, mildly squeezing your navel into your spine without moving the spine.

### Tips for good form

- Avoid momentum—use a slow, controlled movement.
- Avoid hunching your shoulders. Keep your chest open, head and spine neutral, and shoulder blades depressed.
- Avoid tensing your buttocks or forcing your lower back down into the mat. Focus on using your abdominals.

| ANALYSIS OF MOVEMENT | JOINT 1 | JOINT 2 |
|---|---|---|
| Main joints | Knee | Hip |
| Joint movement | Up: extension<br>Down: flexion | Up: slight extension<br>Down: slight flexion |
| Main mobilizing muscles | Quadricep group | Rectus femoris<br>Iliopsoas |

| Main stabilizing muscles |
|---|
| Major stabilization effort is from the Adductor, Quadricep, and Abdominal groups<br>Neck: Sternocleidomastoid<br>Shoulder blades: Serratus anterior, Rhomboids, and Lower trapezius<br>Hips: Iliopsoas and Rectus femoris |

# CABLE HIP ABDUCTIONS

Auxiliary exercise • Isolation/single joint: strong stabilization emphasis
• Pull • Open chain • Cable machine
• Beginner to intermediate

→ This old gym favorite provides a more functional stabilization challenge than the abductor machine.

## Description

Slowly and with control, abduct the hip, moving the outer leg laterally away from your body. Pause, slowly lower the leg, then repeat. Change, and repeat with the other leg.

## Tips for good form

- Use a low weight and focus on contracting from the Gluteus medius and minimus.
- Keep your hips centered over the vertical center-line of your body; engage the abdominals.
- Avoid allowing your thigh to rotate externally, or your hips to twist while lifting your leg.
- Work slowly and avoid momentum.
- Avoid over-abducting your hips.

| ANALYSIS OF MOVEMENT | JOINT 1 |
|---|---|
| Main joints | Hip |
| Joint movement | Lateral: abduction<br>Medial: adduction |
| Main mobilizing muscles | Gluteus medius and minimus<br>Tensor fasciae latae |

Main stabilizing muscles

The main stabilizers of the trunk are the Abdominal group, Erector spinae, Quadratus lumborum, and muscles of the fixed leg

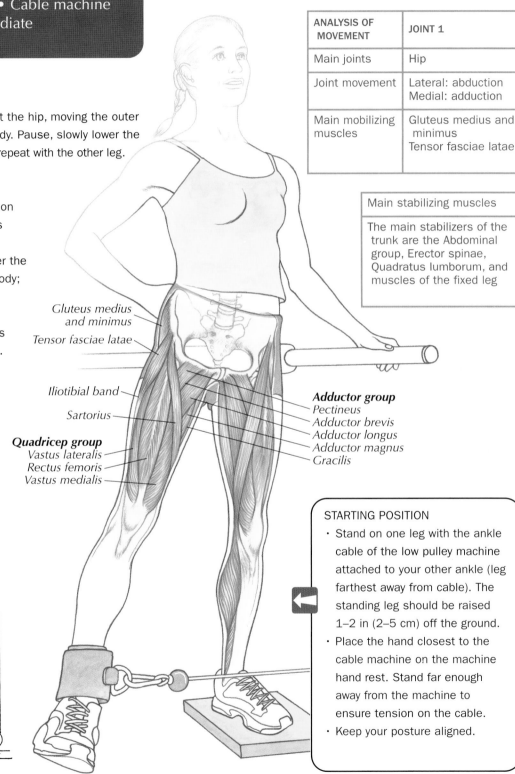

Gluteus medius and minimus
Tensor fasciae latae
Iliotibial band
Sartorius
**Quadricep group**
Vastus lateralis
Rectus femoris
Vastus medialis

**Adductor group**
Pectineus
Adductor brevis
Adductor longus
Adductor magnus
Gracilis

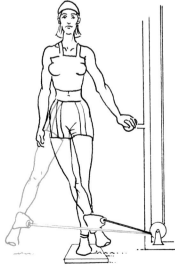

### STARTING POSITION

- Stand on one leg with the ankle cable of the low pulley machine attached to your other ankle (leg farthest away from cable). The standing leg should be raised 1–2 in (2–5 cm) off the ground.
- Place the hand closest to the cable machine on the machine hand rest. Stand far enough away from the machine to ensure tension on the cable.
- Keep your posture aligned.

# PRONE HIP EXTENSIONS

Auxiliary exercise • Isolated/single joint
• Push • Open chain • Body-weight
• Beginner to intermediate

→ The hip-extension range of motion is only 10°–15° beyond vertical. Doing this exercise properly ensures that you effectively isolate and tone your buttocks.

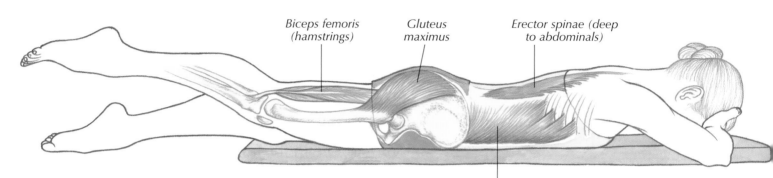

Biceps femoris (hamstrings)

Gluteus maximus

Erector spinae (deep to abdominals)

External obliques (abdominals)

## Description

As you exhale, raise one leg by extending from the hip. Pause, return, and repeat.

### STARTING POSITION

· Lie prone on a mat.
· Keep your legs extended, with your feet on the floor.
· Rest your forehead on both hands, cupped one under the other.

| ANALYSIS OF MOVEMENT | JOINT 1 |
|---|---|
| Main joints | Hip |
| Joint movement | Up: extension<br>Down: flexion |
| Main mobilizing muscles | Gluteus maximus<br>Hamstring |

| Main stabilizing muscles |
|---|
| Most upper body muscles will be involved in stabilizing the trunk, in particular the Erector spinae and Abdominal group. |

## Tips for good form

· Avoid trying to over-extend the hips by compensating with movement from the lower back. The hips should only be able to extend 10°–15°.
· Work slowly and avoid compensating with momentum, or trunk or lumbar movement.
· Keep your trunk and spine stabilized. Focus on abdominal stabilization. Keep your navel mildly squeezed into your spine as you lift your leg.

# MACHINE-LYING LEG CURL

Auxiliary exercise • Isolation/single joint
• Pull • Open chain • Machine
• Intermediate to advanced

Weak hamstring muscles predispose women to increased risk of knee injury during knee extension activities. Additional toning of the hamstrings, together with fat loss in the hip area, will contribute to the appearance of smaller buttocks. This is one of the few isolation exercises for this muscle.

## Tips for good form

· Work slowly, avoiding momentum.
· Avoid over-extending the knee joints, or dropping the weight on the downward phase.
· Focus on abdominal stabilization to avoid lifting the hips and rocking the body and lower back.
· Squeeze from your hamstrings as opposed to lifting from your feet. Avoid pulling on the handles to generate momentum.
· Inhale on the upward phase; exhale on the downward movement.

## Description

Lift your lower legs by flexing your knees. Return, and repeat.

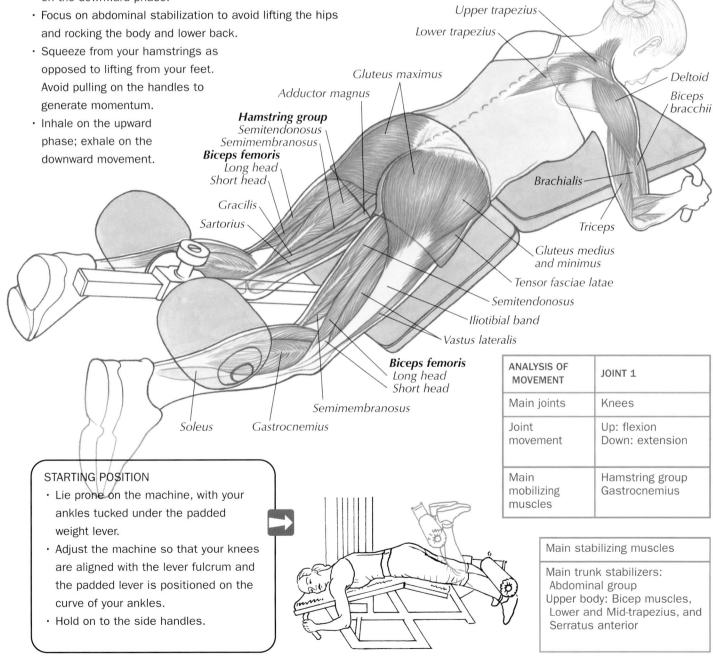

Upper trapezius
Lower trapezius
Gluteus maximus
Adductor magnus
**Hamstring group**
Semitendonosus
Semimembranosus
**Biceps femoris**
Long head
Short head
Gracilis
Sartorius
Deltoid
Biceps bracchii
Brachialis
Triceps
Gluteus medius and minimus
Tensor fasciae latae
Semitendonosus
Iliotibial band
Vastus lateralis
**Biceps femoris**
Long head
Short head
Semimembranosus
Soleus
Gastrocnemius

## STARTING POSITION

· Lie prone on the machine, with your ankles tucked under the padded weight lever.
· Adjust the machine so that your knees are aligned with the lever fulcrum and the padded lever is positioned on the curve of your ankles.
· Hold on to the side handles.

| ANALYSIS OF MOVEMENT | JOINT 1 |
|---|---|
| Main joints | Knees |
| Joint movement | Up: flexion<br>Down: extension |
| Main mobilizing muscles | Hamstring group<br>Gastrocnemius |

| Main stabilizing muscles |
|---|
| Main trunk stabilizers:<br> Abdominal group<br>Upper body: Bicep muscles,<br>Lower and Mid-trapezius, and<br>Serratus anterior |

# SEESAW WITH BALL

Whole body stabilization
• Open chain • Body-weight
• Intermediate to advanced

This is an unusual and demanding exercise that requires some concentration and stability. It benefits stabilization strength, balance, coordination, and proprioceptive skills, and tones the lower back, abdominals, hips, and thighs.

## Description

Slowly lean your weight forward by pivoting forward on your hips. At same time let one extended leg pivot backward as the upper body tilts forward, until you achieve a horizontal line from leg to trunk. Return and repeat, then change sides.

Posterior deltoid

Erector spinae

Gluteus maximus

Lower trapezius
Latissimus dorsi
Serratus anterior
External oblique

**Hamstring group**
Semimembranosus
Semitendonosus
Biceps femoris

Gluteus medius and minimus
Tensor fasciae latae
Iliotibial band
Vastus lateralis

Gastrocnemius
Tibialis anterior
Peroneus longus
Soleus

### STARTING POSITION

· Stand feet shoulder-width apart, with a ball supported between your hands and your arms raised vertically.
· Keep your posture aligned, with your spine neutral.

### Tips for good form

· For easier movement, have your standing leg raised by 1–2 in (2–5 cm) on a weight plate or platform.
· Try to keep your chest and shoulders open.
· Maintain posture stabilization throughout.
· Lengthen out in both directions.

| ANALYSIS OF MOVEMENT | JOINT 1 |
|---|---|
| Main joints | Hips (standing leg) |
| Joint movement | Forward: flexion<br>Return: extension |
| Main mobilizing muscles | Gluteus maximus<br>Hamstring group |

| Main stabilizing muscles |
|---|
| The main stabilizers of the trunk are the Abdominal group, Erector spinae, Quadratus lumborum, and muscles of the fixed leg<br>Hips: Gluteus maximus and Hamstring of moving leg<br>Upper body: Anterior deltoid, Rotator cuff muscles, Serratus anterior, Rhomboids, and Lower trapezius |

# YOGA QUAD STRETCH WITH FORWARD LEAN

## Whole-body stabilization
- Open chain • Body-weight
- Intermediate to advanced

➡️ This exercise combines active balance and proprioception, stretching, stabilization, and mobilization strength work.

### Description

Holding one foot with a hand, extend your opposite arm vertically upward while keeping your shoulders relaxed. Keeping your weight centered through the foot of the supporting leg, slowly lean forward by pivoting on your hips. At same time, let the held leg pivot backward as your upper body tilts forward, until you achieve a 15°–30° lean. Return, and repeat, then change sides.

### Tips for good form

- Try to keep your chest and shoulders open, your posture aligned, and your spine neutral.
- Maintain posture stabilization throughout.
- Lengthen out in both directions.

### STARTING POSITION
- In a standing position, bend one leg at the knee.
- Reach back with your hand on the same side to hold your foot, pulling your heel toward your buttocks.

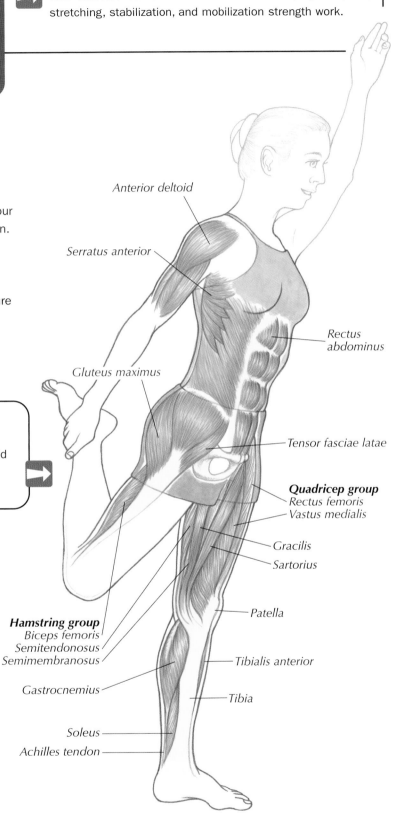

Anterior deltoid
Serratus anterior
Gluteus maximus
Rectus abdominus
Tensor fasciae latae
**Quadricep group**
Rectus femoris
Vastus medialis
Gracilis
Sartorius
Patella
**Hamstring group**
Biceps femoris
Semitendonosus
Semimembranosus
Gastrocnemius
Tibialis anterior
Tibia
Soleus
Achilles tendon

| ANALYSIS OF MOVEMENT | JOINT 1 |
|---|---|
| Main joints | Hips (standing leg) |
| Joint movement | Forward: flexion<br>Return: extension |
| Main mobilizing muscles | Gluteus maximus<br>Hamstring group |

| Main stabilizing muscles |
|---|
| The main stabilizers of the trunk are the Abdominal group, Erector spinae, Quadratus lumborum, and muscles of the fixed leg<br>Hips: Gluteus maximus and Hamstring of moving leg<br>Upper body: Anterior deltoid, Rotator cuff muscles, Serratus anterior, Rhomboids, and Lower trapezius |

# FREE-STANDING CALF RAISE

Auxiliary exercise • Isolation/single joint
• Push • Close chain • Machine
• Beginner to advanced

➡️ You can do this exercise at home by simply using the edge of a step. To increase the weight, work one leg at a time.

## Description

Raise your heels by plantarflexing your ankles as high as possible. Pause and then lower your heels, until your calves are stretched. Repeat.

### STARTING POSITION

• Place the toes and balls of your feet on the foot platform.
• In a standing position, maintain postural alignment and abdominal stabilization.

## Tips for good form

• Avoid bending or hyperextending your knees.
• Emphasis on the calf muscle can be increased by relaxing your toes and taking them out of the effort.

| ANALYSIS OF MOVEMENT | JOINT 1 |
|---|---|
| Main joints | Ankles |
| Joint movement | Up: plantarflexion<br>Down: dorsiflexion |
| Main mobilizing muscles | Gastrocnemius<br>Soleus<br>Tibialis posterior<br>Peroneus longus |

| Main stabilizing muscles |
|---|
| Trunk: Erector spinae, Quadratus lumborum, and Abdominal group<br>Legs and hips: Adductor group, Gluteus medius and minimus, and Quadricep group |

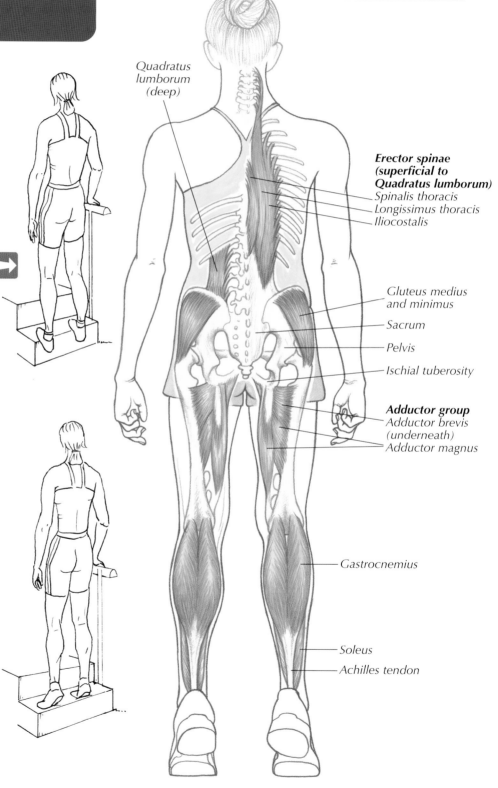

Quadratus lumborum (deep)

**Erector spinae (superficial to Quadratus lumborum)**
Spinalis thoracis
Longissimus thoracis
Iliocostalis

Gluteus medius and minimus

Sacrum

Pelvis

Ischial tuberosity

**Adductor group**
Adductor brevis (underneath)
Adductor magnus

Gastrocnemius

Soleus
Achilles tendon

# SEATED CALF RAISE MACHINE

Auxiliary exercise • Isolation/single joint
• Push • Close chain • Machine
• Intermediate to advanced

➡ This exercise differs from the standing version in that it places emphasis on the Soleus muscle of the calf, while the Gastrocnemius becomes passive due to poor biomechanical advantage created by the knee's flexion.

## Description
Lower your heels until the calves are stretched. Return to starting position, and repeat.

## Tips for good form
· Adjust the machine to give maximum range of movement for the calf muscles.
· Increase emphasis on the calf muscles by relaxing your toes and taking them out of the effort.

Erector spinae
(superficial)

Quadratus lumborum
(deep)

Femur

Gastrocnemius
(tendons cut away)

Fibula

Tibia

Soleus

Achilles tendon
(cut away)

### STARTING POSITION
· Sit on the seat, on your sitting bones, with your spine aligned.
· Place your toes and the balls of your feet on the platform.
· Place your lower thighs under the weight pad, moving it onto your legs by using the machine lever. The machine should be adjusted so that the weight pads offer resistance throughout the full range of motion. Release the support lever.
· Maintain postural alignment and abdominal stabilization.

| ANALYSIS OF MOVEMENT | JOINT 1 |
|---|---|
| Main joints | Ankle |
| Joint movement | Down: dorsiflexion<br>Up: plantarflexion |
| Main mobilizing muscles | Emphasis is on the<br> Soleus muscle<br>Gastrocnemius<br>Tibialis posterior<br>Peroneus longus |

| Main stabilizing muscles |
|---|
| Moderate stabilization is effected by the Abdominal group, Erector spinae, Mid- and Lower trapezius, and Rhomboids |

# BACK AND SHOULDERS

The back and shoulder muscles have four distinct layers and are among the most complex muscles in the body, allowing for a wide variety of movement functions.

A typical female skeleton has a smaller ribcage and wider pelvis than a skeleton of a man. This can predispose women to a smaller upper trunk with rounded shoulders, especially in larger bust sizes. Collapsing at the chest then weakens the mid-back stabilizers, compromises chest strength, and promotes cervical neck pain. With time this affects whole-body posture and stabilization, energy levels through compromised breathing, and digestion.

While the legs are agents of locomotion and base posture, the back muscles together with the abdominals are the foundation of all upper-body movements. These muscles help to anchor the trunk and stabilize it, allowing upper-body movements to occur.

Metaphorically, a collapsed spine and closed chest indicate detachment and separation from the world. When we "open up" and stand firm, we meet life's challenges with more confidence, clarity, and poise. These facts heighten the importance of having a well-conditioned back, one that anchors you and opens you to the world.

## Major Muscles of the Back and Shoulders

| Name | Joints crossed | Origin | Insertion | Action |
|------|---------------|--------|-----------|--------|
| Erector spinae | Length of the spinal column | Posterior iliac crest and sacrum | Angles of ribs, transverse processes of all ribs | Spinal extension |
| Latissimus dorsi | Shoulder | Posterior crest of the ilium, sacrum, spinous processes of the lumbar spine, and lower 6 thoracic vertebrae | Medial side of the humerus | Shoulder: adduction, extension, medial rotation, horizontal abduction |
| Trapezius, consisting of: Upper fibers Mid-fibers Lower fibers | Cross from vertebral column onto the scapula | Occipital bones, spinous processes of cervical and thoracic vertebrae | Acromion process and spine of the scapula | Together, the main action is scapular retraction. Separately: upper fibers—scapula elevation; mid-fibers—scapula adduction (retraction); lower fibers—scapula depression, upward rotation |
| Rhomboids | Cross from vertebral column onto the scapula | Spinous processes of the last cervical and the first 5 thoracic vertebrae | Medial border of the scapula, below the scapula spine | Scapular: adduction (retraction); downward rotation |
| Levator scapulae | Cervical spine to scapula | Transverse processes of the first 4 cervical vertebrae | Medial border of the scapula | Scapular elevation |
| Teres major | Shoulder | Posterior, inferior lateral border of the scapula | Medial humerus | Shoulder: extension, medial rotation, adduction |
| Deltoid, consisting of: Posterior fibers Mid-fibers Anterior fibers | Shoulder | Posterior fibers: inferior edge of the spine of the scapula; mid-fibers lateral: aspect of the acromion; anterior fibers: anterior lateral third of the clavicle | Lateral side of the humerus | Shoulder abduction. Also: posterior fibers—shoulder extension, horizontal abduction, and lateral rotation; mid-fibers—shoulder abduction; anterior fibers—shoulder flexion, horizontal adduction, and medial rotation. |

| Name | Joints crossed | Origin | Insertion | Action |
|------|----------------|--------|-----------|--------|
| Serratus anterior | Shoulder | Upper 8 ribs at the side of the chest | Anterior aspect of the entire medial border of the scapula | Scapula: abduction (protraction), upward rotation |
| Quadratus lumborum | From the spine to the pelvis | Posterior inner surface of the iliac crest | Transverse processes of the upper 4 lumbar vertebrae and the lower border of the 12th rib | Trunk lateral flexion; elevation of the pelvis (while standing) |

## Muscles of the Rotator Cuff

| Name | Joints crossed | Origin | Insertion | Action |
|------|----------------|--------|-----------|--------|
| Supraspinatus | Shoulder | Supraspinous fossa | Around the greater tubercle of the humerus | Shoulder abduction (first 15°) |
| Infraspinatus | Shoulder | Scapular posterior surface on the medial aspect of the infraspinatus fossa, just below the scapula spine | Around the greater tubercle of the humerus | Shoulder: lateral rotation, horizontal abduction, extension |
| Teres minor | Shoulder | Posterior, upper, and middle aspect of the lateral border of the scapula | Around the greater tubercle of the humerus | Shoulder: lateral rotation, horizontal abduction, extension |
| Subscapularis | Shoulder | Along the anterior surface of the subscapular fossa | Lesser tubercle of the humerus | Shoulder: medial rotation, adduction, extension |

**Notes** Collectively, these muscles give extra stability to the shoulder joints. Specifically, they work in the following examples:
· Lateral raises with slight medial rotation of the arm will strengthen the Supraspinatus.
· Any pull-down action uses the Infraspinatus and Teres minor muscles, e.g. lateral pull-downs and chin-ups.
· Medial rotation against resistance with the arms down beside the body will strengthen the Subscapularis.

## Exercises

1. Machine Cable Front Lateral Pull-down, page 94
2. Chin-up Assist Machine, page 96
3. Standing Cable Pull-over, page 97
4. Standing Reverse Grip Cable Rows, page 98
5. Seated Low Cable Pulley Rows, page 99
6. Supported Bent-over Row Machine, page 100
7. Dumb-bell Bent-over Rows, page 101
8. Prone Back Extension on Ball, page 102
9. Back Extension Apparatus, page 103
10. Alternate Arm and Leg Raises on Ball, page 104
11. Machine Shoulder Press, page 106
12. Dumb-bell Seated Shoulder Press, page 107
13. Dumb-bell Standing Lateral Raise, page 108
14. Rear Deltoid Machine, page 109
15. Seated Bent-over Dumb-bell Raises on Ball, page 110
16. Rotator Cuff Stabilization with Theraband, page 111

# MACHINE CABLE FRONT LATERAL PULL-DOWN

Core exercise • Compound/multi-joint
• Pull • Open chain • Machine
• Beginner to advanced

The lateral pull-down is one of the most complete upper-body exercises, with many variations possible. It is more of a functional exercise than its traditional counterpart, which involves pulling the bar down to the back of the neck.

## Description

With a slight lean back, pull the bar down to your upper chest. Pause, return, and repeat.

## Tips for good form

· Avoid momentum—use a slow, controlled, full range of movement.
· Avoid hunching or rounding your shoulders during the exercise. Keep your chest open and your shoulder blades depressed.
· Leaning slightly backward from the sitting bones will give better clearance for the bar, and will activate the abdominal stabilizers.
· Inhale on the down-phase.

### STARTING POSITION
· Sit on the sitting bones, with your chest open and your spine aligned.
· Place your knees under the roll-pad restraint.
· Hold the bar with a wide grip.
· Sit with your legs underneath the machine supports.

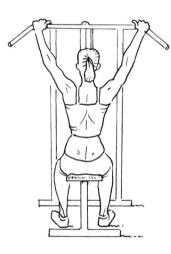 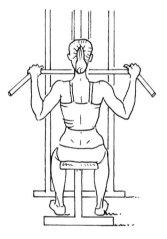

| Main stabilizing muscles |
| --- |
| Trunk: Abdominal group and Erector spinae<br>Shoulder joint: Rotator cuff muscles<br>Shoulder blades: Serratus anterior, Rhomboids, and<br> Lower trapezius<br>Forearms: Wrist flexors |

| ANALYSIS OF MOVEMENT | JOINT 1 | JOINT 2 | JOINT 3 |
| --- | --- | --- | --- |
| Main joints | Elbow | Shoulder | Scapulothoracic |
| Joint movement | Down: flexion<br>Up: extension | Down: adduction, partial extension<br>Up: abduction, partial flexion | Down: downward rotation, adduction (retraction), depression<br>Up: upward rotation, abduction (protraction), elevation |
| Main mobilizing muscles | Biceps brachii<br>Brachialis<br>Brachoradialis | Latissimus dorsi<br>Teres major<br>Pectoralis major<br>Posterior deltoid | Rhomboids, Trapezius |

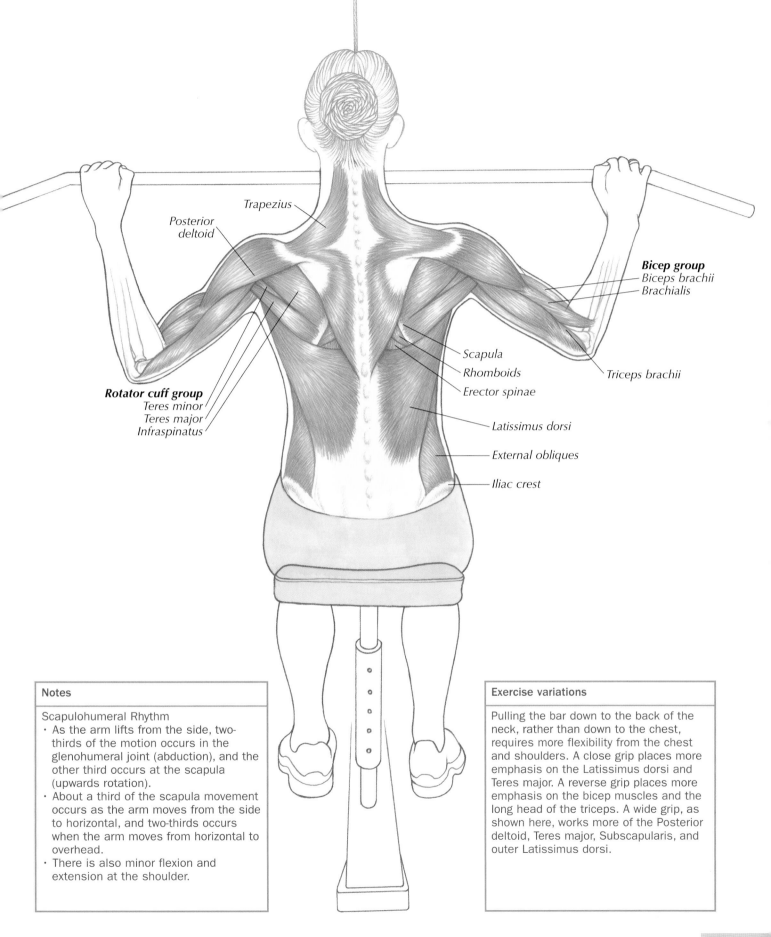

Trapezius

Posterior
deltoid

Bicep group
Biceps brachii
Brachialis

Scapula

Rhomboids

Erector spinae

Triceps brachii

Rotator cuff group
Teres minor
Teres major
Infraspinatus

Latissimus dorsi

External obliques

Iliac crest

**Notes**

Scapulohumeral Rhythm
· As the arm lifts from the side, two-thirds of the motion occurs in the glenohumeral joint (abduction), and the other third occurs at the scapula (upwards rotation).
· About a third of the scapula movement occurs as the arm moves from the side to horizontal, and two-thirds occurs when the arm moves from horizontal to overhead.
· There is also minor flexion and extension at the shoulder.

**Exercise variations**

Pulling the bar down to the back of the neck, rather than down to the chest, requires more flexibility from the chest and shoulders. A close grip places more emphasis on the Latissimus dorsi and Teres major. A reverse grip places more emphasis on the bicep muscles and the long head of the triceps. A wide grip, as shown here, works more of the Posterior deltoid, Teres major, Subscapularis, and outer Latissimus dorsi.

# CHIN-UP ASSIST MACHINE

Core exercise • Compound/multi-joint • Pull • Open chain • Machine • Intermediate to advanced

➡ This unique machine allows you to select weight to compensate for your body weight. The more weight you choose, the easier it is. As you progress and get fitter, you can slowly use less supporting body weight and lift more of your own body weight.

## Description

Leaning back slightly, leading with the upper chest, pull yourself toward the machine. Pause, return, and repeat.

## Tips for good form

· Avoid momentum—use a slow, controlled, full range of movement.
· Avoid hunching or rounding your shoulders. Keep your chest open, your shoulder blades depressed.
· Leaning slightly backward will give better clearance and activate the abdominal stabilizers.
· Inhale on the down-phase.

Posterior deltoid
Upper trapezius
Brachioradialis
Biceps brachii
Brachialis
**Triceps**
Lateral head
Long head
**Rotator cuff group**
Teres minor
Teres major
Infraspinatus
Rhomboids
Lower trapezius
Erector spinae
Latissimus dorsi
Erector spinae (superficial)
Quadratus lumborum (underneath)
Iliac crest

**FINISHING POSITION**

### STARTING POSITION

· Step onto the machine platform, then place one knee on the support pad. Put your hands on the grips, pull yourself up, and bring the other knee onto the support pad.
· Lower yourself gently into the ready position with your arms extended, shoulders relaxed, and shoulder blades drawn down and against the ribs.

| Main stabilizing muscles |
|---|
| Trunk: Abdominal group and Erector spinae<br>Shoulder joints: Rotator cuff muscles<br>Shoulder blades: Serratus anterior,<br> Rhomboids, and Lower trapezius<br>Forearms: Wrist flexors |

| ANALYSIS OF MOVEMENT | JOINT 1 | JOINT 2 | JOINT 3 |
|---|---|---|---|
| Main joints | Elbow | Shoulder | Scapulothoracic |
| Joint movement | Down: flexion<br>Up: extension | Down: adduction, partial extension<br>Up: abduction, partial flexion | Down: downward rotation, adduction (retraction), depression<br>Up: upward rotation, abduction (protraction), elevation |
| Main mobilizing muscles | Biceps brachii<br>Brachialis<br>Brachioradialis | Latissimus dorsi<br>Teres major<br>Pectoralis major<br>Posterior deltoid | Rhomboids<br>Trapezius |

# STANDING CABLE PULL-OVER

Auxiliary exercise with significant stabilization emphasis • Isolated • Pull • Close chain • Machine • Intermediate to advanced

➡ This exercise, also known as a Straight-arm Pull-down, is particularly useful for strengthening the postural stabilizers such the abdominals, Serratus anterior, and Lower trapezius. Quality of work is more important than quantity of weight lifted.

## Description

Keeping your arms straight, pull the bar down by extending your shoulders until they are in line with your sides. Return with control, and repeat.

## Tips for good form

- Avoid momentum—use a slow, controlled, full range of movement.
- Avoid hunching or rounding your shoulders. Keep your chest open, and your shoulder blades depressed.
- Keep your elbows soft, not locked, and hyperextended.
- Keep your trunk stable, your posture aligned, and your spine neutral. You should feel your abdominal stabilizers engaging strongly in the mid-range of movement.

Pectoralis major

Wrist flexors

Posterior deltoid
Trapezius
Teres major
Triceps brachii
Serratus anterior
Latissimus dorsi
Erector spinae (deep)

### Main stabilizing muscles

Hips and legs: Gluteus maximus and main leg muscles
Trunk: Abdominal group and Erector spinae
Shoulder joints: Rotator cuff muscles
Shoulder blades: Serratus anterior, Rhomboids, and Lower trapezius
Arms: Triceps
Forearms: Wrist flexors

### STARTING POSITION

- Stand facing the high cable pulley, one leg in front of the other for better balance, weight 70 percent on the front leg.
- Take hold of the bar with a medium grip (slightly wider than shoulder-width).
- Keep your posture aligned, maintaining a neutral spine.

| ANALYSIS OF MOVEMENT | JOINT 1 |
|---|---|
| Main joints | Shoulder |
| Joint movement | Down: extension Up: flexion |
| Main mobilizing muscles | Latissimus dorsi Teres major Pectoralis major Posterior deltoid |

# STANDING REVERSE GRIP CABLE ROWS

Auxiliary exercise • Isolated • Pull
• Close chain • Machine
• Intermediate to advanced

This functional back exercise combines leg and abdominal stabilization effort with back and arm strength. It also uses more bicep group muscles than conventional cable rows and lateral pull-downs.

## Description
Pull the bar towards your lower chest by bending at your elbows. Return with control, and repeat.

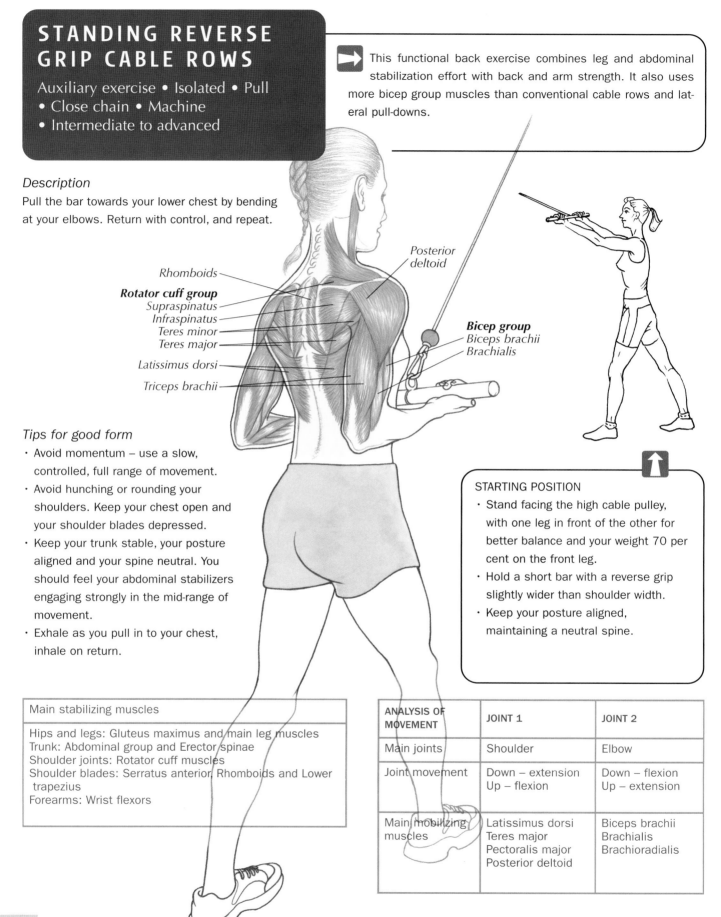

Rhomboids

**Rotator cuff group**
Supraspinatus
Infraspinatus
Teres minor
Teres major

Latissimus dorsi

Triceps brachii

Posterior deltoid

**Bicep group**
Biceps brachii
Brachialis

## Tips for good form
· Avoid momentum – use a slow, controlled, full range of movement.
· Avoid hunching or rounding your shoulders. Keep your chest open and your shoulder blades depressed.
· Keep your trunk stable, your posture aligned and your spine neutral. You should feel your abdominal stabilizers engaging strongly in the mid-range of movement.
· Exhale as you pull in to your chest, inhale on return.

### STARTING POSITION
· Stand facing the high cable pulley, with one leg in front of the other for better balance and your weight 70 per cent on the front leg.
· Hold a short bar with a reverse grip slightly wider than shoulder width.
· Keep your posture aligned, maintaining a neutral spine.

| Main stabilizing muscles |
| --- |
| Hips and legs: Gluteus maximus and main leg muscles<br>Trunk: Abdominal group and Erector spinae<br>Shoulder joints: Rotator cuff muscles<br>Shoulder blades: Serratus anterior, Rhomboids and Lower trapezius<br>Forearms: Wrist flexors |

| ANALYSIS OF MOVEMENT | JOINT 1 | JOINT 2 |
| --- | --- | --- |
| Main joints | Shoulder | Elbow |
| Joint movement | Down – extension<br>Up – flexion | Down – flexion<br>Up – extension |
| Main mobilizing muscles | Latissimus dorsi<br>Teres major<br>Pectoralis major<br>Posterior deltoid | Biceps brachii<br>Brachialis<br>Brachioradialis |

# SEATED LOW CABLE PULLEY ROWS

Core exercise • Compound/multi-joint
• Pull • Open chain • Machine
• Intermediate to advanced

The first low cable pulley rows were developed in the late 1940s. This exercise is one of the mainstays of an effective compound back workout.

## Description

Pull the bar to your waist, keeping your chest open, and your shoulders and elbows back. Return, and repeat.

## Tips for good form

• Avoid momentum—use a slow, controlled, full range of movement.
• Avoid hunching or rounding your shoulders during the exercise. Keep your chest open and your shoulder blades depressed.
• Avoid rounding your mid- and lower back.
• Inhale on the backward phase.

SUPERFICIAL MUSCLES
Trapezius
Posterior deltoid

**Bicep group**
Biceps brachii
Brachialis
Brachioradialis

DEEP MUSCLES
Levator scapuli
Supraspinatus
Rhomboids

**Rotator cuff group**
Infraspinatus
Teres minor
Teres major

Serratus anterior
Latissimus dorsi
Quadratus lumborum
External oblique
Pelvis

Sacrum

Femur

### STARTING POSITION

• Sit on the platform and take a close grip on the bar; bend from the knees.
• Sit back on your sitting bones, chest open, and spine aligned.
• Keep your knees slightly bent.

| ANALYSIS OF MOVEMENT | JOINT 1 | JOINT 2 | JOINT 3 |
|---|---|---|---|
| Main joints | Elbow | Shoulder | Scapulothoracic |
| Joint movement | Back: flexion<br>Forward: extension | Back: extension<br>Forward: flexion | Back: adduction (retraction)<br>Forward: abduction (protraction) |
| Main mobilizing muscles | Biceps brachii<br>Brachialis<br>Brachioradialis | Latissimus dorsi<br>Teres major<br>Posterior deltoid | Rhomboids<br>Trapezius |

Main stabilizing muscles

Hips and legs: Hamstrings, Gluteal muscles, and Adductors
Trunk: Abdominal group and Erector spinae
Shoulder joints: Rotator cuff muscles
Shoulder blades: Serratus anterior, Rhomboids, and Lower trapezius
Arms: Wrist flexors

# SUPPORTED BENT-OVER ROW MACHINE

Core exercise • Compound/multi-joint
• Pull • Open chain • Machine
• Intermediate to advanced

This exercise offers the effectiveness of a free-weight exercise with the support of a machine.

## Description

Pull the bar toward your chest, keeping your chest open, and your shoulders and elbows back. Return, and repeat.

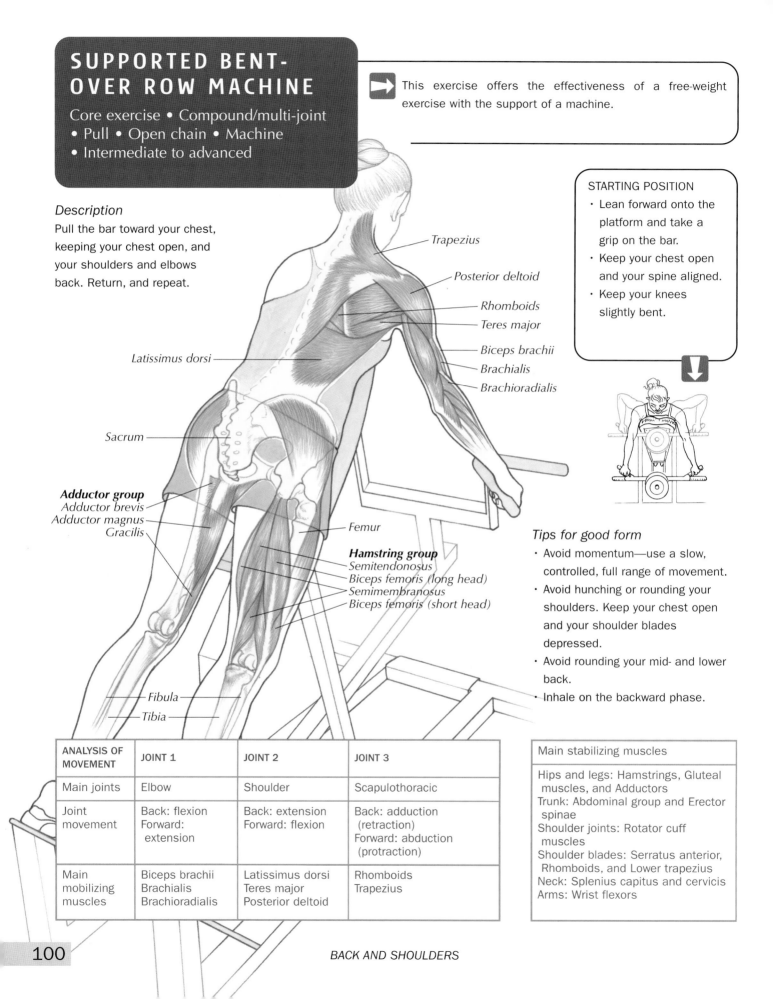

Trapezius

Posterior deltoid

Rhomboids

Teres major

Biceps brachii

Brachialis

Brachioradialis

Latissimus dorsi

Sacrum

**Adductor group**
Adductor brevis
Adductor magnus
Gracilis

Femur

**Hamstring group**
Semitendonosus
Biceps femoris (long head)
Semimembranosus
Biceps femoris (short head)

Fibula

Tibia

### STARTING POSITION

· Lean forward onto the platform and take a grip on the bar.
· Keep your chest open and your spine aligned.
· Keep your knees slightly bent.

## Tips for good form

· Avoid momentum—use a slow, controlled, full range of movement.
· Avoid hunching or rounding your shoulders. Keep your chest open and your shoulder blades depressed.
· Avoid rounding your mid- and lower back.
· Inhale on the backward phase.

| ANALYSIS OF MOVEMENT | JOINT 1 | JOINT 2 | JOINT 3 |
|---|---|---|---|
| Main joints | Elbow | Shoulder | Scapulothoracic |
| Joint movement | Back: flexion Forward: extension | Back: extension Forward: flexion | Back: adduction (retraction) Forward: abduction (protraction) |
| Main mobilizing muscles | Biceps brachii Brachialis Brachioradialis | Latissimus dorsi Teres major Posterior deltoid | Rhomboids Trapezius |

Main stabilizing muscles

Hips and legs: Hamstrings, Gluteal muscles, and Adductors
Trunk: Abdominal group and Erector spinae
Shoulder joints: Rotator cuff muscles
Shoulder blades: Serratus anterior, Rhomboids, and Lower trapezius
Neck: Splenius capitus and cervicis
Arms: Wrist flexors

# DUMB-BELL BENT-OVER ROWS

Core exercise with significant stabilization emphasis • Compound/multi-joint • Pull • Close chain • Dumb-bell • Intermediate to advanced

➡️ When done correctly, this exercise is one of the most valuable and complete upper body exercises of all, challenging both postural stabilizer and mobilizing muscles.

## Description
Pull the dumb-bells to your upper waist, retracting your shoulder blades. Return, and repeat.

## Tips for good form
· Avoid momentum—use a slow, controlled, full range of movement.
· Avoid hunching or rounding your shoulders during the exercise. Keep your chest open and your shoulder blades depressed.
· Avoid rounding your mid- and lower back. Keep your pelvis neutral and your spine aligned.
· Inhale on the up-phase.

### STARTING POSITION
· Take a stable squat position with the dumb-bells in your hands held with an overhand grip. ➡️

Upper trapezius
Lower trapezius
Rhomboids
Erector spinae
Latissimus dorsi
Serratus anterior
External obliques (abdominals)
Gluteus medius and minimus
Gluteus maximus

Posterior deltoid
**Rotator cuff group**
Infraspinatus
Teres minor
Teres major
Pectoralis major
**Bicep group**
Biceps brachii (left)
Brachialis (right)

**Hamstring group**
Biceps femoris
Semitendonosus
Semimembranosus

Gastrocnemius
Soleus

## Women-specific training tip—rounded shoulders
If you have typically rounded shoulders, it is important that you strengthen the rhomboids and Middle and Lower trapezius, as well as stretch the Pectoralis major and minor. This is an ideal exercise for rounded shoulders.

| ANALYSIS OF MOVEMENT | JOINT 1 | JOINT 2 | JOINT 3 |
|---|---|---|---|
| Main joints | Elbow | Shoulder | Scapulothoracic |
| Joint movement | Up: flexion Down: extension | Up: extension, horizontal abduction Down: flexion, horizontal adduction | Up: adduction (retraction) Down: abduction (protraction) |
| Main mobilizing muscles | Bicep group (partial work) | Latissimus dorsi Teres major Posterior deltoid Infraspinatus Teres minor | Rhomboids Trapezius |

| Main stabilizing muscles |
|---|
| Legs: Hamstrings, Gluteal muscles, Adductors, and Rectus femoris |
| Trunk: Abdominal group and Erector spinae |
| Shoulder joints: Rotator cuff muscles |
| Shoulder blades: Serratus anterior, Rhomboids, and Lower trapezius |
| Forearms: Wrist flexors |
| Neck: Splenius capitus and cervicis |

# PRONE BACK EXTENSION ON BALL

Auxiliary exercise • Compound/ multi-joint • Pull • Open chain • Body- weight • Intermediate to advanced

➡ The original manufacturing birthplace of the gym equipment known as a "stability ball" (see also page 38) was in Consani plastics in Italy in the early 1960s.

## Description

Without the ball moving, extend your upper body up from your hips. The emphasis is on the spinal movement. Return, and repeat. To make the exercise easier, position the ball under your waist. To make it harder, place the ball under your buttocks, or put your arms behind your head.

### Tips for good form

- Avoid momentum—use a slow, controlled, full range of movement.
- Inhale on the up-phase.

| ANALYSIS OF MOVEMENT | JOINT 1 |
|---|---|
| Main joints | Spine |
| Joint movement | Up: extension<br>Down: flexion |
| Main mobilizing muscles | Erector spinae |

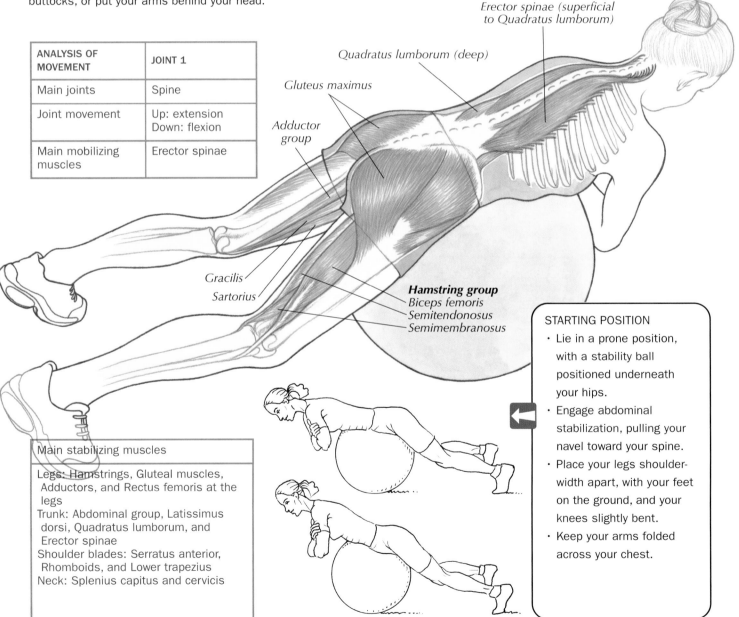

Erector spinae (superficial to Quadratus lumborum)

Quadratus lumborum (deep)

Gluteus maximus

Adductor group

Gracilis

Sartorius

**Hamstring group**
Biceps femoris
Semitendonosus
Semimembranosus

### Main stabilizing muscles

Legs: Hamstrings, Gluteal muscles, Adductors, and Rectus femoris at the legs
Trunk: Abdominal group, Latissimus dorsi, Quadratus lumborum, and Erector spinae
Shoulder blades: Serratus anterior, Rhomboids, and Lower trapezius
Neck: Splenius capitus and cervicis

⬅ STARTING POSITION
- Lie in a prone position, with a stability ball positioned underneath your hips.
- Engage abdominal stabilization, pulling your navel toward your spine.
- Place your legs shoulder- width apart, with your feet on the ground, and your knees slightly bent.
- Keep your arms folded across your chest.

# BACK EXTENSION APPARATUS

Auxiliary exercise • Compound/multi-joint • Pull • Open chain • Body-weight • Intermediate to advanced

The Back Extension Apparatus allows for two different, but equally effective exercises. Because they both act on the back muscles, both are shown here. Folding the arms across the chest, as shown in the line drawings, makes the exercises harder.

*Erector spinae*

*Ribcage*

*Gluteus maximus*

*Biceps femoris (hamstrings)*

## Description

**Version 1** Lower your body to the ground by flexing at the waist, keeping your back straight (see line drawings below). Return by raising your body until your trunk is parallel with your legs. Repeat.

**Version 2** Lower your body to the ground by rounding your spine, and then flexing your hips (see left). The emphasis here is on the spinal movement. Return in reverse order, and repeat.

### STARTING POSITION
· Lie in a prone position.
· Place your heels under the padded brace, your upper thighs against the pad.
· Position your hip bones above the pad.
· Inhale on the up-phase.

## Tips for good form
· Avoid momentum—use a slow, controlled, full range of movement.
· Engage abdominal stabilization, pulling your navel in toward your spine.
· Inhale on the up-phase.

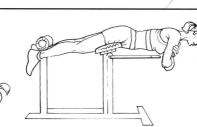

### Main stabilizing muscles

**Version 1** Legs: Rectus femoris at the legs
Trunk: Abdominal group and Erector spinae
Shoulder blades: Serratus anterior, Rhomboids, and Lower trapezius
Neck: Splenius capitus and cervicis
**Version 2** Legs: Hamstrings, Gluteal muscles, Adductors, and Rectus femoris
Trunk: Abdominal group and Erector spinae
Neck: Splenius capitus and cervicis

| ANALYSIS OF MOVEMENT | JOINT 1 | JOINT 2 | JOINT 3 |
|---|---|---|---|
| | Version 1 | Version 2 | |
| Main joints | Hips | Spine | Hips |
| Joint movement | Up: extension Down: flexion | Up: extension Down: flexion | Up: extension Down: flexion |
| Main mobilizing muscles | Gluteus maximus Hamstring group | Erector spinae | Gluteus maximus Hamstring group |

# ALTERNATE ARM AND LEG RAISES ON BALL

Core exercise • Compound/multi-joint
• Push • Close chain • Body-weight
• Intermediate to advanced

Chronic lower back pain is ranked as the number one cause of disability in the general population of the United States. This exercise may be used in a guided rehabilitation program for mechanical lower back injury, and is also excellent for preventing this same condition.

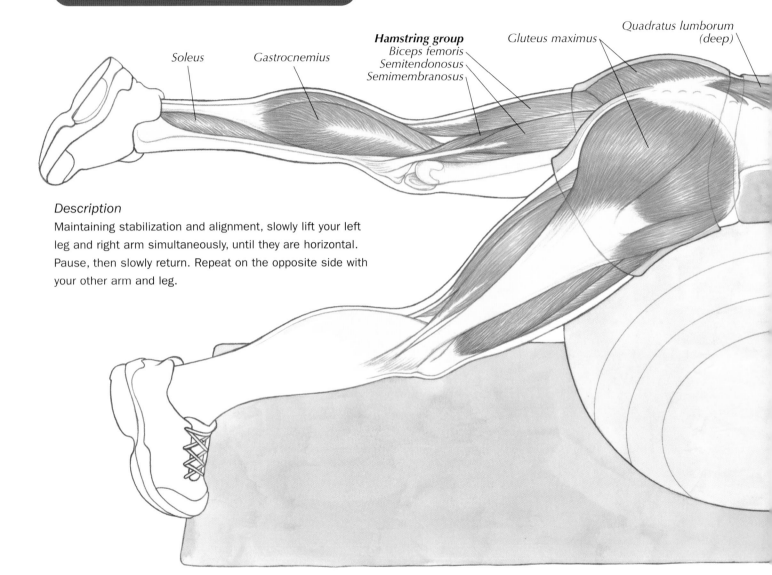

Soleus     Gastrocnemius     **Hamstring group** / Biceps femoris / Semitendonosus / Semimembranosus     Gluteus maximus     Quadratus lumborum (deep)

## Description

Maintaining stabilization and alignment, slowly lift your left leg and right arm simultaneously, until they are horizontal. Pause, then slowly return. Repeat on the opposite side with your other arm and leg.

| ANALYSIS OF MOVEMENT | JOINT 1 | JOINT 2 |
|---|---|---|
| Main joints | Shoulder (lifting arm) | Hips (lifting leg) |
| Joint movement | Up: flexion Down: extension | Up: extension Down: flexion |
| Main mobilizing muscles | Posterior deltoid | Gluteus maximus Hamstring group |

Main stabilizing muscles

Muscles in opposing arm (mainly triceps) and leg
Trunk: Abdominal group, Quadratus lumborum, Erector spinae, Adductor group, and Gluteus medius, and minimus
Shoulder joints: Rotator cuff muscles
Shoulder blades: Serratus anterior, Rhomboids, and Trapezius
Neck: Splenius capitus and cervicis

**Rotator cuff group**
*Infraspinatus*
*Teres minor*
*Teres major*

*Trapezius*

*Latissimus dorsi*

*Posterior deltoid*

*Biceps brachii*

*Brachialis*

*Brachioradialis*

*Tips for good form*
- Avoid momentum—use a slow, controlled, full range of movement.
- Avoid rounding, arching, or twisting your mid- and lower back. Keep your pelvis neutral and your spine aligned.
- Keep your legs relaxed, and push slightly forward from your waist into the ball.
- Keep your chest open and your shoulder blades depressed.
- If you cannot stabilize your trunk, do the exercise lying prone, or work your legs and arms separately.
- Inhale on the up-phase.

STARTING POSITION
- Lie prone on a stability ball (the ball should be at waist-level). Place your hands directly under your shoulders, with your knees bent, and your feet on the floor shoulder-width apart. A slightly smaller ball than normal is best.
- Maintain a neutral spine and engage abdominal stabilization, pulling your navel toward your spine.
- Keep your chest open. Aim to depress and widen your shoulder blades against your back, activating the Serratus anterior.

# MACHINE SHOULDER PRESS

Core • Compound/multi-joint • Push
• Close chain • Machine
• Intermediate to advanced

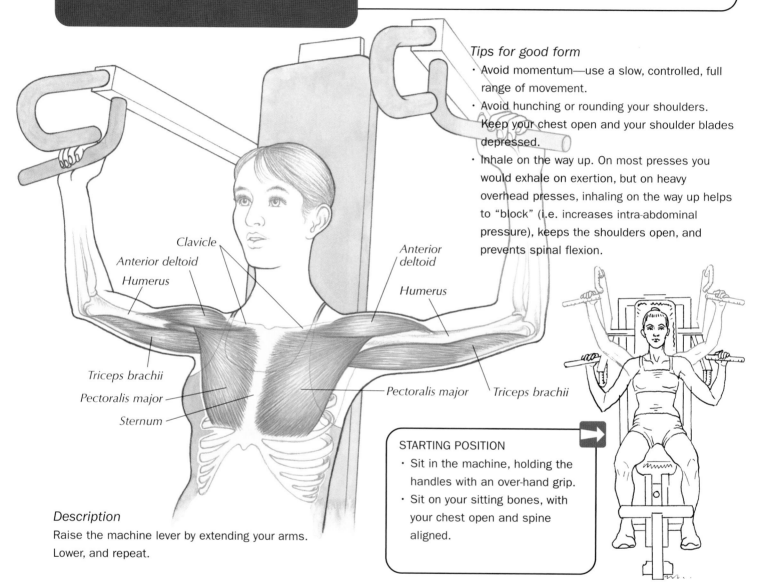

The risk of shoulder injury increases when the arm moves from horizontal to abducted and extended. For this reason, overhead presses should be introduced gradually. The Machine Shoulder Press is a good option for beginners.

*Tips for good form*
· Avoid momentum—use a slow, controlled, full range of movement.
· Avoid hunching or rounding your shoulders. Keep your chest open and your shoulder blades depressed.
· Inhale on the way up. On most presses you would exhale on exertion, but on heavy overhead presses, inhaling on the way up helps to "block" (i.e. increases intra-abdominal pressure), keeps the shoulders open, and prevents spinal flexion.

*Clavicle*
*Anterior deltoid*
*Humerus*
*Anterior deltoid*
*Humerus*
*Triceps brachii*
*Pectoralis major*
*Sternum*
*Pectoralis major*
*Triceps brachii*

STARTING POSITION
· Sit in the machine, holding the handles with an over-hand grip.
· Sit on your sitting bones, with your chest open and spine aligned.

## Description
Raise the machine lever by extending your arms. Lower, and repeat.

| Main stabilizing muscles |
| --- |
| Trunk: Abdominal group and Erector spinae<br>Shoulder joints: Rotator cuff muscles at the shoulder joints<br>Shoulder blades: Serratus anterior, Rhomboids, and Upper and Lower trapezius<br>Forearms: Wrist flexors |

| ANALYSIS OF MOVEMENT | JOINT 1 | JOINT 2 | JOINT 3 |
| --- | --- | --- | --- |
| Main joints | Elbow | Shoulder | Scapulothoracic |
| Joint movement | Up: extension<br>Down: flexion | Up: abduction, flexion<br>Down: adduction, extension | Up: upward rotation<br>Down: downward rotation |
| Main mobilizing muscles | Triceps brachii<br>Anconeus | Deltoid<br>Pectoralis major (clavicular aspect) | Serratus anterior<br>Trapezius |

# DUMB-BELL SEATED SHOULDER PRESS

Core • Compound/multi-joint • Push
• Close chain • Dumb-bell
• Beginner to advanced

→ Compared to the machine version, this exercise incorporates more work from the back and shoulder stabilizers while also allowing the shoulder muscles to work through a slightly greater range of movement.

## Description

Raise the dumb-bells by extending your arms, keeping your forearms parallel, i.e. do not let the weights meet. Lower, and repeat.

## Tips for good form

• Avoid momentum—use a slow, controlled, full range of movement.
• Avoid hunching or rounding your shoulders. Keep your chest open and your shoulder blades depressed.
• Inhale on the way up. On most presses you would exhale on exertion, but on heavy overhead presses, inhaling on the way up helps to "block" (i.e. increases intra-abdominal pressure), keeps the shoulders open, and prevents spinal flexion.

Pectoralis major

Anterior deltoid

Anterior deltoid

Biceps brachii

Biceps brachii

Brachialis

Triceps brachii

Triceps brachii

Brachialis

Coracobrachialis

### STARTING POSITION

• Sit on a bench, holding the dumb-bells at shoulder-height, palms facing forward.
• Sit on your sitting bones, keeping your chest open and your spine aligned.

### Main stabilizing muscles

Trunk: Abdominal group and Erector spinae
Shoulder joints: Rotator cuff muscles at the shoulder joints
Shoulder blades: Serratus anterior, Rhomboids, and Upper and Lower trapezius
Forearms: Wrist flexors

| ANALYSIS OF MOVEMENT | JOINT 1 | JOINT 2 | JOINT 3 |
|---|---|---|---|
| Main joints | Elbow | Shoulder | Scapulothoracic |
| Joint movement | Up: extension Down: flexion | Up: abduction, flexion Down: adduction, extension | Up: upward rotation Down: downward rotation |
| Main mobilizing muscles | Triceps brachii Anconeus | Deltoid Pectoralis major (clavicular aspect) | Serratus anterior Trapezius |

# DUMB-BELL STANDING LATERAL RAISE

Auxiliary exercise • Isolated/single joint
• Pull • Close chain • Dumb-bell
• Beginner to advanced

➡️ This very simple method is one of the most biomechanically misunderstood exercises. It is often performed with too much weight and momentum, but when done correctly it is an excellent isolation exercise for the deltoids.

## Description

Maintaining a fixed elbow angle of about 10°, raise your arms laterally to shoulder-height. Keep your wrists, elbows, and shoulders in line. Lower, and repeat.

DEEP MUSCLES

Humerus

SUPERFICIAL MUSCLES

Upper trapezius

Deltoid

Lower trapezius

**Rotator cuff group**
Teres minor
Teres major
Infraspinatus
Supraspinatus

## Tips for good form

· Avoid momentum, especially arching from your lower back. Use a slow, controlled, full range of movement.
· Avoid rounding your chest and shoulders: keep them open. Aim to depress and widen your shoulder blades against your back, activating the Serratus anterior.
· Doing the exercise with heavier weights and bent elbows is deceiving. By bending the elbows you shorten the effective lever, compensating for the additional weight being lifted.
· Inhale on the up-phase.

### STARTING POSITION

· Stand with your feet shoulder-width apart.
· Keep your posture aligned, with a neutral spine.
· Keep your knees soft.
· Hold the dumb-bells with your hands at your sides.

| ANALYSIS OF MOVEMENT | JOINT 1 |
|---|---|
| Main joints | Shoulder |
| Joint movement | Up: abduction Down: adduction |
| Main mobilizing muscles | Deltoid Supraspinatus |

| Main stabilizing muscles |
|---|
| General leg muscles Trunk: Abdominal group and Erector spinae Shoulder joints: Rotator cuff muscles Shoulder blades: Serratus anterior, Rhomboids, and Upper and Lower trapezius Forearms: Wrist extensors |

# REAR DELTOID MACHINE

Auxiliary exercise • Isolated/single joint
• Pull • Close chain • Machine
• Beginner to advanced

→ Common postural syndromes generally lead to an imbalance between the Anterior and Posterior deltoids, with the former tending to tighten and the latter tending to functional weakness. The Rear Deltoid Machine strengthens the Posterior deltoid.

## Description
Maintaining a fixed elbow angle of about 10°, pull the levers backward until your elbows are just behind the line of your trunk. Return, and repeat.

## Tips for good form
· Avoid momentum, especially arching from the lower back. Use a slow, controlled movement.
· Avoid hunching or rounding your shoulders. Keep your chest open and your shoulder blades depressed.
· Inhale when pulling back.

### STARTING POSITION
· Sit facing the machine.
· Position the pads behind your upper arms, maintaining the arms in a horizontal position. (Some machines have handles instead.)
· Sit on your sitting bones, with your chest open and your spine aligned.

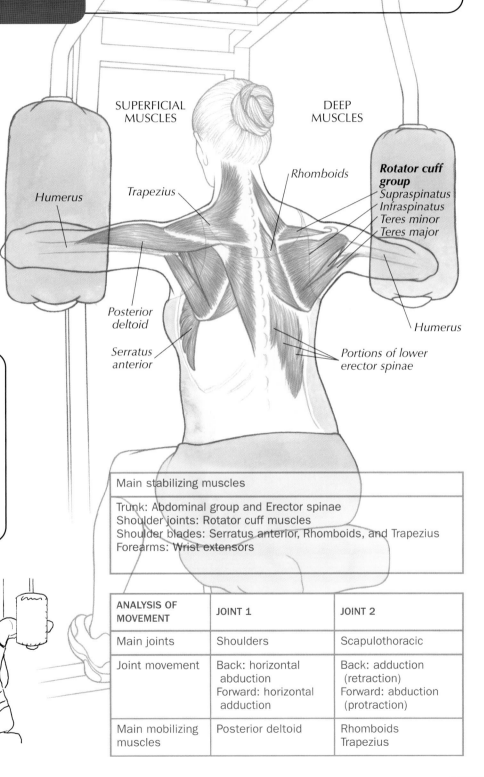

SUPERFICIAL MUSCLES

DEEP MUSCLES

Humerus

Trapezius

Rhomboids

Rotator cuff group
Supraspinatus
Infraspinatus
Teres minor
Teres major

Posterior deltoid

Serratus anterior

Humerus

Portions of lower erector spinae

**Main stabilizing muscles**

Trunk: Abdominal group and Erector spinae
Shoulder joints: Rotator cuff muscles
Shoulder blades: Serratus anterior, Rhomboids, and Trapezius
Forearms: Wrist extensors

| ANALYSIS OF MOVEMENT | JOINT 1 | JOINT 2 |
|---|---|---|
| Main joints | Shoulders | Scapulothoracic |
| Joint movement | Back: horizontal abduction<br>Forward: horizontal adduction | Back: adduction (retraction)<br>Forward: abduction (protraction) |
| Main mobilizing muscles | Posterior deltoid | Rhomboids<br>Trapezius |

# SEATED BENT-OVER DUMB-BELL RAISES ON BALL

Auxiliary exercise with significant stabilization emphasis • Isolated/single joint • Pull • Close chain • Dumb-bell • Intermediate to advanced

➡ The Posterior deltoid is often overlooked in strength-training programs. This is an ideal exercise to include in a training program to fill this gap.

## Description

Maintaining a fixed elbow angle of 10°–20°, raise your arms perpendicularly to your trunk, to shoulder-height. Your elbows will be above the line of your wrists. Lower, and repeat.

## Tips for good form

· Avoid momentum, especially lifting the trunk. Use a slow, controlled, full range of movement.
· Keep your chest and shoulders open. Aim to depress and widen your shoulder blades against your back.
· Doing the exercise with heavier weights and bent elbows is deceiving. By bending your elbows you shorten the effective lever, compensating for additional weight being lifted.
· Inhale on the up-phase.

*Trapezius*

*Posterior deltoid*

*Posterior deltoid*

**Rotator cuff group**
*Teres minor*
*Teres major*
*Infraspinatus*

*Rhomboids*

*Quadratus lumborum (deep)*

*Serratus anterior*

*Iliac crest*

### STARTING POSITION
· Sit with your sitting bones centered on a stability ball. A slightly smaller ball than normal is best.
· Position your feet farther forward than your knees.
· Bring your trunk forward to rest on your knees, as close to horizontal as possible.
· Hold the dumb-bells at your sides, under your legs.

| ANALYSIS OF MOVEMENT | JOINT 1 | JOINT 2 |
|---|---|---|
| Main joints | Shoulder | Scapula |
| Joint movement | Up: horizontal abduction<br>Down: horizontal adduction | Up: adduction (retraction)<br>Down: abduction (protraction) |
| Main mobilizing muscles | Posterior deltoid | Rhomboids Trapezius |

| Main stabilizing muscles |
|---|
| Trunk: Abdominal group<br>Hips: Gluteus medius and minimus, Adductor group, and Quadratus lumborum<br>Shoulder joints: Rotator cuff muscles<br>Shoulder blades: Serratus anterior, Rhomboids, and Trapezius<br>Forearms: Wrist extensors<br>Neck: Splenius capitus and cervicis |

# ROTATOR CUFF STABILIZATION WITH THERABAND

Auxiliary exercise • Isolation single joint
• Pull • Close chain • Theraband
• Beginner to advanced

Rotator cuff weakness and imbalance is often a limiting factor in training performance, and predisposes many common injury syndromes. Usually, there is weakness of the lateral rotators (Supraspinatus, Infraspinatus, and Teres minor), tightness of the medial rotator (Subscapularis), and poor stabilization in general.

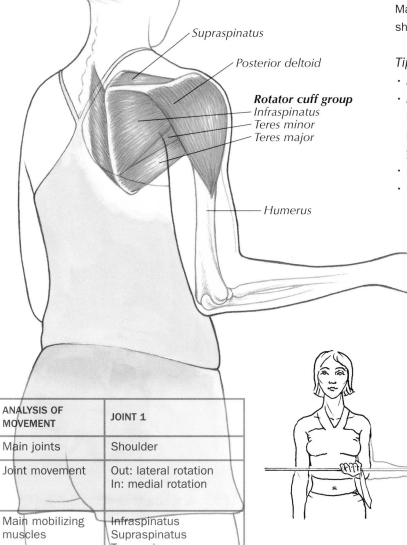

Supraspinatus

Posterior deltoid

**Rotator cuff group**
Infraspinatus
Teres minor
Teres major

Humerus

### Description
Maintaining elbow flexion, laterally rotate your shoulders. Return, and repeat.

### Tips for good form
· Avoid momentum—use a slow, controlled motion.
· Avoid rounding your chest and hunching your shoulders. Keep your chest open, and aim to depress and widen your shoulder blades against your back.
· Keep your elbows at your sides.
· Use moderate/low weight and focus on technique.

### STARTING POSITION
· Place one foot in front of the other, shoulder-width apart. Keep the knees soft.
· Keep your posture aligned, maintaining a neutral spine.
· Hold one end of the theraband in one hand, with your elbow flexed at 90°. Anchor the other end in your other hand, held at the same height.

| ANALYSIS OF MOVEMENT | JOINT 1 |
|---|---|
| Main joints | Shoulder |
| Joint movement | Out: lateral rotation In: medial rotation |
| Main mobilizing muscles | Infraspinatus Supraspinatus Teres minor Posterior deltoid |

| Main stabilizing muscles |
|---|
| Trunk: Abdominal group and Erector spinae Shoulder blades: Serratus anterior, Rhomboids, and Trapezius Forearms: Wrist flexors |

### Women-specific training tip—unstable shoulders
The shoulder joint is the most mobile of all ball-and-socket joints, making it susceptible to injury, especially when the arm is extended and abducted above 90°. In women, weakness of these muscles will predispose dislocation and neck pain in overhead exercises. If you are at risk, use rotator cuff exercises to build up better shoulder joint stability and leave overhead presses to the intermediate stage. Also start with moderate repetitions and sets, and progress slowly.

# ARMS

Although there is currently a trend for women to have well toned and defined arms, many women are concerned that arm training will result in bulky, unattractive arm muscles, as it can in men. However, due to fundamental differences in the hormonal balances of men and women, this is unlikely.

Hormones act as cell messengers, activating and limiting certain physiological functions such as growth, menstrual cycles, and blood-sugar balance. In fact, most physiological functions in the body are impacted by hormones. Women have more estrogen hormones, and men more androgenic hormones such as testosterone and human growth hormone. The hormones that promote muscle growth and size in men are limited in women, thus limiting the potential hypertrophy a woman's arm can achieve.

A woman's muscle-tissue quality is, however, the same as that of a man, so that pound for pound, arm training can result in more toned and defined arms in a woman.

In women, there is a small storage site for fat tissue in the upper arm at the back of the tricep muscle. However, this will usually only increase as overall body fat increases. If a woman leads a sedentary lifestyle, it is also quite likely to enlarge after the menopause.

In the upper arm, at least two-thirds is occupied by the tricep muscle, and one-third by the bicep muscle. Strengthening both these muscles with a variety of exercises will tone and fill the arm compartments, resulting in shapelier and more attractive-looking arms.

## *Major Muscles of the Forearm*
**Note** For purposes of simplicity, other significant muscles are not detailed here.

| Name | Joints crossed | Origin | Insertion | Joint |
|------|------|------|------|------|
| **Wrist flexor group** | | | | |
| Flexor carpi radialis | Wrist | Medial epicondyle of the humerus | Anterior surface (palm-side) of the 2nd and 3rd metacarpals | Wrist: flexion; abduction (also assists elbow flexion) |
| Flexor carpi ulnaris | Wrist | Medial epicondyle of the humerus, posterior proximal ulna | Base of the 5th metacarpal, pisiform, and hamate bones | Wrist: flexion; adduction (also assists in weak flexion of the elbow) |
| Palmaris longus | Wrist | Medial epicondyle of the humerus | Aponeurosis of the palm in the 2nd to 5th metacarpals | Wrist flexion |
| **Wrist extensor group** | | | | |
| Extensor carpi ulnaris | Wrist | Lateral epicondyle of the humerus | 5th metacarpal dorsal surface (back of the hand) | Wrist: extension; adduction (also assists elbow extension) |
| Extensor carpi radialis brevis | Wrist | Lateral epicondyle of the humerus | Dorsal surface of the 3rd metacarpal | Wrist: extension; abduction (also assists in elbow extension) |
| Extensor carpi radialis longus | Wrist | Lateral epicondyle of the humerus | Base of the dorsal surface of the 2nd metacarpal | Wrist: extension; abduction (also assists in weak elbow extension) |
| Forearm supinator | Elbow | Lateral condyle of the humerus and the posterior part of the adjacent ulna | Lateral surface of the proximal radius | Forearm supination |

| Name | Joints crossed | Origin | Insertion | Joint |
|---|---|---|---|---|
| Forearm pronators | | | | |
| Pronator teres | Elbow | Distal medial epicondyle of the humerus, and medial side of the ulna | One-third of the way down the lateral surface of the radius | Forearm pronation (also assists in elbow flexion) |
| Pronator quadratus | Radioulnar junction | Distal anterior side of the ulna | Distal anterior side of the radius | Forearm pronation |

## Major Muscles of the Upper arm

| Name | Joints crossed | Origin | Insertion | Joint |
|---|---|---|---|---|
| Bicep group | | | | |
| Biceps brachii | Shoulder and elbow | The muscle has two heads: long head: supraglenoid tubercle, above the glenoid fossa; short head: coracoid process of the scapula and the upper lip of the glenoid fossa | Tuberosity of the radius | Elbow flexion (best when forearm is supinated); forearm supination; assists in shoulder flexion |
| Brachialis | Elbow | Distal half of the anterior humerus | Coranoid process of the ulna | Elbow flexion |
| Brachioradialis | Elbow | Distal section of the lateral supra condylar ridge of the humerus | Lateral surface of the distal radius, at the styloid process | Elbow flexion; pronation from supinated position to neutral; supination from pronated position to neutral |
| Triceps brachii, consisting of three divisions with a single insertion: long head; lateral head; medial head | All cross the elbow; the long head also crosses the shoulder | Long head: lateral side of the inferior lip of the glenoid fossa of the scapula; lateral head: proximal half of the posterior humerus; medial head: distal two-thirds of the posterior humerus | Olecranon process of the ulna | Elbow extension; the long head also performs shoulder extension |
| Anconeus | Elbow | Posterior lateral condyle of the humerus | Posterior surface of the olecranon process of the ulna | Elbow extension |
| **Note** Rotator cuff muscles are listed in Section 3, Back and Shoulders. | | | | |

## List of Exercises

1. Seated Overhead Tricep Extension on Ball with Theraband, page 114
2. Supine Barbell French Curl, page 115
3. Tricep Machine, page 116
4. Cable Tricep Push-down, page 117
5. Tricep Rope Pull-down, page 118
6. Standing Barbell Curl, page 119
7. Seated Incline Dumb-bell Curl with Supination, page 120
8. Dumb-bell Concentration Curl, page 121

# SEATED OVERHEAD TRICEP EXTENSION ON BALL WITH THERABAND

Core • Isolation/single joint • Push
• Close chain • Flexiband
• Intermediate to advanced

➡ This conventional gym exercise is transformed into a more complete and functionally orientated exercise by the use of a stability ball, increasing the role of the stabilizing muscles such as the abdominals and Erector spinae.

## Description
Keeping your elbow close to your head, raise the theraband by extending your elbow. Return, and repeat.

### Tips for good form
· Use a slow, controlled motion, and avoid momentum.
· Keep your abdominals engaged; pull your navel in to your spine.
· Avoid dropping or flaring your elbow outward. Your upper arm must stay stationery, as if it was part of the spine.
· Keep your chest open, and avoid rounding your shoulders.
· Inhale on the downward phase, exhale on the upward movement.

Triceps brachii
Posterior deltoid
Teres major
Latissimus dorsi
Serratus anterior

Anterior deltoid
Coracobrachialis
Pectoralis minor
Pectoralis major

**Abdominal group**
Rectus abdominus
External obliques

### STARTING POSITION
· Sit on a stability ball, with your posture aligned and stabilized, and with a neutral spine.
· With one arm extended at the shoulder, elbow bent, grasp one end of the theraband with your hand. Anchor the lower end of the theraband in the other hand, folded behind the back.

| ANALYSIS OF MOVEMENT | JOINT 1 |
|---|---|
| Main joints | Elbow (moving arm) |
| Joint movement | Up: extension<br>Down: flexion |
| Main mobilizing muscles | Triceps brachii (emphasis on long head)<br>Anconeus |

| Main stabilizing muscles |
|---|
| General leg muscles<br>Trunk and hips: Abdominals, Latissimus dorsi, Erector spinae, Quadratus lumborum, and Tensor fasciae latae<br>Shoulders: Deltoid, Rotator cuff group, and Pectoralis major<br>Shoulder blades: Serratus anterior, Rhomboids, and Lower trapezius<br>Forearms: Wrist flexors |

# SUPINE BARBELL FRENCH CURL

Core • Isolated/single joint • Push
• Open chain • Barbell
• Intermediate to advanced

→ This effective tricep exercise is often affectionately known as the "headbanger" or "skullcrusher," although this term is not meant to be taken literally—it is one of the most effective arm exercises that there is.

## Description

Lower the bar toward your forehead by flexing your elbows. Stop just before head level, return, and repeat. Once you have achieved good form and stabilization, you can increase the range of movement by extending your elbows slightly, and allowing the bar to clear the curvature of your head.

*Triceps brachii*

*Anconeus*

*Triceps brachii*

*Pectoralis major*

| Main stabilizing muscles |
| --- |
| Abdominals, Latissimus dorsi, Teres major at trunk and shoulders<br>Shoulders: Deltoid, Rotator cuff group, and Pectoralis major<br>Shoulder blades: Serratus anterior, Rhomboids, and Lower trapezius<br>Forearms: Wrist flexors |

## Tips for good form

· Use a slow, controlled motion, and avoid momentum.
· Avoid dropping or flaring your elbows outward during movement. Your upper arm must stay stationery.
· Avoid arching your lower back during the movement, and keep your navel drawn in toward your spine.
· Keep your chest open, and avoid rounding your shoulders.
· Inhale on the downward phase, exhale on the upward movement.

↑

## STARTING POSITION

· Lie supine on a bench.
· Position your arms shoulder-width apart or slightly narrower, with an over-grip on the barbell.
· Place the barbell in line with your forehead, with your arms extended.

| ANALYSIS OF MOVEMENT | JOINT 1 |
| --- | --- |
| Main joints | Elbow |
| Joint movement | Up: extension<br>Down: flexion |
| Main mobilizing muscles | Triceps brachii (emphasis on long head)<br>Anconeus |

# TRICEP MACHINE

Auxiliary exercise • Isolated/single joint • Push • Close chain • Machine • Beginner to advanced

Various tricep machines exist. Some feature sitting or kneeling starting positions; others use bars, handles, or pads. However, all employ the same arm movements, with the movement principles shown in this exercise.

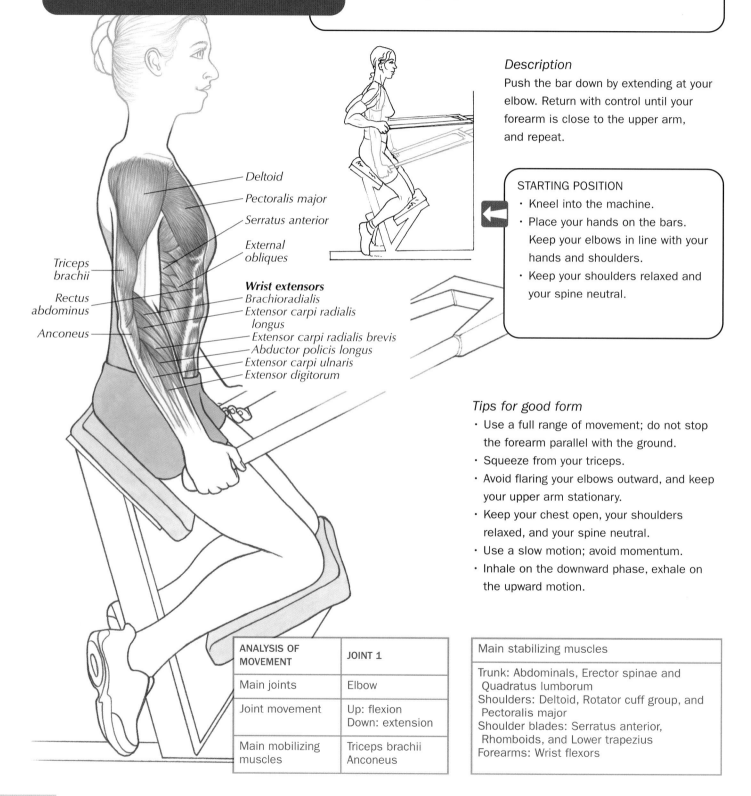

*Deltoid*

*Pectoralis major*

*Serratus anterior*

*External obliques*

*Triceps brachii*

*Rectus abdominus*

*Anconeus*

***Wrist extensors***
*Brachioradialis*
*Extensor carpi radialis longus*
*Extensor carpi radialis brevis*
*Abductor policis longus*
*Extensor carpi ulnaris*
*Extensor digitorum*

## Description

Push the bar down by extending at your elbow. Return with control until your forearm is close to the upper arm, and repeat.

### STARTING POSITION
· Kneel into the machine.
· Place your hands on the bars. Keep your elbows in line with your hands and shoulders.
· Keep your shoulders relaxed and your spine neutral.

## Tips for good form
· Use a full range of movement; do not stop the forearm parallel with the ground.
· Squeeze from your triceps.
· Avoid flaring your elbows outward, and keep your upper arm stationary.
· Keep your chest open, your shoulders relaxed, and your spine neutral.
· Use a slow motion; avoid momentum.
· Inhale on the downward phase, exhale on the upward motion.

| ANALYSIS OF MOVEMENT | JOINT 1 |
|---|---|
| Main joints | Elbow |
| Joint movement | Up: flexion Down: extension |
| Main mobilizing muscles | Triceps brachii Anconeus |

| Main stabilizing muscles |
|---|
| Trunk: Abdominals, Erector spinae and Quadratus lumborum |
| Shoulders: Deltoid, Rotator cuff group, and Pectoralis major |
| Shoulder blades: Serratus anterior, Rhomboids, and Lower trapezius |
| Forearms: Wrist flexors |

# CABLE TRICEP PUSH-DOWN

Auxiliary exercise • Isolated/single joint
• Push • Close chain • Machine
• Beginner to advanced

One of the most basic gym exercises for triceps work, the Cable Tricep Push-down places emphasis on the medial aspect of the tricep muscle. To effectively work all portions of this muscle you will need to use increasingly heavy resistance.

*Description*

Push the bar down by extending at the elbow. Return with control until the forearm is close to the upper arm, and repeat.

*Tips for good form*

· Use a full range of movement; do not stop your forearm parallel with the ground.
· Squeeze from your triceps rather than pushing from your hands.
· For better balance and form with heavy weights, lean forward slightly on to your front leg.
· Avoid flaring your elbows outward, and keep your upper arms stationary as though they are part of your spine.
· Keep your chest open, your shoulders relaxed, and your spine neutral.
· Use a slow, controlled motion, and avoid momentum.
· Inhale on the downward phase, exhale on the upward motion.

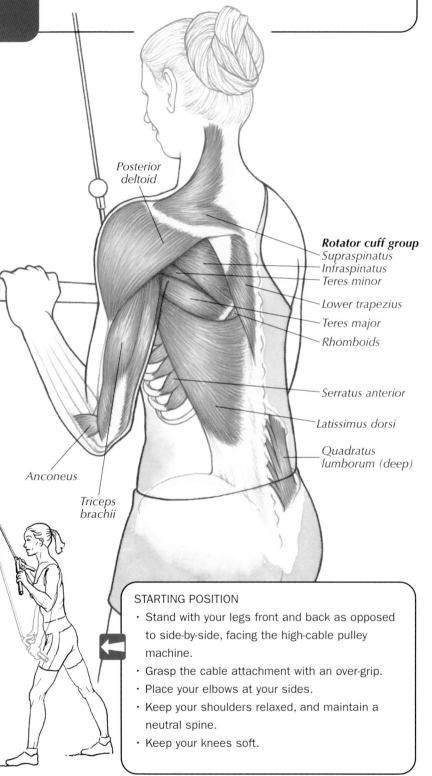

Posterior deltoid

**Rotator cuff group**
Supraspinatus
Infraspinatus
Teres minor

Lower trapezius

Teres major

Rhomboids

Serratus anterior

Latissimus dorsi

Quadratus lumborum (deep)

Anconeus

Triceps brachii

| ANALYSIS OF MOVEMENT | JOINT 1 |
|---|---|
| Main joints | Elbow |
| Joint movement | Up: flexion Down: extension |
| Main mobilizing muscles | Triceps brachii Anconeus |

| Main stabilizing muscles |
|---|
| Trunk: Abdominals, Erector spinae, and Quadratus lumborum Shoulders: Deltoid, Rotator cuff group, and Pectoralis major Shoulder blades: Serratus anterior, Rhomboids, and Lower trapezius Forearms: Wrist flexors |

STARTING POSITION
· Stand with your legs front and back as opposed to side-by-side, facing the high-cable pulley machine.
· Grasp the cable attachment with an over-grip.
· Place your elbows at your sides.
· Keep your shoulders relaxed, and maintain a neutral spine.
· Keep your knees soft.

# TRICEP ROPE PULL-DOWN

Auxiliary exercise • Isolated/single joint
• Push • Close chain • Machine
• Beginner to advanced

This tricep exercise tends to emphasize the lateral aspect of the Triceps brachii.

## Description

Pull the rope down by extending your elbow using a curvilinear motion, so that your forearms go down to your hips first, and then curve laterally away, brushing past your sides. At the end point, your small finger should point away from your body and your thumbs should be against your sides. Return with control and repeat.

## Tips for good form

· Use a full range of movement; do not stop your forearm parallel with the ground.
· Keep your posture aligned, and maintain a neutral spine.
· Keep your chest open, and avoid rounding your shoulders.
· Avoid flaring your elbows outward during movement. The upper arms should be stationery, as though they are part of the spine.
· Use a slow, controlled motion, and avoid momentum.
· Squeeze from the triceps rather than pushing from the hands.
· Inhale on the downward phase, exhale on the upward motion.

Deltoid

Triceps brachii

Humerus

Olecranon process

Anconeus

Ulna

Radius

STARTING POSITION
· Stand facing the high-cable pulley machine.
· Grasp the rope attachment with an over-grip.
· Keep your wrists neutral, with the thumbs pointing to each other.
· Position your elbows at your sides.
· Keep your shoulders relaxed, and maintain a neutral spine.
· Keep your knees soft.

| ANALYSIS OF MOVEMENT | JOINT 1 |
| --- | --- |
| Main joints | Elbow |
| Joint movement | Extension |
| Main mobilizing muscles | Triceps brachii, emphasis on lateral aspect |

Main stabilizing muscles

Trunk: Abdominals, Erector spinae, and Quadratus lumborum
Shoulders: Deltoid, Rotator cuff group, and Pectoralis major
Shoulder blades: Serratus anterior, Rhomboids, and Lower trapezius
Forearms: Wrist flexors

# STANDING BARBELL CURL

Core • Isolated/single joint • Pull • Close chain • Barbell • Beginner to advanced

This exercise is one of the most effective general bicep exercises. Here, the elbow flexion challenges the Biceps brachii best when the forearm is supinated.

## Description

Lift the bar by flexing your elbows until your forearms almost touch your upper arms. Return, lowering the bar until your arms are fully extended, and repeat.

## Tips for good form

- Keep your posture aligned, and maintain a neutral spine.
- Use a slow, controlled motion. Avoid momentum (typically with a rocking motion pivoting on the lower back).
- Use a full range of movement, and do not stop your forearm parallel with the ground.
- Keep your chest open, and avoid rounding or hunching your shoulders.
- Your upper arms should stay stationery throughout the movement, as though they are part of the spine. When your elbows are fully flexed, they should only travel forward slightly so that the forearms are no more than vertical.
- Squeeze from the biceps rather than pulling from the hands, or rocking the lower back.
- Keep your weight directly over your heel to mid-foot. Avoid lifting your heels.
- Inhale on the upward phase, exhale on the downward motion.

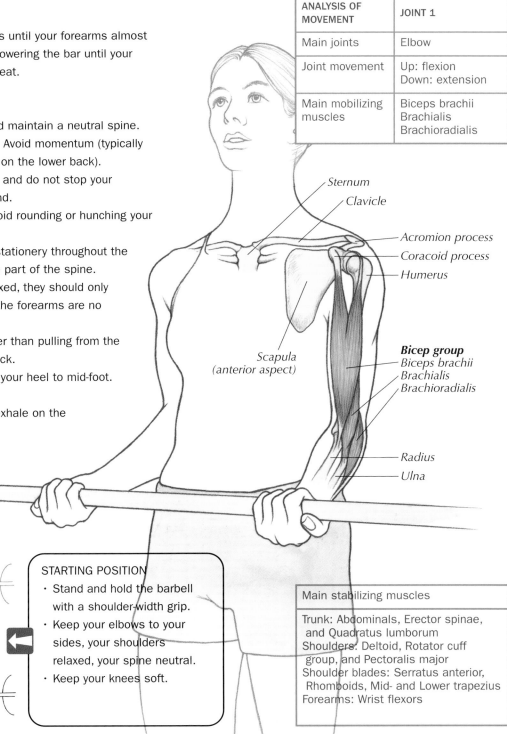

| ANALYSIS OF MOVEMENT | JOINT 1 |
|---|---|
| Main joints | Elbow |
| Joint movement | Up: flexion<br>Down: extension |
| Main mobilizing muscles | Biceps brachii<br>Brachialis<br>Brachioradialis |

Sternum
Clavicle
Acromion process
Coracoid process
Humerus
Scapula (anterior aspect)

**Bicep group**
Biceps brachii
Brachialis
Brachioradialis

Radius
Ulna

STARTING POSITION
- Stand and hold the barbell with a shoulder-width grip.
- Keep your elbows to your sides, your shoulders relaxed, your spine neutral.
- Keep your knees soft.

Main stabilizing muscles

Trunk: Abdominals, Erector spinae, and Quadratus lumborum
Shoulders: Deltoid, Rotator cuff group, and Pectoralis major
Shoulder blades: Serratus anterior, Rhomboids, Mid- and Lower trapezius
Forearms: Wrist flexors

# SEATED INCLINE DUMB-BELL CURL WITH SUPINATION

Core exercise • Isolation/single joint •
Pull • Close chain • Dumb-bell •
Beginner to advanced

➡️ When using a barbell in bicep work, it is possible to compensate with the stronger arm. Using separate dumb-bells has the advantage of preventing "cheating" by the weaker arm. By using a slightly inclined sitting position, you will increase the range of motion on the bicep group as well as the stabilization effort.

## Description

Lift one dumb-bell by flexing your elbow. Supinate until your forearm is vertical and your palm faces your shoulder. Return, and repeat, alternating your arms.

## Tips for good form

- Keep your posture aligned, and maintain a neutral spine.
- Use a slow, controlled motion, and avoid momentum.
- Use a full range of movement, and do not stop your forearm parallel with the ground.
- Keep your chest open; avoid hunching your shoulders.
- Your upper arm must stay stationery throughout the movement. Squeeze from your biceps.
- Inhale on the upward phase, exhale on the downward motion.

Sternocleidomastoid

Sternum

Pectoralis minor

Serratus anterior

Rectus abdominus

External obliques

Clavicle

Anterior deltoid

**Bicep group**
Biceps brachii
Brachialis
Brachioradialis

Triceps brachii

**Wrist flexors (inside forearm)**

| ANALYSIS OF MOVEMENT | JOINT 1 |
|---|---|
| Main joints | Elbow |
| Joint movement | Up: flexion Down: extension |
| Main mobilizing muscles | Biceps brachii Brachialis Brachioradialis |

| Main stabilizing muscles |
|---|
| Trunk: Abdominals, Erector spinae, and Quadratus lumborum Shoulders: Deltoid, Rotator cuff group, Latissimus, and Pectoralis major Shoulder blades: Serratus anterior, Rhomboids, and Mid- and Lower trapezius Forearms: Wrist flexors |

⬅️ **STARTING POSITION**
- Sit on the bench at about 15° from vertical.
- Hold a dumb-bell in each hand so that your arms hang vertically with a 15° shoulder extension.
- Position your arms at your sides with your palms facing inward, and keep your feet flat.

# DUMB-BELL CONCENTRATION CURL

Auxiliary exercise • Isolated/single joint
• Pull • Close chain • Dumb-bell
• Intermediate to advanced

➡ The name of this exercise emphasizes both the focus and the intensity of the work placed on the bicep muscles.

## Description

Lift the dumb-bell to the front of your shoulder by flexing your elbow. Return, lowering the dumb-bell until your arm is fully extended. Repeat. Continue with the opposite arm.

Deltoid
Pectoralis major
Triceps brachii

**Bicep group**
Biceps brachii
Brachialis
Brachioradialis

Pronator teres

Anconeus

**Forearm flexors**
Flexor carpi ulnaris
Flexor carpi radialis

⬆ STARTING POSITION

· Sit on the bench with your legs angled 45° outward, and your feet flat. Lean forward slightly from the hips.
· Take a single dumb-bell from between your feet. Position the back of your elbow into your inner thigh.
· Your opposite arm should be internally rotated, hand palm-down on your leg to counterbalance your frame.
· Maintain a neutral spine.

Main stabilizing muscles

Trunk: Abdominals, Erector spinae, and Quadratus lumborum
Shoulders: Deltoid, Rotator cuff group, Latissimus, and Pectoralis major
Shoulder blades: Serratus anterior, Rhomboids, and mid- and Lower trapezius
Forearms: Wrist flexors

| ANALYSIS OF MOVEMENT | JOINT 1 |
|---|---|
| Main joints | Elbow |
| Joint movement | Up: flexion<br>Down: extension |
| Main mobilizing muscles | Biceps brachii<br>Brachialis<br>Brachioradialis |

## Tips for good form

· Keep your posture aligned, and maintain a neutral spine.
· Use a slow, controlled motion, and avoid momentum.
· Keep your chest open, and avoid rounding or hunching your shoulders.
· Squeeze from the bicep—avoid pulling from your hand.
· Inhale on the upward phase, exhale on the downward motion.

# STRETCHES AND FLEXIBILITY

Flexibility is commonly defined as the range of motion (ROM) around a joint. For each joint there is a degree of flexibility that is considered normal and optimum for daily function. Many activities, such as gymnastics, sprinting, dance, and martial arts, require a greater degree of ROM than is normal for the activities of daily living.

Exercise manuals commonly refer to four types of stretching: static stretching, mobilization stretching, Proprioceptive Neuromuscular Facilitation (PNF), and ballistic stretching (see opposite). In static stretching, a progressive mild stretch takes place in a set position. Most of the stretches analyzed in this section are static stretches. Mobilization stretching uses a full-range movement around a joint. The PNF technique involves a partner and uses a specific technique to stimulate the golgi tendon organ in the muscle for increased range work. Ballistic stretching, which incorporates mild bouncing in the statically stretched position, is often unfairly maligned, but is useful for elastic strength warm-ups. Static stretching is relatively safe and easy to start with. It also makes an ideal cool-down after a workout. Mobilization stretching is the most functional. PNF and ballistic stretching are more advanced, higher risk, and not generally recommended without specialist assessment and instruction.

## Benefits of Flexibility Training

While opinions differ about the benefits of improved flexibility, lack of flexibility is a significant factor in postural compensation, reduced freedom of movement, increased risk of muscle tension, and injury.

Some people are naturally more flexible than others due to factors such as gender, genetics, age, and level of physical activity. People who are less active tend to be less flexible, and sedentary people tend to lose flexibility as they age. The benefits of regular stretching include ease of movement and better postural alignment, the ability to offset age-related loss of flexibility, and a reduced risk of injury and tension.

Conflicting research on stretching may be missing the essential relationship between strength and flexibility. Muscles work in agonistic and antagonistic relationships: that is, some muscles work together and some oppose each other. In opposing groups, an imbalance in one muscle will affect the opposite muscle. For example, tightness in the Erector spinae will inhibit the ability of the abdominal muscles to fully contract, while tight biceps will leave the triceps in a slightly elongated position.

Where there is significant postural imbalance, some muscles will be tight and others weak. The tight muscles will need stretching and the weak muscles will require strengthening. Many training experts agree that one of the best ways of stretching a tight muscle affected by postural imbalance is to functionally strengthen the opposing muscle group. Adequate assessment is necessary to determine precisely which stretch and strength exercises are necessary for each individual.

## Guidelines for Static Stretching

- Stretching is best done on warm muscles, as this significantly reduces the risk of injury.
- Ensure proper position and alignment in the starting position.
- Breathe in a relaxed manner; avoid holding the breath, forcing the stretch, or tensing the muscles.
- The stretch should be 4–7 on a scale of 1–10. At this level you should feel mild or pleasant discomfort. Above 7 equates to stabbing pain.
- Feel the muscle being stretched, relaxed, and softened. Static stretches should be held for 30–90 seconds.

## Stretches

1. Neck and Shoulder Stretch, page 124
2. Standing Chest and Anterior Shoulder Stretch, page 125
3. Ball Shoulder Stretch, page 126
4. Seated Side Stretch on Ball, page 127
5. Full-body Stretch, page 128
6. Supine Hip Flexion Stretch, page 129
7. Spine Roll, page 130
8. Side-to-side Hip Rolls, page 131
9. Supine Lying Gluteus Stretch, page 132
10. Supine Lying Single Leg Hamstring Stretch, page 133
11. Seated Stride into Saw Stretch, page 134
12. Supine Lying Deep External Rotators Stretch, page 135
13. Standing Iliopsoas Stretch, page 136
14. Gastrocnemius Stretch, page 137
15. Plank to Downward-facing Dog, page 138
16. Child Stretch, page 139

Static

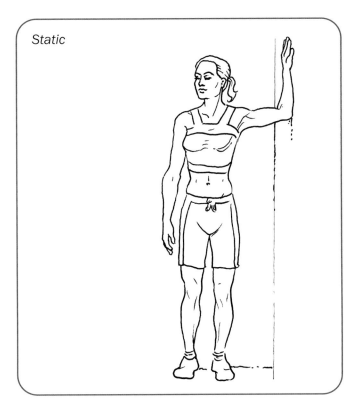

Mobilization

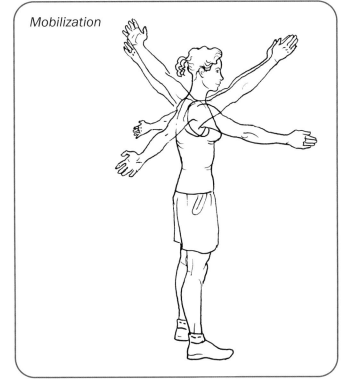

Proprioceptive Neuromuscular
Facilitation (PNF)

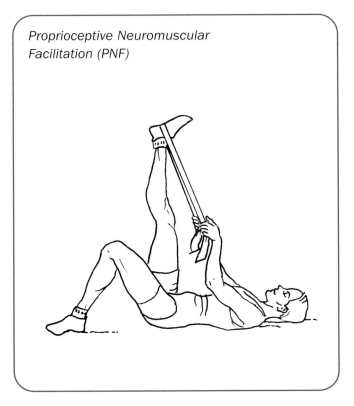

Ballistic

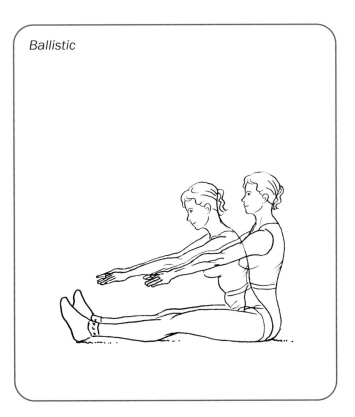

# NECK AND SHOULDER STRETCH

Static • Isolation/single joint • Close chain • Body-weight • Beginner to advanced

With the tension of modern living, multi-tasking with telephones, and countless bags to carry, it is easy to feel that your shoulders are stuck to your head at the end of the day. Done gently and regularly, this stretch wonderfully relaxes that tension.

## Description

Stand, and place both arms behind your back, holding one wrist with the opposite hand and pulling toward the opposite side. Let your neck side flex to the side the arm is being pulled toward. Hold the stretch without forcing (4–7 on a scale of 1–10). Repeat on the opposite side. For an easier version, try this exercise without arm involvement. For a version that adds more of a trunk stabilization challenge, do the exercise sitting on a stability ball.

## Tips for good form

- Avoid forcing the stretch. Focus on pulling your neck with your hand, letting it simply guide the natural pull of gravity on your neck and shoulder. Also concentrate on keeping your shoulder down. Relax into the stretch.
- Breathe in a relaxed manner.
- Avoid hunching or rounding your shoulders. Keep your chest open, shoulders relaxed, and shoulder blades depressed.

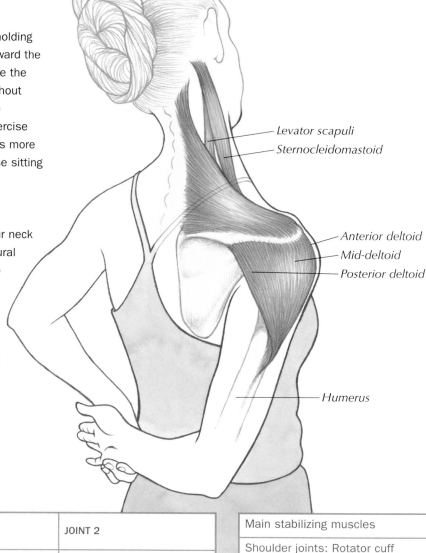

- Levator scapuli
- Sternocleidomastoid
- Anterior deltoid
- Mid-deltoid
- Posterior deltoid
- Humerus

| ANALYSIS OF MOVEMENT | JOINT 1 | JOINT 2 |
|---|---|---|
| Active joints | Neck, i.e. cervical spine | Shoulder joint |
| Joint position | Lateral flexion | Extended and adducted |
| Main stretching muscles | Upper trapezius*<br>Splenius<br>Sternocleidomastoid<br>Levator scapulae*<br>Rectus capitis lateralis<br>*Across cervical spine but attached to scapula (all on side being stretched) | Deltoid, emphasis on the anterior aspect<br>Clavicular portion of Pectoralis major<br>Coracobrachialis<br>Biceps brachii (long head) |

**Main stabilizing muscles**

Shoulder joints: Rotator cuff group
Scapula: Rhomboids and Lower trapezius
Trunk: Abdominals, Erector spinae, and Quadratus lumborum
Legs and hips: Gluteal group, Hamstring group, Rectus femoris, Adductors, and other leg muscles

# STANDING CHEST AND ANTERIOR SHOULDER STRETCH

Static • Isolation/single joint
• Close chain • Body-weight
• Beginner to advanced

➡ Decreased range of motion (ROM) of the pectorals increases the injury risk of exercises performed behind the head, especially when combined with decreased ROM in shoulder external rotation and excessively protracted scapulae. This inflexibility can also limit the effectiveness of various chest exercises and increase the risk of rotator cuff injury.

## Description

Stand with your feet shoulder-width apart and your knees soft, not locked. Keep your posture aligned, and stabilized. Extend your arm at shoulder height, placing your palm on a doorway. Gently turn your body until you feel the stretch in your chest muscles (4–7 on a scale of 1–10). Hold the stretch. Repeat with the opposite arm.

## Tips for good form

- Avoid forcing the stretch. Relax into it.
- Breathe in a relaxed manner.
- Avoid hunching or rounding your shoulders. Keep your chest open, shoulders relaxed, and shoulder blades depressed.
- Avoid locking your elbows. Keep them extended with a roughly 10° bend.

Biceps brachii

Anterior deltoid

Sternocleidomastoid

Brachialis

Triceps

Coracobrachialis

Pectoralis major

Serratus anterior

Rectus abdominus

External obliques

| ANALYSIS OF MOVEMENT | JOINT 1 | JOINT 2 |
|---|---|---|
| Active joints | Shoulders | Trunk |
| Joint position | Horizontally abducted and laterally rotated | Rotation |
| Main stretching muscles | Pectoralis major Anterior deltoid Coracobrachialis | External oblique on the side of the arm being stretched |

Main stabilizing muscles

Abdominal group
Trunk and hips: Quadratus lumborum, Erector spinae, Adductor group, and Gluteus medius and minimus
Legs: Rectus femoris, Hamstring group and general leg muscles
Shoulder joints: Rotator cuff group
Shoulder blades: Serratus anterior, Rhomboids, and Lower trapezius

# BALL SHOULDER STRETCH

Static • Compound/multi-joint • Close chain • Body-weight • Beginner to advanced

→ This deep, relaxing stretch helps to ease the tension in the shoulders and upper back, as well as realigning the shoulder joint into its socket.

## Description

Kneel on a mat with a stability ball in front of you. Place your hands on the sides of the ball. Lean your buttocks back to your hips, going into a kneeling position while rolling the ball forward with your hands, so that your head and trunk become horizontal, face looking down. Hold the stretch at 4–7 on a scale of 1–10.

## Tips for good form

· Avoid hunching or rounding your shoulders. Keep your chest open, shoulders relaxed, and shoulder blades depressed.
· Avoid arching your neck: keep your eyes toward the floor.
· Avoid forcing the stretch. Relax into it.
· Breathe in a relaxed manner.

| Main stabilizing muscles |
|---|
| Trunk: Abdominal group, Erector spinae and Quadratus lumborum
Scapula: Lower trapezius, Rhomboids, and Serratus anterior
Shoulders: Rotator cuff
Neck: Splenius capitus and cervicis |

*Gluteus maximus*

*Trapezius*

*Rhomboids*

*Latissimus dorsi*

*Deltoid*

*Infraspinatus*

*Teres minor*

*Teres major*

| ANALYSIS OF MOVEMENT | JOINT 1 | JOINT 2 | JOINT 3 | JOINT 4 |
|---|---|---|---|---|
| Active joints | Shoulder | Scapula | Hip | Knee |
| Joint position | Flexed and internally rotated | Depressed | Flexed | Flexed |
| Main stretching muscles | Pectoralis major, Latissimus dorsi, Anterior deltoid, Rotator cuff group, Biceps brachii | Pectoralis minor Teres major Teres minor Mid- and Lower trapezius Lower rhomboids | Gluteus maximus Hamstring group | Quadricep group |

*STRETCHES AND FLEXIBILITY*

# SEATED SIDE STRETCH ON BALL

Static • Compound/multi-joint
• Close chain • Body-weight
• Beginner to advanced

➡ This beautiful stretch eases the tension along the sides of the body. The use of the ball enhances the functional nature of the exercise, while allowing for deep hip stretches when shifting the hips away from the side being stretched.

## Description

Sit centered on the stability ball with your feet flat on the ground. Sit tall from the sitting bones, with abdominal stabilization active. Place one hand on the opposite knee. Raise the opposite arm, and with a lateral curve of the spine, stretch over to the opposite side, 4–7 on a scale of 1–10. Hold the stretch. Change, and repeat on the opposite side.

## Tips for good form

· Avoid forcing the stretch. Relax into it.
· Breathe in a relaxed manner.
· Avoid hunching or rounding your shoulders. Keep your chest open, shoulders relaxed, and shoulder blades depressed.
· Keep your weight centered through the middle of the ball.

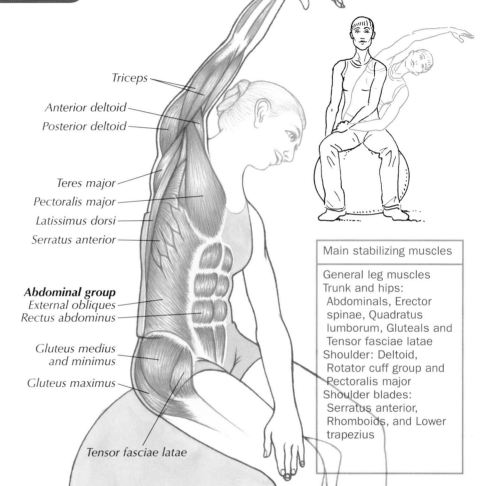

Triceps
Anterior deltoid
Posterior deltoid
Teres major
Pectoralis major
Latissimus dorsi
Serratus anterior
**Abdominal group**
External obliques
Rectus abdominus
Gluteus medius and minimus
Gluteus maximus
Tensor fasciae latae

### Main stabilizing muscles

General leg muscles
Trunk and hips:
 Abdominals, Erector spinae, Quadratus lumborum, Gluteals and Tensor fasciae latae
Shoulder: Deltoid, Rotator cuff group and Pectoralis major
Shoulder blades: Serratus anterior, Rhomboids, and Lower trapezius

| ANALYSIS OF MOVEMENT | JOINT 1 | JOINT 2 | JOINT 3 | JOINT 4 |
|---|---|---|---|---|
| Active joints | Spine (side of raised arm) | Scapula (side of raised arm) | Shoulder (side of raised arm) | Neck, i.e. cervical spine |
| Joint position | Laterally flexed | Upwardly rotated | Abducted | Laterally flexed |
| Main stretching muscles | Erector spinae group Quadratus lumborum Latissimus dorsi Abdominal group | Lower aspect of Rhomboids Lower trapezius Teres major Teres minor | Latissimus dorsi Rotator cuff group Pectoralis major, emphasis on the sternal and abdominal portion Deltoid with emphasis on posterior aspect Long head of Triceps Coracobrachialis | Upper trapezius* Splenius Sternocleidomastoid Levator scapulae* Rectus capitis lateralis * Across cervical spine but attached to scapula (all on side being stretched) |

# FULL-BODY STRETCH

Static • Compound/multi-joint • Body-weight • Beginner to advanced

➡️ This stretch, adapted from Yoga, is simpler than it looks. It is a surprising and wonderful full-body stretch that can be done almost anywhere.

## Description

Sit slightly forward on a bench with your feet flat and knees bent, positioned above your feet. Leaning forward from your hips, twist your spine to one side, placing the back of your elbow against your inside knee. As you twist, open your chest, and raise and extend your other arm. Turn your head to look at the upper hand. Hold at 4–7 on a scale of 1–10. Return, and repeat on the other side.

## Tips for good form

- Lengthen both arms away from each other, expending your chest.
- Avoid forcing the stretch. Relax into it.
- Breathe in a relaxed manner.
- Avoid hunching or rounding your shoulders. Keep your chest open, shoulders relaxed, and shoulder blades depressed.
- If you find you can reach your ankle comfortably, try using a wooden block to support the lower hand.

| Main stabilizing muscles |
| --- |
| General leg muscles<br>Trunk and hips: Abdominals, Erector spinae, Quadratus lumborum, and Tensor fascia late<br>Shoulders: Deltoid, Rotator cuff group, and Pectoralis major<br>Shoulder blades: Serratus anterior, Rhomboids, and Lower trapezius<br>Neck: Sternocleidomastoid and Rectus capitis lateralis |

Biceps brachii
Triceps
Anterior deltoid
Pectoralis major
Serratus anterior
External obliques
Gluteus medius and minimus
Tensor fasciae latae
Biceps femoris (Hamstrings)

Pectoralis major
Anterior deltoid
Triceps brachii
Biceps brachii

| ANALYSIS OF MOVEMENT | JOINT 1 | JOINT 2 | JOINT 3 |
| --- | --- | --- | --- |
| Active joints | Hips, on open side | Spine | Shoulder (top arm) |
| Joint position | Flexed | Horizontal rotation to open side | Horizontally abducted and laterally rotated |
| Main stretching muscles | Gluteus maximus Hamstring group, emphasis on upper portion | Abdominal group, emphasis on external oblique Quadratus lumborum Latissimus dorsi Lower erector spinae | Pectoralis major Corcobrachialis Anterior deltoid Long head of Triceps |

*STRETCHES AND FLEXIBILITY*

# SUPINE HIP FLEXION STRETCH

Static • Isolation/single joint
• Body-weight • Beginner to advanced

➡ This simple stretch is ideal for releasing the typical lower back tension that accumulates from the postural stressors of modern-day living. It is also a good warm-up stretch for other supine lying lower body stretches.

## Description

Lie supine, maintaining a neutral spine. Pull one leg up to your chest, bending your hips, and knees while maintaining abdominal stability. Keep the opposite leg down and flat. You should feel a slight pull at the front of that hip. Hold at an intensity of 4–7 on a scale of 1–10. As a variation, you can do the exercise with both legs hugged to your chest.

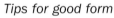

Abdominals

Sternocleidomastoids

Biceps brachii

**Hamstrings**
Semitendonosus

Biceps femoris

Latissimus dorsi

Spinal column (lumbar vertebrae)

Iliac crest

Iliopsoas

Greater trochanter

Femur

Gluteus maximus

Ischial tuberosities

## Tips for good form

· Avoid rounding your back, tensing, or lifting your buttocks. If you lack flexibility, release the hip stretch, and hold the leg underneath the knee.
· Avoid forcing the stretch. Relax into it.
· Breathe in a relaxed manner.
· Avoid hunching your shoulders. Keep your chest open, shoulders relaxed, and shoulder blades depressed.

### Main stabilizing muscles

Neck: Sternocleidomastoid
Arms: Bicep group
Shoulder joints: Posterior deltoid, Latissimus dorsi, Teres major, and Rotator cuff muscles
Abdominal group
Shoulder blades: Serratus anterior, Rhomboids, and Lower trapezius

| ANALYSIS OF MOVEMENT | JOINT 1 | JOINT 2 | JOINT 3 |
|---|---|---|---|
| Active joints | Hip (on side being stretched) | Knee (on side being stretched) | Opposite hip |
| Joint position | Flexed | Flexed | Mild extension |
| Main stretching muscles | Gluteus maximus Hamstring group | Quadricep group | Rectus femoris of the Quadricep group Iliopsoas |

# SPINE ROLL

Static • Compound/multi-joint
• Body-weight • Beginner to advanced

➡️ This simple stretch is ideal for releasing the typical lower back tension that tends to accumulate from the postural stressors of modern-day living. It is also a good warm-up stretch for other supine lying lower body stretches.

## Description

Kneel on all fours over a stability ball, as shown. Maintain a neutral spine, keeping abdominal stabilization engaged, and pulling your navel into your spine. Round your spine up to the ceiling, rounding as much as possible on the full length of the spine. Relax, and lower your spine back to neutral. Dip your abdominals forward, lifting your head.

## Tips for good form

· Avoid forcing the stretch. Relax into it.
· Breathe in a relaxed manner.
· Avoid hunching your shoulders. Keep your chest open, shoulders relaxed, and shoulder blades depressed.

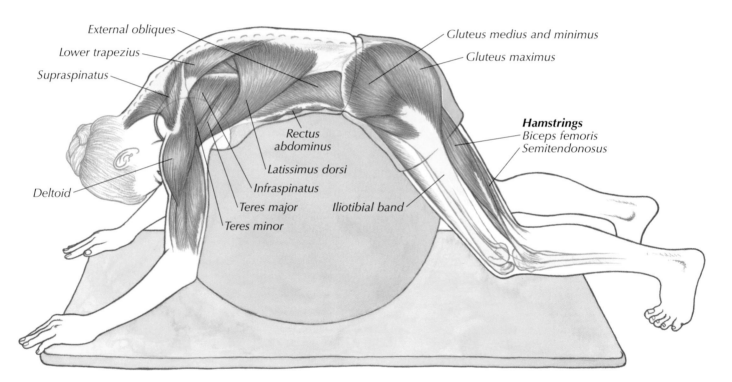

| ANALYSIS OF MOVEMENT | JOINT 1 | JOINT 2 |
|---|---|---|
| Active joints | Spine | Hips |
| Joint position | Flexed | Mild flexion |
| Main stretching muscles | Erector spinae Lower and Mid-trapezius Rhomboids Quadratus lumborum Latissimus dorsi | Gluteus maximus Hamstring group (upper portion) |

| Main stabilizing muscles |
|---|
| Arms: Tricep and forearm muscles Shoulder joints: Posterior deltoid, Latissimus dorsi, Teres major, and Rotator cuff muscles Abdominal group Shoulder blades: Serratus anterior, Rhomboids, and Lower trapezius |

# SIDE-TO-SIDE HIP ROLLS

Static • Compound/multi-joint
• Body-weight • Beginner to advanced

➡ This is another easy stretch that helps to reduce the accumulation of lower back tension. It can be done as part of your exercise routine, or even on its own at the end of a long day.

## Description

Lie supine with your knees bent and your feet flat on the floor. Gently let your knees roll to the floor on one side, carrying your hips over. Hold the stretch. Return, and repeat on the other side.

## Tips for good form

· Keep your feet in the same place as you roll to the side.
· Avoid forcing the stretch. Relax into it.
· Breathe in a relaxed manner.
· Avoid hunching your shoulders. Keep your chest open, shoulders relaxed, and shoulder blades depressed.

Iliotibial band
Tensor fasciae latae
Gluteus medius and minimus
Iliac crest
External obliques
Serratus anterior
Latissimus dorsi
Gluteus maximus
Erector spinae (deep layer)

| ANALYSIS OF MOVEMENT | JOINT 1 | JOINT 2 |
|---|---|---|
| Active joints | Spine on side of leg rolled over | Hip on side of leg rolled over |
| Joint position | Rotation | Mild internal rotation and adduction |
| Main stretching muscles | Abdominals, especially external obliques<br>Lower erector spinae<br>Quadratus lumborum | Gluteus maximus, medius, and minimus<br>Tensor fascia latae and Iliotibial band |

| Main stabilizing muscles |
|---|
| Mild stabilization from Erector spinae, abdominals, and other upper body muscles. |

# SUPINE LYING GLUTEUS STRETCH

Static • Compound/multi-joint • Body-weight • Intermediate to advanced

The Gluteus maximus is prone to tightness and weakness, an unusual combination. The tightness increases the risk of lower back strain and injury during hip flexion in knee flexion exercises such as squats and leg presses.

*Tips for good form*
- Avoid forcing the stretch. Relax into it.
- Breathe in a relaxed manner.
- Avoid hunching or rounding your shoulders. Keep your chest open, shoulders relaxed, and shoulder blades depressed.
- If it is not possible to pull your legs to your chest, leave out this step until your flexibility improves. Keep your right leg crossed over, and push your right knee away slightly with your right hand.

*Description*
Lie supine with your knees bent and your feet flat. Cross your right leg over the left, so that your right foot is across your left knee. Place both hands around your left upper thigh, and pull towards your chest, until you feel a stretch at 4–7 on a scale of 1–10. Hold, and then repeat with the other leg.

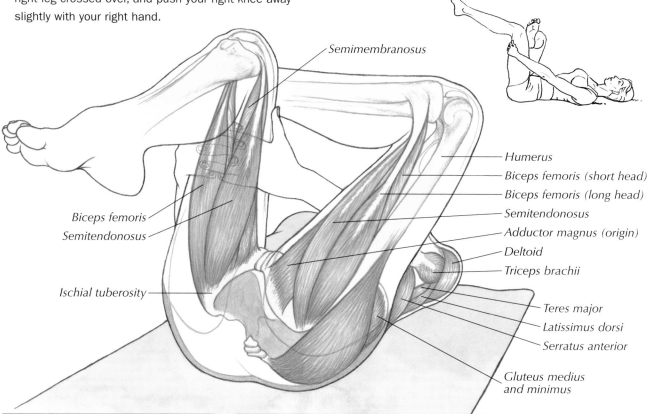

- Semimembranosus
- Biceps femoris
- Semitendonosus
- Ischial tuberosity
- Humerus
- Biceps femoris (short head)
- Biceps femoris (long head)
- Semitendonosus
- Adductor magnus (origin)
- Deltoid
- Triceps brachii
- Teres major
- Latissimus dorsi
- Serratus anterior
- Gluteus medius and minimus

| Main stabilizing muscles |
|---|
| Arms: Bicep group<br>Shoulder joints: Posterior deltoid, Latissimus dorsi, Teres major, and Rotator cuff muscles<br>Shoulder blades: Serratus anterior, Rhomboids, and Lower trapezius<br>Abdominal group |

| ANALYSIS OF MOVEMENT | JOINT 1 | JOINT 2 |
|---|---|---|
| Active joints | Hip (right thigh) | Hip (left thigh) |
| Joint position | Flexed, adducted and externally rotated | Flexed |
| Main stretching muscles | Gluteus maximus<br>Hamstring group on lateral aspect | Gluteus maximus<br>Hamstring group |

# SUPINE LYING SINGLE LEG HAMSTRING STRETCH

Static • Compound/multi-joint
• Open chain • Body-weight
• Beginner to advanced

Hamstring inflexibility—which this exercise helps—increases the risk of lower back strain, particularly in exercises where the knees are extended, and the hips flexed.

## Description

Sit on a mat and place a strap around the underneath of the middle of your right foot. Holding the strap evenly in both hands, lie back into a supine position, and raise your right leg. Pull the leg vertically, keeping the knee extended without hyper-extending it. Keep your opposite leg down and flat on the ground. You should felt a slight pull at the front of the hip of that leg. Feel the stretch at 4–7 on a scale of 1–10. Hold, and then repeat with the opposite leg.

## Tips for good form

· Avoid forcing the stretch. Relax into it.
· Breathe in a relaxed manner.
· Avoid hunching or rounding your shoulders. Keep your chest open, shoulders relaxed, and shoulder blades depressed.
· If your hamstrings are tight, flex the knee of the stretched leg.

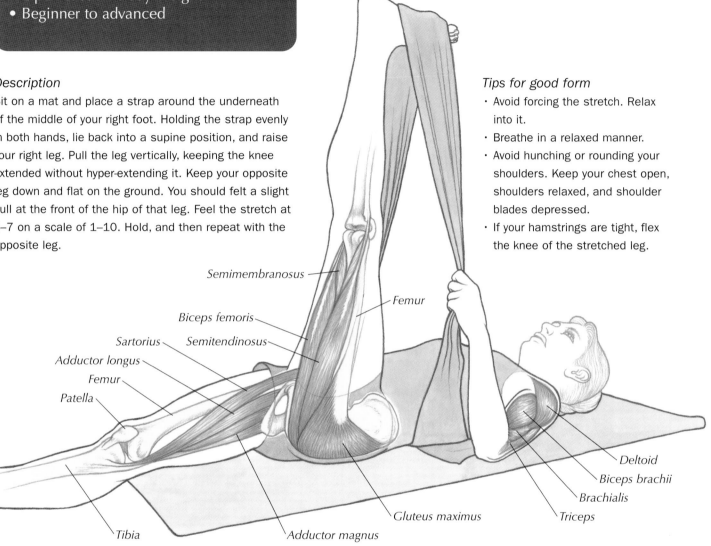

Semimembranosus
Biceps femoris
Sartorius
Semitendinosus
Adductor longus
Femur
Patella
Femur
Gluteus maximus
Deltoid
Biceps brachii
Brachialis
Triceps
Tibia
Adductor magnus

| ANALYSIS OF MOVEMENT | JOINT 1 | JOINT 2 | JOINT 3 |
|---|---|---|---|
| Active joints | Hip | Knee | Opposite hip |
| Joint position | Flexed | Extended | Mild extension |
| Main stretching muscles | Hamstring group Gluteus maximus | Hamstring group Gastrocnemius | Rectus femoris of the Quadricep group Iliopsoas |

| Main stabilizing muscles |
|---|
| Arms: Bicep group<br>Shoulder joints: Posterior deltoid, Latissimus dorsi, Teres major, and Rotator cuff muscles<br>Shoulder blades: Serratus anterior, Rhomboids, and Lower trapezius<br>Abdominal group<br>Active hip: Iliopsoas<br>Stretched leg: Quadricep and Adductor groups<br>Opposite leg: Adductor group |

# SEATED STRIDE INTO SAW STRETCH

Static • Isolation • Body-weight
• Beginner to advanced

➡ This is another total body stretch, this time focused on the lower body.

## Description

Sit tall on your sitting bones with your legs flat at a 60° angle apart. Hold your arms horizontally with your chest open. Twisting your upper body from the waist, let your arms turn with your chest. Exhale, reaching your arms and trunk forward, and down toward one leg so that the opposite hand touches your inside lower leg. Hold the stretch at 4–7 on a scale of 1–10. Return, and then repeat on the opposite side.

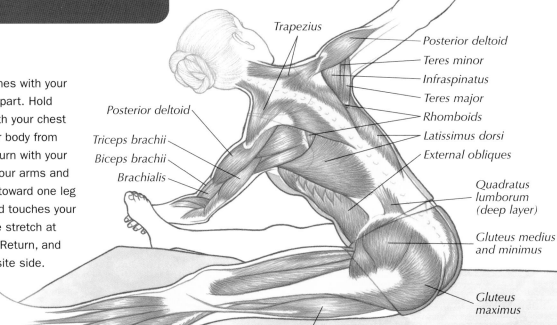

Trapezius
Posterior deltoid
Teres minor
Infraspinatus
Teres major
Rhomboids
Latissimus dorsi
External obliques
Quadratus lumborum (deep layer)
Gluteus medius and minimus
Gluteus maximus

Posterior deltoid
Triceps brachii
Biceps brachii
Brachialis

Biceps femoris (Hamstrings)

## Tips for good form

· Avoid forcing the stretch. Relax into it.
· Breathe in a relaxed manner.
· Avoid hunching or rounding your shoulders. Keep your chest open, shoulders relaxed, and shoulder blades depressed.
· If your hips are too tight, modify the exercise by sitting on a small cushion or folded towel.

| ANALYSIS OF MOVEMENT | JOINT 1 | JOINT 2 | JOINT 3 |
|---|---|---|---|
| Active joints | Hips | Spine | Scapula |
| Joint position | Flexed and abducted | Rotated | Abducted (protracted) |
| Main stretching muscles | In both legs: Gluteus maximus, Hamstring group, Adductor group, namely Pectineus, Adductor brevis, Adductor longus, Adductor magnus, and Gracilis<br>On side being stretched: Tensor fasciae latae and Gluteus minimus | Mainly on side being stretched: Abdominal group, especially Obliques, Latissimus dorsi, Quadratus lumborum, Erector spinae (lower aspect) | Rhomboids, Mid- and Lower trapezius |

### Main stabilizing muscles

Trunk: Abdominal group, Erector spinae, and Quadratus lumborum
Shoulder blades: Serratus anterior, Rhomboids, and Lower trapezius
Shoulders: Rotator cuff group and Deltoid

# SUPINE LYING DEEP EXTERNAL ROTATORS STRETCH

Static • Isolation • Body-weight
• Beginner to advanced

Tightness of the deep lateral rotators of the hips is usually experienced in the dominant leg, where it can impinge on the main leg nerve (sciatic nerve), causing numbness and a tingling sensation down the leg, or sciatica. There are many variants of this stretch—the most common form is shown here.

## Description

Lie supine with your legs straight and your arms out to the sides. Flex your right knee and hip and, placing your left hand on the outside of your right knee, pull the right leg over to the left until you feel a stretch of 4–7 on a scale of 1–10. Your right knee should be in line or slightly below your left hip. Hold, and then repeat with the opposite leg.

## Tips for good form

· This stretch is advanced, so avoid forcing it. Relax into it.
· If it is not possible to pull over with your arm, let the weight of the leg determine how far it can stretch.
· Make sure that the major rotation occurs at your hip before you start to rotate at the lower spine.
· Avoid hunching or rounding your shoulders. Keep your chest open, shoulders relaxed, and shoulder blades depressed.
· Breathe in a relaxed manner.

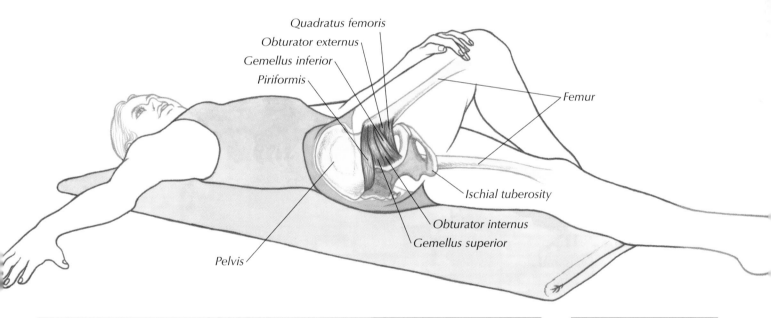

| ANALYSIS OF MOVEMENT | JOINT 1 | JOINT 2 |
|---|---|---|
| Active joints | Hips | Pelvis and spine |
| Joint position | Flexed and horizontally adducted | Rotated |
| Main stretching muscles | Deep lateral hip rotators, namely Piriformis, Gemellus superior and inferior, Obturator externus and internus, and Quadratus femoris Tensor faciae latae and Iliotibial band Gluteus maximus, medius and minimus | Erector spinae (lower aspect) Abdominal obliques Latissimus dorsi Quadratus lumborum |

**Main stabilizing muscles**

Arms: Tricep group
Shoulder joints: Posterior deltoid. Latissimus dorsi, Teres major, and Rotator cuff muscles
Shoulder blades: Serratus anterior, Rhomboids, and Lower trapezius
Abdominal group

# STANDING ILIOPSOAS STRETCH

Static • Isolation • Close chain • Body-weight • Intermediate to advanced

→ Tightness of the hip flexors, especially the Iliopsoas, can pull the lumbar spine into greater extension during exercise done in a standing position, and this is exacerbated if the abdominal stabilization is weak. This exercise is an important precise stretch that must be done slowly, with proper attention to technique.

## Description

Stand with one foot in front of the other, feet shoulder-width apart. Face a wall, placing your arms on the wall or an exercise bar. Your front foot should be flat and underneath or slightly forward of the front knee, your back leg extended back. Your hips should be square with the spine aligned and stabilized. Lean the hips gently forward and tilt the pelvis backward. Hold at an intensity of 4–7 on a scale of 1–10. Repeat with the opposite leg.

## Tips for good form

- Avoid forcing the stretch. Relax into it. You should feel it as a small, tight pull on the front of the hip of your back leg, deep near the fold of the leg.
- Breathe in a relaxed manner, and keep your posture aligned and stabilized.
- Avoid hunching or rounding your shoulders. Keep your chest open, shoulders relaxed, and shoulder blades depressed.
- Keep your front knee from passing over the vertical line of your toes.

Iliopsoas
Psoas
Ilium
Iliacus
Spine
Pelvis
Greater trochanter
Pectineus
Rectus femoris
Vastus lateralis
Vastus medius
Adductor longus
Adductor magnus
Femur
Gracilis
Patella
Fibula
Tibia

| Main stabilizing muscles |
| --- |
| Abdominal group |
| Trunks and hips: Quadratus lumborum, Erector spinae, Adductor group, and Gluteus medius and minimus |
| Legs: Rectus femoris, Adductors, and Hamstring group |
| Shoulder blades: Serratus anterior, Rhomboids, and Lower trapezius |

| ANALYSIS OF MOVEMENT | JOINT 1 |
| --- | --- |
| Active joints | Hips |
| Joint position | Extended |
| Main stretching muscles | Iliopsoas Rectus femoris |

# GASTROCNEMIUS STRETCH

Static • Isolation • Close chain
• Body-weight • Beginner to advanced

The calf muscles have a dense, compact structure. Relative to their size, they are one of the strongest muscles in the body. Tight calves limit ankle dorsiflexion, and this can, in turn, inhibit knee flexion and exaggerate hip flexion, and also be problematic in exercises such as leg presses and squats.

## Description

Stand facing a wall with one foot in front of the other, shoulder-width apart. Your front foot should be directly under your slightly bent knee, and your back leg should extend behind. Lean forward and place both arms on the wall at upper chest height. Keeping your feet flat and your posture stabilized, lean your hips into the wall until you feel a stretch of 4–7 on a scale of 1–10 in the calf. Hold, and then repeat with the opposite leg.

## Tips for good form

· Avoid forcing the stretch. Relax into it.
· Breathe in a relaxed manner.
· Avoid hunching or rounding your shoulders. Keep your chest open, shoulders relaxed, and shoulder blades depressed.
· Avoid over-extending your elbows and tensing your shoulders. Keep your elbows extended with a roughly 10° bend.

Semitendonosus

Biceps femoris

Semimembranosus

Gastrocnemius

Soleus

| ANALYSIS OF MOVEMENT | JOINT 1 | JOINT 2 |
| --- | --- | --- |
| Active joints | Ankles | Knee (back leg) |
| Joint position | Dorsiflexed | Extended |
| Main stretching muscles | Gastrocnemius Soleus | Gastrocnemius |

| Main stabilizing muscles |
| --- |
| Trunk: Abdominal group and Erector spinae<br>Hips: Adductor group, and Gluteus medius and minimus<br>Shoulder joints: Anterior deltoid, Pectoralis major, and Rotator cuff muscles<br>Shoulder blades: Serratus anterior, Rhomboids, and Lower trapezius<br>Arms: Tricep muscles<br>General leg muscles: Rectus femoris and Hamstring group |

# PLANK TO DOWNWARD-FACING DOG

Static/dynamic • Compound/multi-joint
• Close chain • Body-weight
• Intermediate to advanced

➡ The Downward-facing Dog forms part of the Sun Salutation, a Yoga sequence of 12 postures performed in a single, graceful flow, done in coordination with the breath.

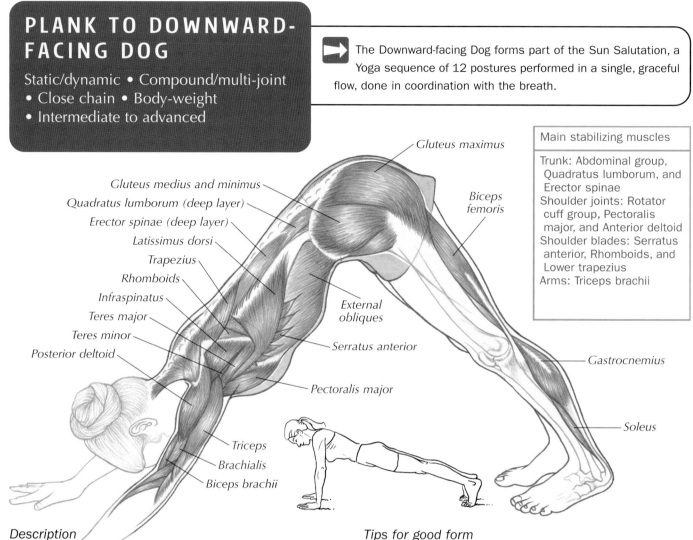

Gluteus maximus

Gluteus medius and minimus
Quadratus lumborum (deep layer)
Erector spinae (deep layer)
Latissimus dorsi
Trapezius
Rhomboids
Infraspinatus
Teres major
Teres minor
Posterior deltoid

Biceps femoris

External obliques

Serratus anterior

Pectoralis major

Triceps
Brachialis
Biceps brachii

Gastrocnemius

Soleus

**Main stabilizing muscles**

Trunk: Abdominal group, Quadratus lumborum, and Erector spinae
Shoulder joints: Rotator cuff group, Pectoralis major, and Anterior deltoid
Shoulder blades: Serratus anterior, Rhomboids, and Lower trapezius
Arms: Triceps brachii

## Description

Raise your body, supporting yourself on your hands and feet. Extend your arms slightly more than shoulder-width apart, at the level of your upper chest. Maintain a neutral spine, with abdominal stabilization engaged, squeezing your navel into your spine. Exhale, lift from the hips, then push them back and up. Keep your chest open.

## Tips for good form

· At first keep your knees slightly bent and your heels lifted off the floor.
· Try to lift your sitting bones to the ceiling; settle back toward a flat foot.
· Depress and widen your shoulder blades.
· Keep your hands flat, with the palms spread out and the index fingers parallel to each other.

| ANALYSIS OF MOVEMENT | JOINT 1 | JOINT 2 | JOINT 3 | JOINT 4 |
|---|---|---|---|---|
| Active joints | Ankle | Knees | Hips and pelvis | Shoulders |
| Joint position | Dorsiflexed | Extended | Flexed | Full flexion and internal rotation |
| Main stretching muscles | Gastrocnemius Soleus Plantaris Tibialis posterior Flexor digitorum longus Flexor hallucis longus | Gastrocnemius Hamstring group Popliteus | Gluteus maximus Hamstring group Quadratus lumborum Latissimus dorsi Erector spinae | Triceps brachii Biceps brachii Rotator cuff group Latissimus dorsi Teres major Deltoid Pectoralis major, emphasis on abdominal (lower) aspect |

# CHILD STRETCH

Static/dynamic • Compound/multi-joint • Close chain • Body-weight • Beginner to advanced

This Child pose derives from Yoga. It can provide a calming end to an intense workout or series of intense exercises or stretches.

### Description
Kneel prone on an exercise or Yoga mat with your knees slightly apart. Rest your arms at your sides. Let your head lie on the mat, to the side, or on your forehead, whichever is more comfortable.

### Tip for good form
The key in this stretch is to relax. Let you body naturally soften and be comfortable.

### Breathing and relaxation tip
Relaxed or diaphragmatic breathing is the body's natural breathing response. Chronic stress can condition a shallow, limited breath into the body's neural responses, which brings in up to 90 percent less oxygen than relaxation breathing. That is why stress breathing can promote fatigue and poor concentration (poor oxygen-supply to the brain), poor digestion (collapsed chest), and increased muscle tension (from mild hypoxia effect). Use relaxation or deep-breathing practices on a regular basis. Start with as little as three deep breaths. Breathe in through the nose and let the air passively escape through the mouth. Relaxation breathing can be done anywhere and can help promote a state of relaxation, clarity, and alertness.

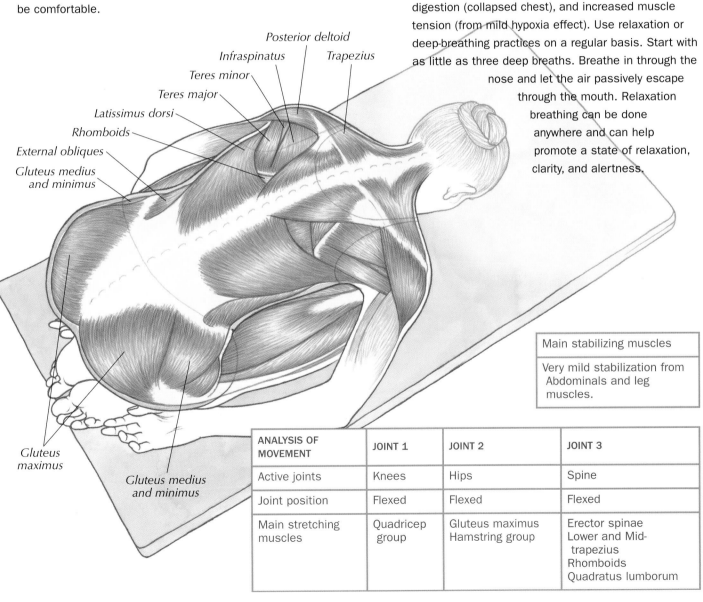

Posterior deltoid
Infraspinatus
Teres minor
Teres major
Latissimus dorsi
Rhomboids
External obliques
Gluteus medius and minimus
Trapezius
Gluteus maximus
Gluteus medius and minimus

| Main stabilizing muscles | | |
|---|---|---|
| Very mild stabilization from Abdominals and leg muscles. | | |

| ANALYSIS OF MOVEMENT | JOINT 1 | JOINT 2 | JOINT 3 |
|---|---|---|---|
| Active joints | Knees | Hips | Spine |
| Joint position | Flexed | Flexed | Flexed |
| Main stretching muscles | Quadricep group | Gluteus maximus Hamstring group | Erector spinae Lower and Mid-trapezius Rhomboids Quadratus lumborum |

# GLOSSARY

**Abduction** Movement of a limb away from the center line, such as lifting a straight arm laterally from your side.

**Adduction** Movement of a limb toward the mid-line of the body, such as pulling a straight arm toward your side.

**Agonist** A muscle that causes motion.

**Anterior** (ventral) The front of the body.

**Anterior pelvic tilt** If the pelvis is a bucket of water, it is tilted so water is falling toward the front.

**Antagonist** A muscle that moves the joint opposite to the movement produced by the agonist.

**Auxiliary** Optional exercise to supplement a core exercise. Auxiliary exercises place greater relative intensity on a specific muscle, or on the head of a muscle.

**Circumduction** Circular movement (combining flexion, extension, adduction, and abduction) with no shaft rotation

**Compound exercises** Involving two or more joint movements.

**Concentric** A muscle contraction, resulting in its shortening.

**Core** A principal exercise.

**Closed chain** An exercise in which the end segment of the exercised limb is fixed, or supporting the weight. Most compound exercises are closed-chain movements.

**Deep lateral rotators of the hip** The group name of the Piriformis, Gemelli, Obturator, and Quadratus femoris muscles, deep to the Gluteus maximus.

**Distal** Farther away from the center of the body.

**Dynamic stabilizer** A biarticulate muscle that simultaneously shortens at the target joint and lengthens the adjacent joint with no appreciable difference in length. Dynamic stabilization occurs during many compound movements.

**Eccentric** The contraction of a muscle during its lengthening.

**Eversion** Moving the foot away from the medial plane.

**Extension** Straightening, extending, or opening out a joint, resulting in an increase of the angle between two bones.

**External rotation** Outward (lateral) rotation of a joint within the transverse plane of the body. The resulting movement will be toward the posterior (back) of the body.

**Flexion** Bending a joint, resulting in a decrease of angle.

**Functional** An exercise which allows you to gain motor development or strength in a manner in which it is used in the execution of a particular task (eg: specific sport skill, occupational task, or daily activity).

**High-impact** Type of exercise with a high gravitational impact on the skeletal system, for example, running.

**Hyperextension** Extending a joint beyond its normal anatomical position.

**Inferior** Movement away from the head.

**Intensity** The amount of weight used, percentage of one repetition maximum, or degree of effort used during exercise.

**Internal rotation** Inward medial rotation of a joint within the transverse plane of the body. Movement is directed toward the anterior (front) surface of the body.

**Inversion** Moving the sole of the foot toward the medial plane.

**Isolated** An exercise that involves just one discernible joint movement.

**Isometric** Contracting a muscle without significant movement; also referred to as static tension

**Isotonic** Muscle contraction with movement against a natural resistance.

**Kyphosis** A backward curve of the spine.

**Lateral** Away from sagittal mid-line of body

**Lordosis** A forward curve of the spine.

**Low-impact** Type of exercise with a relatively low gravitational impact on the skeletal system, for example, walking.

**Medial** Toward sagittal mid-line of body

**Non-weight bearing** Exercise in which the body's weight against gravity is reduced, for example, swimming.

**Open chain** An exercise in which the end segment of the exercised limb is not fixed, or is not supporting the weight. Most isolated exercise are open-chain movements.

**Overload** Stimulation beyond the body's present capacity, in order to elicit a longer-term physiological change.

**Posterior (dorsal)** Located behind or to the back of the body.

**Posterior pelvic tilt** If the pelvis is a bucket of water, it is tilted so water is falling toward the back.

**Pronation** Internal rotation of the foot or forearm.

**Proximal** Closer to the center or core of the body.

**ROM** Range of Motion. The amount of movement at each joint. Every joint in the body has a "normal" range of motion.

**Rotation** Circular (rotary) movement around the longitudinal axis of the bone.

**Sagittal plane** A division that separates the body into a left and a right half. Movements in the sagittal plane are in the forward-backward direction.

**Spotter** Someone to assist you with technique, usually to load and unload the barbell from its resting position.

**Synergist** A muscle that assists another muscle to accomplish a movement.

**Stabilizer** A muscle that contracts with no significant movement.

**Superior** Above, on top, or toward the head.

**Supination** External rotation of the foot or forearm, resulting in appendage facing upward.

**Transverse plane** Division separating the body into an upper and lower half. Movements in this plane are horizontal.

**Valgus** An outward turning of a bone, for instance, in the hips, knees, or feet.

**Weight-bearing** Activities in which the body's weight acts directly against gravity, for example, walking.

# INDEX

Page numbers in **bold** indicate references to illustrations.

abdominal exercises 40–55
abdominal muscles 38, 39, **41**
abdominal stabilization 46–47
abduction 12
abductors 69
adduction 12
adductors 69
aerobic machines **36**, 36–37
aerobic training 24, 28–37
  aerobic test 17
  duration 29
  frequency 28
  types of 29
aerobics 34
Alternate Arm and Leg Raises on Ball
  104–105
anatomical position 9–10
anatomical terms 9–10
Anconeus 113
ankle movements 12
anterior 10
Anterior deltoid 56
aqua-aerobics 35
arm exercises 114–121
arm muscles 112–113

**B**
back and shoulder exercises 94–111
back and shoulder muscles 92–93
Back Extension Apparatus 103
back muscles 38
back pain 44, 104
balance 38–39, 42
Ball Bridge 80
Ball Shoulder Stretch 126
Barbell Bench Press 59, 62–63
Barbell exercises
  Bench Press 59, 62–63
  Free-standing Plié Squats 71
  Free-standing Squats 72–73
  Modified Bent Leg Deadlift 78
  Reverse Lunge 75
  Standing Curl 119

  Supine French Curl 115
Barbell Reverse Lunge 75
Bench Press Machine 59, 60
Bench Step 77
Biceps brachii 113, 119–121
Biceps femoris 68
BMI (body mass index) 16, 18
body types 14, 17
Body-weight Oblique Crunches with Ball
  50
Body-weight Dips 64
Body-weight Modified Push-ups 57
Borg CR10 scale 28
BOSU balls 38
boxing classes 34
Brachialis 113

**C**
Cable Cross-over 67
Cable Hip Abductions 85
Cable Tricep Push-down 117
calf muscles 137
cardiovascular exercise *see* aerobic
  training
chest exercises 56–67
chest muscles 56
Child Stretch 139
Chin-up Assist Machine 96
circumduction 12
Combination Crunch 51
conditioning programs 22–23
connective tissues 11
cycling classes 34

**D**
deep lateral rotators 69
deltoids 92, 108–110
depression 12
devising programs 16–20
Diastasis recti 46
dorsiflexion 12
Double Leg Bridge with Shoulder
  Flexion 79

Dumb-bell Bent-over Rows 101
Dumb-bell Concentration Curl 121
dumb-bell exercises
  Bench Press 59, 60–61
  Bent-over Rows 101
  Concentration Curl 121
  Flat Bench Flyes 66
  Incline Bench Press 59, 60–61
  Seated Shoulder Press 107
  Standing Lateral Raise 108
Dumb-bell Flat Bench Flyes 66
Dumb-bell Seated Shoulder Press 107
Dumb-bell Standing Lateral Raise 108

**E**
ectomorphs 14, 17
elevation 12
endomorphs 14, 17
Erector spinae 92, 122
Extensor carpi radialis brevis 112
Extensor carpi radialis longus 112
exercise analysis 14
exercise balls 38, 42, 44, 45, 48, 50
exercise principles 15
exercise programs 21–27
extension 12
Extensor carpi radialis 112
Extensor carpi ulnaris 112

**F**
fat tissue 11
fitness tests 16–20
FITT principle 15
flexibility 25–26, 122
flexibility test 17
flexion 12
Flexor carpi radialis 112
Flexor carpi ulnaris 112
floor exercises
  Abdominal Stabilization Program
    46–47
  Alternate Arm and Leg Raises on Ball
    104–105

Ball Bridge 80

Barbell Reverse Lunge 75

Bench Step 77

Body-weight Oblique Crunch 50

Cable Hip Abductions 85

Child Stretch 139

Combination Crunch 51

Double Leg Bridge with Shoulder
    Flexion 79

Dumb-bell Bent-over Rows 101

Dumb-bell Standing Lateral Raise 108

Free-standing Barbell Plié Squats 71

Free-standing Barbell Squats 72–73

Free-standing Calf Raise 90

Free–standing Lateral Lunge 76

Gastrocnemius Stretch 137

Kneeling Heel Touch 54–55

Modified Barbell Bent Leg Deadlift 78

Plank Pose Stabilization on Ball 44

Plank to Downward-facing Dog 138

Prone Back Extension on Ball 102

Prone Hip Extensions 86

Rotator Cuff Stabilization with
    Theraband 111

Seated Bent-over Dumb-bell Raises on
    Ball 110

Seated Overhead Tricep Extension on
    Ball with Theraband 114

Seated Stride into Saw Stretch 134

Seesaw with Ball 88

Shell Prone Ball Roll-Up 45

Side-lying Ball Lift 81

Side-to-side Hip Rolls 131

Spine Roll 130

Squats with Ball Between Legs 70

Standing Barbell Curl 119

Standing Iliopsoas Stretch 136

Supine Adductor Stabilization with
    Ball 84

Supine Hip Flexion Stretch 129

Supine Lying Deep External Rotators
    Stretch 135

Supine Lying Gluteus Stretch 132

Supine Lying—Neutral Spine with
    Scapula Release 40

Supine Lying Single Leg Hamstring
    Stretch 133

Transverse Activation in 4-point
    Kneeling 43

Two-stage Crunch 48

Yoga Quad Stretch with Forward
    Lean 89

forearm movements 12

forearm muscles 112–113

Free-standing Barbell Plié Squats 71

Free-standing Barbell Squats 72–73

Free-standing Calf Raise 90

Free-standing Lateral Lunge 76

Full-body Stretch 128

functional exercises 26, 38, 57–58, 78,
    84, 85, 94

functional training 15, 21

G

Gastrocnemius 68, 91

Gastrocnemius Stretch 137

Gemellus 69

Gluteus maximus 69, 132

Gluteus medius 69

Gracilis 69

gym programs 22–26

H

hamstrings 68, 87, 133

heart-rate monitors 29

heart rates 17, 19, 28

height 16

high-impact exercises 29

Hip Abductor Machine 82

Hip Adductor Machine 83

hip exercises 127, 131, 135, 136

Hip Flexor Apparatus 52

hip joints and muscles 10, 38, 41,
    68–69

home programs 27

I

Iliopsoas 69, 136

Incline Dumb-bell Bench Press 59,
    60–61

Infraspinatus 93

intensity 21, 28

J

jogging 32–33

joint
    movements 10–11, 12–13, **13**
    types of 10

K

Karvonen formula 29

Kneeling Heel Touch 54–55

L

Lateral Pull-downs 94–95

lateral rotation 12

Latissimus dorsi 92

leg and hip exercises 69–91, 137

leg and hip muscles 38, 41, 68–69,
    137

Levator scapula 92

Low-impact exercises 29

Lower trapezius 56

lunges 75–76

M

Machine Cable Front Lateral Pull-down
    94–95

machine exercises 36–37
    Back Extension Apparatus 103
    Bench Press Machine 59, 60
    Cable Cross-over 67
    Cable Front Lateral Pull-down 94–95
    Cable Hip Abductions 85
    Cable Tricep Push-down 117
    Chin-up Assist Machine 96
    Hip Abductor Machine 82
    Hip Adductor Machine 83
    Hip Flexor Apparatus 52
    Incline Leg Press 74
    Incline Pec Deck Machine 65
    Lying Leg Curl 87
    Rear Deltoid Machine 109
    Seated Calf Raise Machine 91
    Seated Low Cable Pulley Rows 99
    Shoulder Press 106
    Standing Cable Pull-over 97
    Standing Reverse Grip Cable Rows 98
    Supported Bent-over Row Machine
        100

Tricep Machine 116
Machine Incline Leg Press 74
Machine Lying Leg Curl 87
Machine Shoulder Press 106
marathons 32, 33
Maximal Heart Rate (MHR) 28–29
medial 10
medial rotation 12
medication 29
mesomorphs 14, 17
mobilizers 8
Modified Barbell Bent Leg Deadlift 78
motivation phases 14
muscles 8, **9**, 9
   man/woman comparison 11
musculoskeletal system 9

**N**
Neck and Shoulder Stretch 124
neutral spine **41**
Neutral Spine—Stand and Breathe 41
non-weight-bearing exercises 29
nutrition 15

**O**
obliques 39
Obturator externus 69
older adult programmes 27
origin 9
overload principle 15

**P**
Palmaris longus 112
Pec Deck Machine 65
Pectoralis major 56
Pectoralis minor 56
pectorals 125
pelvic floor 46
pelvis 10
Piriformis 69
Plank Pose Stabilization on Ball 44
Plank to Downward-facing Dog 138
plantarflexion 12
position and direction 9, 10
postural programs 25–26
posture 40–41, 122
Predicted Maximal Heart Rate (PMHR)

28–29
pregnancy 46
progression principle 15
pronation 12
Pronator quadratus 113
Pronator teres 113
prone 10
Prone Back Extension on Ball 102
Prone Hip Extensions 86
pulse rates 29
push-ups 57–58

**Q**
Quadratus femoris 69
Quadratus lumborum 93
Quadriceps 68

**R**
range of motion (ROM) 122
Rated Perceived Exertion (RPE) scale 28
Rear Deltoid Machine 109
Rectus abdominis 39
Rectus femoris 68
rest/effort principle 15
resting heart rate 17, 19, 29
Reverse Incline Bench Sit-ups 49
reversibility principle 15
Rhomboids 92
rotator cuff muscles 93
Rotator Cuff Stabilization 111
rowing machines 36–37
running 32–33

**S**
sacroilliac joint 10
SAID principle 15
scapula movements 12
Seated Bent-over Dumb-bell Raises on
   Ball 110
Seated Calf Raise Machine 91
Seated Incline Dumb-bell Curl with
   Supination 120
Seated Low Cable Pulley Rows 99
Seated Overhead Tricep Extension on
   Ball with Theraband 114
Seated Side Stretch on Ball 127
Seated Stride into Saw Stretch 134

Seesaw with Ball 88
Semimembranosus 68
Semitendinosus 68
Serratus anterior 40, 56, 93
Shell Prone Ball Roll-Up 45
shoulder joints and muscles 10, 38,
   40, 56
shoulder movements 13
Side-lying Ball Lift 81
Side-to-side Hip Rolls 131
sit-and-reach test 17
sit-ups 49
6-mile runs 33
Soleus 68, 91
Spine Roll 130
Squats with Ball Between Legs 70
stability balls 38, 102
stabilization muscles 38, 39
Standing Barbell Curl 119
Standing Cable Pull-over 97
Standing Chest and Anterior Shoulder
   Stretch 125
Standing Iliopsoas Stretch 136
Standing Reverse Grip Cable Rows 98
step test 17, 19
Straight-arm Pull-down 97
strength endurance test 17
strength programs 25–26
strength-training guidelines 21
stretching 122, **123**, 124–139
Subscapularis 93
supination 12
Supine Adductor Stabilization with
   Ball 84
Supine Barbell French Curl 115
Supine Hip Flexion Stretch 129
Supine Lying Deep External Rotators
   Stretch 135
Supine Lying Gluteus Stretch 132
Supine Lying—Neutral Spine with
   Scapula Release 40
Supine Lying Single Leg Hamstring
   Stretch 133
Supported Bent-over Row Machine 100
Supraspinatus 93
synovial joints 10, 11

**T**

Talk Test 28

Tensor fasciae latae 69

Teres major 92

Teres minor 93

3-minute step test 17

tone and strength programs 25

Training Heart Rate method (THR) 28

Transverse abdominus 39, 43

Transverse Activation (4-point
   kneeling) 43

Trapezius 40, 56, 92

Tricep Machine 116

Tricep Rope Pull-down 118

Triceps 113, 115–118

Two-stage Crunch 48

**U**

upper arm muscles 113

**W**

walking **30**, 30–31, 33

Wall Push-ups on Bar 58

weight 16, 18

weight-loss programs 24

weights 21

wrist muscles 112

**Y**

Yoga Quad Stretch 89

# REFERENCES

**Further Reading**

ACSM, *ACSM's Guidelines for Exercise Testing and Prescription*, 7th edition, 2005, Lippincott, Williams and Wilkins, USA

Anatomical Chart Company, *Women's Health and Wellness: an illustrated Guide*, 2002, Lippincott, Williams and Wilkins, USA

Craig, Colleen, *Pilates on the Ball*, 2001, Healing Arts Series, Vermont

Craig, Colleen, *Strength Training on the Ball*, 2005, Healing Arts Series, Vermont

Dealvier, Frederic, *Women's Strength Training Anatomy*, 2003, Human Kinetics

Dufton, Jennifer, *The Pilates Difference*, 2005, Bounty, London

Endacott, Jan, *Fitball Workout*, 2004, Bounty, London

Floyd, R.T. and Thompson, Clem W., *Manual of Structural Kinesiology*, 14th edition, 2003, McGraw Hill, USA

Viljoen, Wayne, *Weight Training Handbook*, 2004, New Holland, London

Wyatt, Tanya, *Be Your Own Personal Trainer*, 2004, New Holland, London

Wyatt, Tanya, *Stretch Routines*, 2005, New Holland, London

**Websites**

www.acefitness.org

www.acsm.org

www.anatomical.com

www.exerciseacademy.com

www.exrx.net

www.fitnesszone.co.za

www.womenfitness.net

www.womenshealth.com

www.4women.gov